LIGHT
ON THE
MAHĀBHĀRATA

THE OXFORD CENTRE FOR HINDU STUDIES MANDALA PUBLISHING SERIES

The Oxford Centre for Hindu Studies Mandala Publishing Series offers authoritative yet accessible introductions to a wide range of subjects in Hindu Studies. Each book in the series aims to present its subject matter in a form that is engaging and readily comprehensible to persons of all backgrounds – academic or otherwise – without compromising scholarly rigor. The series thus bridges the divide between academic and popular writing by preserving and utilising the best elements of both.

LIGHT
ON THE
MAHĀBHĀRATA

A Guide to India's Great Epic

Nicholas Sutton

MANDALA
San Rafael Los Angeles London

CONTENTS

Introduction

The *Mahābhārata* is a truly vast work of early Sanskrit literature that reflects on a wide range of issues which have concerned people throughout different epochs. Within the context of Indian culture, the significance of the *Mahābhārata* cannot be overstated, as its themes, characters, narratives, and preoccupations have reverberated across the region for centuries. It is probably accurate to say that, apart perhaps from the very young, every inhabitant of India will have some knowledge of the *Mahābhārata* and many will have a detailed appreciation of the various narratives that cross and re-cross each other throughout its meandering course of exposition. One must hasten to add, however, that the significance of the *Mahābhārata,* and the lessons it offers, are by no means relevant solely to persons conditioned by Indian culture, for the questions it raises and seeks to answer are those of a universal nature relating to the human condition, human interactions, and the great conundrums of our existence in this world.

My previous work on the *Mahābhārata, Religious Doctrines in the Mahābhārata* (Motilal Banarsidass, 2000), had the primary aim of chronicling the different religious ideas and teachings that are located within its eighteen books, or *parvans*. The principal aim of the present work is to build on that earlier endeavour by delving more deeply into the discussions one encounters in the *Mahābhārata* and to review the diverse responses it provides to the complex questions it presents before the reader. We can thereby consider in greater detail why the main characters behave in the manner that they do, what is the vision of life that motivates them, and the extent to which they are able to prioritise enlightened wisdom over narrow self-interest. And, of course, as these questions and the responses are considered, we will naturally enough reflect on our own lives and the ways in which we ourselves confront such issues.

It is well-known that the whole of the *Mahābhārata* is structured around a central narrative that tells of an ancient conflict between two branches of the same royal house, referred to as the Pāṇḍavas and Kauravas. Within this narrative form, we have a range of different protagonists, all of whom display differing character traits, some saintly, some admirable, and some less so. We are hence urged to reflect on the subtleties of right and wrong action, and whether or not pragmatism should take precedence over pure virtue in certain situations; and it is certain that all of human life revolves to a significant degree around the conclusions we draw on such issues. Then we come on to the question of religion and spirituality in our lives and in our world. What is the goal we should seek to pursue? Is it success and prosperity in the here and now? Is it righteous living based on service to the world? Or is it spiritual liberation from mundane existence? All of these possibilities, and combinations of them as well, are explored within the *Mahābhārata,* both by means of its narrative accounts and also through lengthy tracts of direct instruction.

We start off with a consideration of the extent and range of the content, looking at the main narrative and the associated subplots, before considering the male and female characters in order to determine the lessons that are imparted through the differing ways in which they conduct themselves. On the basis of this discussion of the characters, we are then able to move on to try to make sense of what the *Mahābhārata* is saying about *dharma*, which really means the proper ways in which human beings should live their lives, and the goals that they should seek to pursue.

Whilst the main narrative and its associated subplots certainly hold a central position for any understanding of the *Mahābhārata*, we must be aware that around half of the chapters and verses are given over to material of a purely didactic nature. The principal characters frequently encounter sagacious and enlightened individuals who respond to the questions put to them by imparting revealed wisdom on a huge range of subjects. This element of the *Mahābhārata*'s structure is most evident after the great battle is over when the surviving warriors approach the dying Bhīṣma and receive instruction from him on a variety of subjects, both spiritual and mundane. This element of the *Mahābhārata*'s content is quite frequently given less prominence when the work is discussed or reviewed, but my feeling is that a more complete study of the *Mahābhārata* must focus on the content in its entirety, and hence I have devoted as much attention as space allows to considering the various lines of direct instruction on issues as diverse as charity, diet, Yoga, and religious philosophy. Moreover, we also have the presence of Kṛṣṇa striding across the narrative stage, and at times providing further passages of instruction on spiritual and ethical issues. As a divine *avatāra*, Kṛṣṇa transcends humanity: his very presence in the *Mahābhārata* offers a further revelation with regard to the nature of the Supreme Deity and the complex theology of Indian theistic thought.

Anyone who has some knowledge of the *Rāmāyaṇa* will quickly recognise the difference between the two works with regard to the manner in which the main characters are portrayed. In the *Rāmāyaṇa*, Rāma, Lakṣmaṇa, Sītā, and Hanumān are supremely virtuous, never straying from the path of *dharma* or appearing to be overly taxed by difficult questions as to how *dharma* should be best pursued or what the true nature of *dharma* might be. The great strength of Vālmīki's work is the simplicity of its message, as it portrays the stark contrast between right and wrong, light and dark, *dharma* and *adharma*, and thereby guides us beyond the darkness towards the light, as the *Bṛhad-āraṇyaka Upaniṣad* (1.3.28) puts it (*tamaso mā jyotir gamaya*).

This apparent strength might, however, also be regarded as a weakness, for the reality of life is rarely so simple, and within the *Mahābhārata* we find a very obvious contrast inasmuch as none of the main characters, including Kṛṣṇa, the *avatāra*, can be regarded as being beyond reproach. The result is that we are deprived of a straightforward message that urges us towards virtue, but in its place we have a more accurate depiction of the realities of human life in which we may indeed strive for virtue but be forced to make compromises due to the exigencies of the human condition. All of these points are considered in the review of the *Mahābhārata*'s insights into the nature of *dharma* and the manner in which it focuses on the subtle questions relating to how we live in this world, the righteous and unrighteous use of violence, tolerance, and assertive action, and how we reconcile spiritual aspirations with the necessity of living within the world and fully meeting the obligations and responsibilities each of us has. These are highly complex questions and the *Mahābhārata* does not try to fob us off with simplistic answers or creedal formulae. *Dharma* is more subtle than that.

The *Mahābhārata* can be likened in some ways to a great conference in which different authoritative speakers come forward to express their views on the complex issues raised by the dilemmas which confront the main characters. There are conflicts and disagreements, but also enlightening insights based on the powerful wisdom of the speakers. It does not give us the simple answers we might hanker for, but rather ideas that can form the basis for our own quest for knowledge and understanding of the world, of human beings, and of human society. Ultimately, each of us will take his or her own message from the *Mahābhārata,* following the form of inspiration that comes to us by reflecting on the issues it draws to our attention, and it is hoped that the present work can be of some assistance in that line of reflection.

B.G. Sharma

I
SCOPE OF THE *MAHĀBHĀRATA*

In this opening chapter, I want to begin by conveying a sense of the size and scope of the *Mahābhārata*. This is truly a work of vast proportions that not only presents a complex narrative with many different strands and subplots, but also contains extensive passages of religious, philosophical, moral, and practical instruction. So the main aim here is to provide an outline of the contents of the text by presenting a review of all of its eighteen books, which are known as *parvans*, meaning 'limb' or 'section'. Before that, however, there are a few points of a more general nature to be considered, such as what sort of text this is, who wrote it, when it was written, and why it was written. What is it really about and what are its principal roles in the religious, cultural, and social life of India? It is to these primary questions that we must first turn our attention.

As many readers will know, the *Mahābhārata* is a great epic tale from the Hindu tradition that tells of the quarrel and conflict between two branches of the same royal family, the Pāṇḍavas and the Kauravas, culminating in the sanguinary conflict at Kurukṣetra in North India. It is, however, much more than an epic tale. The *Mahābhārata* is not just the story of an inter-dynastic conflict, it is also about the struggle between good and evil, and whilst many Indian people will regard it as historical truth, some commentators, ancient and modern, have taken it as an allegory for the confrontation between right and wrong that takes place within each and every individual.

Moreover, the conflict between the two sides is by no means a straightforward triumph of virtue over iniquity: on the righteous Pāṇḍava side we have both the gentle virtue of Yudhiṣṭhira and the assertive aggression of his younger brother, Bhīma, which leads to clashes and debates of a more subtle nature.

Then on the other side, amongst the Kauravas, we have the sagacious Bhīṣma, a great warrior and teacher of religion, and the mighty Droṇa, a brahmin who takes up arms and who, like Bhīṣma, disapproves of the vicious conduct of Duryodhana and the other leaders of his faction. Set in the middle are Karṇa, a righteous man who is forced to do evil out of a sense of duty to Duryodhana, and Dhṛtarāṣṭra, the blind elder of the dynasty who longs to be virtuous but is led astray by his intense attachment to his son, Duryodhana. Alongside these male protagonists, we also have the women of the dynasty, Gāndhārī, Draupadī, and Kuntī, who frequently bewail their impotence in the face of the misdeeds wrought by their male counterparts, but show little hesitation in coming forward to offer words of advice and even condemnation towards them.

This mighty tale of conflict, virtue, loyalty, and iniquity is on a vast scale, consisting of around 80,000 verses of metrical Sanskrit poetry written for the most part in the *śloka,* or *anuṣṭubh,* form.[1] This size makes it possibly the longest work ever composed, several times longer than the Iliad and Odyssey combined. Why is it so long? First of all, the story itself is told at length with numerous twists and turns and extensive descriptions of individual confrontations on the battlefield where most of the heroes are shot down one by one, their deaths each due to a complex set of circumstances which are narrated in full detail.

---

1 The most common metrical form in Classical Sanskrit, in which a stanza consists of four *pādas,* or quarter-verses, of eight syllables each.

Alongside this extensive central narrative, we also have numerous subplots revealing how each of the main characters was forced to accept his or her own fate. Then there are other stories, generally narrated by sages of the forest, which are not directly related to the principal characters but which provide instruction based on persons of the past who faced similar dilemmas. In this category, we find well-known tales such as that of Nala and Damayantī, and that of Sāvitrī and Satyavān. Here is a list of the main 'sub-narratives' which appear at different points in the *Mahābhārata*. It is illustrative rather than exhaustive, and there are other instructive tales told that are not mentioned here:

1. The story of Śakuntalā and Duḥṣanta, and the birth of their son Bharata;
2. The story of Kaca, Śukra, and Devayānī;
3. The story of Yayāti and Devayānī;
4. The story of the conflict between Viśvāmitra and Vasiṣṭha;
5. A description of the assembly halls of the Gods;
6. The story of Nala and Damayantī;
7. The story of Agastya;
8. The story of the descent of the Gaṅgā to Earth;
9. The story of Ṛśyaśṛṅga;
10. The story of Paraśurāma;
11. The story of Cyavana and Sukanyā;
12. The story of Aṣṭavakra;
13. The story of the birth of Kārttikeya;
14. An abbreviated version of the story of the *Rāmāyaṇa*;
15. The story of Sāvitrī and Satyavān;
16. The story of Indra's sin and his release from sin;
17. The story of Gālava, Garuḍa, and Yayāti;
18. The story of the origin of Death;
19. Nārada's account of the great kings of the past;

20. The story of Śiva's destruction of the Three Cities (Tripura);
21. The story of Śiva's destruction of Dakṣa's Yajña;
22. The story of King Rantideva.

Furthermore, at least half of the content of the *Mahābhārata* is given over to passages of religious and ethical debate which, it could be argued, provide us with a basis for most strands of Hindu religious thought. In the later books, we find the dying Bhīṣma giving instruction to the Pāṇḍavas on subjects such as the duties of a king, the philosophy of Sāṁkhya, the practice of Yoga, and numerous other topics as well. The text itself declares that whatever exists is covered in this work and if anything is not here, then it does not exist. Undoubtedly this is an exaggeration, nevertheless if one is looking for sources for Hindu doctrines, beliefs, and practices, then it is advisable to turn first to the pages of the *Mahābhārata*. Here is a list of some of the main passages of instruction that appear at various junctures within the central narrative:

a. Description of holy places (*tīrthas*) and the merit achieved by visiting them;
b. Draupadī's teachings on a woman's *dharma*;
c. Mārkaṇḍeya's extensive teachings on the identity of Viṣṇu as the Supreme Deity;
d. Yudhiṣṭhira's teachings on *dharma* to free his brothers from a *yakṣa*, or spirit, and from a serpent;
e. Vidura's teachings on morality – the *Vidura-nīti*;
f. Sanatsujāta's teachings on religious philosophy;
g. The *Bhagavad-gītā* instructed by Kṛṣṇa;
h. Saṁjaya's account of the geography of the world and of past kings;

i. Bhīṣma's teachings on the descent of *avatāras*;
j. Vyāsa's teachings on the divine nature of Śiva;
k. Kṛṣṇa's teachings on the true nature of *dharma*;
l. A description of the holy *tīrthas* along the banks of the River Sarasvatī.

Furthermore, when the battle is over, and when Duryodhana is finally slain and his death has been avenged by Aśvatthāman, the story is completely suspended. In the *Śānti, Anuśāsana,* and *Aśvamedhika-parvans* (Books 12, 13, and 14), the story is hardly taken forward at all and instead we have a huge block of religious teachings covering a remarkable range of topics. The principal speaker here is Bhīṣma, who is still lying on the field of battle, mortally wounded and awaiting an auspicious moment to die. Yudhiṣṭhira repeatedly questions his grandfather and listens to the innumerable discourses that are then presented to him. This section of the text contains almost 500 chapters and constitutes about one-third of the *Mahābhārata*'s entire content. Bhīṣma's teachings are divided into four sections, the first three of which constitute the *Śānti-parvan,* and, like other subsections of the main 18 books, are also also referred to as *parvans*:

i. The *Rāja-dharma*
ii. The *Āpad-dharma*
iii. The *Mokṣa-dharma*
iv. The *Anuśāsana*

The *Rāja-dharma* teaching is actually begun by Vyāsa before the Pāṇḍavas approach Bhīṣma and focuses primarily on the appropriate way for a king to rule his domain. These teachings contain a number of stories of the lives of kings, which illustrate the point under discussion. Here we find the following topics being considered:

1. Vyāsa's teachings on *dharma* and destiny to pacify the grieving Yudhiṣṭhira;
2. Bhīṣma's teachings on the four social classes (*varṇas*) and the four stages of life (*āśramas*);
3. *Kṣatriya-dharma*, the essential duties of a king;
4. Respect for the brahmins;
5. Appropriate forms of punishment;
6. How to appoint reliable ministers and advisors;
7. How to construct cities and fortresses;
8. The times to make war and to seek peace;
9. The efficient use of spies;
10. How to form battle arrays and command armies;
11. How to deal with the nobility, internal enemies, and treason;
12. The need to protect the citizens of the kingdom;
13. How to act if one suffers a defeat.

The *Āpad-dharma* literally refers to *dharma* during times of emergency, when the rules that would generally govern a person's conduct, in this case a king's, are relaxed and they are permitted to behave in a manner that would otherwise be regarded as adharmic. In fact, apart from in the opening few chapters, there is not that much difference of emphasis here from the teachings given under the heading of *Rāja-dharma*. Here are some of the topics discussed in this section:

1. How to acquire wealth and power;
2. Rules of taxation for the kingdom;
3. How to deal with enemies of different types;
4. How to make alliances and when they should be broken;
5. How to deceive a rival over one's intentions;
6. Who should be trusted and who should not;
7. Giving protection to the citizens;
8. The sword as a weapon of war.

In the *Mokṣa-dharma*, after the teachings on kingship, at Yudhiṣṭhira's request, Bhīṣma then speaks extensively on the subject of gaining *mokṣa*, liberation from rebirth. This marks a dramatic change of emphasis in the discourse away from the proper way to live in this world towards a world-denying philosophy of renunciation and spiritual absorption. The *Mokṣa-dharma-parvan* is the final section of the *Śānti-parvan*. It is followed by the *Anuśāsana-parvan*, literally the 'Book of Instruction', which follows the same pattern of Bhīṣma giving teachings to Yudhiṣṭhira, although on occasion he asks Kṛṣṇa to speak on a subject on which he is not an expert. Here the topics covered are far more wide-ranging but the emphasis is more towards the execution of religious ritual and the rules governing the working of society. We will look in more detail at the *Mokṣa-dharma-parvan* and the *Anuśāsana-parvan* in later chapters, but at this point I wanted to give some insight into the diverse types of material contained within the *Mahābhārata* in addition to the better known passages which form a part of the central narrative.

Another important point to notice is that the *Mahābhārata* cannot simply be regarded as a single piece of literature. It is much more than one book. First of all, we have the issue of the differing manuscript sources. As early as the thirteenth century CE, the great Vedāntist Madhvācārya was bewailing the fact that he could not arrive at any definitive version of the *Mahābhārata*, as he obtained the text in different manuscript forms, each of which differed from all of the others. This textual diversity existed down to the twentieth century when the task of compiling a Critical Edition of the Sanskrit text was undertaken by a team of mainly Indian scholars who worked on comparing all the available manuscript versions and determining as far as possible which passages were authentic and which were later additions.[2] This task took several decades to complete but the result is that today we have a single version of the Sanskrit text, which can be referred to. The problem with this is that there are a large number of important passages that were excluded from the Critical Edition on text-critical grounds but which have for centuries held a significant position in the *Mahābhārata* tradition, the prayers of the Pāṇḍavas to the Goddess being one notable example.

But beyond the issue of arriving at an agreed textual form for the written *Mahābhārata*, we must also be aware that the *Mahābhārata* exists as a wider tradition that permeates most layers of Indian culture. The fact is that many Indian people will have a detailed knowledge of the *Mahābhārata* without ever having read a single word of the textual version. Rather, the tradition is passed on primarily through parents and grandparents telling stories, through comic books, through dance and drama, and, more latterly, through film and television. Hence when we speak of the *Mahābhārata* we cannot think purely in terms of a single written text but of a much wider tradition that is passed on primarily through oral means of transmission and which may include episodes that are nowhere to be found in the manuscript versions. Many a time I have had Hindu friends refer me to episodes of the *Mahābhārata*, which I know do not appear in the Critical Edition, or, as far as I am aware, in any of the extant manuscripts.

2 *The Mahābhārata for the First Time Critically Edited*, 19 vols, edited by Vishnu S. Sukthankar et al. (Poona: Bhandarkar Oriental Research Institute). Available online at: https://sanskritdocuments.org/mirrors/mahabharata/mahabharata-bori.html. It should be noted that the digital version does not include the critical apparatus of the printed edition.

There are several English versions of the *Mahābhārata* currently available, all abbreviated to a greater or lesser extent. These provide a valuable insight into the progression of the central narrative, but in almost all cases the extensive passages of religious and ethical instruction are omitted. There are also two full English translations, one completed in the nineteenth century by Kisari Mohan Ganguli[3] and the other more recently by Bibek Debroy.[4] The Critical Edition of the text was not available in Ganguli's time and so his translation is of the manuscript used by Nīlakaṇṭha, a sixteenth-century commentator on the *Mahābhārata*, but Bibek Debroy has presented us with a translation that corresponds to the chapters of the Critical Edition.[5]

When we come to consider when and why the *Mahābhārata* was composed, and the genre of literature to which it should be assigned, then some discussion of trends in scholarly debate must be referred to. The traditional Hindu view is that

---

3 Kisari Mohan Ganguli, trans., *The Mahabharata of Krishna-Dwaipayana Vyasa, Translated into English Prose* (Delhi: Munshiram Manoharlal, 2004; first published Calcutta: Bharata Press, 1883–1896).

4 *The Mahabharata*, trans. Bibek Debroy (India Penguin, 2015).

5 Also worth mentioning is the *Mahābhārata* translation project at Chicago University Press, which is not yet complete but has published important volumes; see J. A. B. van Buitenen, trans. and ed., *The Mahābhārata*, 3 vols. (Chicago: University of Chicago Press, 1973–1978); and James L. Fitzgerald, trans. and ed., *The Mahābhārata*, Volume 7, Book 11, The Book of the Women; and Book 12, The Book of Peace, Part 1 (Chicago: University of Chicago Press, 2004). Additionally, much of the *Mahābhārata* has been translated in the Clay Sanskrit Library series by various scholars, although this collective translation is based on the 'vulgate' (i.e. Nīlakaṇṭha's version) rather than the Critical Edition; see Paul Wilmot et al., trans., *Mahābhārata*, Clay Sanskrit Library (New York: New York University Press, 2005–2009).

the *Mahābhārata* was composed by the sage Vyāsa around 5,000 years ago, shortly after the events it describes took place, and many Hindus hold firmly to that view. Modern scholarship has suggested a later date, though without a clear consensus emerging. Early in the twentieth century, E. Washburn Hopkins[6] argued that the *Mahābhārata* was not composed as a single work but began as an oral warrior epic that was gradually expanded and added to over a period of centuries. In Hopkins' view, the original *Bhārata* was a secular work, composed around 400 bce, telling epic tales of kings, warriors, and battles. Over the ensuing centuries, a religious and spiritual dimension was added to the original story, with Kṛṣṇa being later represented as a manifestation of God on Earth. Then, later still, the lengthy passages of religious, philosophical, and ethical instruction, including the famous *Bhagavad-gītā*, were inserted into the text so that it became a sort of library of ancient wisdom. This whole process, it was hypothesised, took place over a period of around 800 years so that the *Mahābhārata* as we know it today was more or less complete by around 400 ce. Furthermore, Hopkins regarded the didactic passages as not integral to the *Mahābhārata* and categorised them as the 'pseudo-epic', a designation that will appear to many people to be somewhat ridiculous.

Subsequent scholarship, with some notable exceptions, has tended to accept Hopkins' opinion that the *Mahābhārata* was not composed as a single unit but took shape over a period of several hundred years, a process that was concluded by around 400 or 500 ce. Moreover, a text-critical approach was adopted in order to gain insight into the structure and meaning of its content. The exceptional work of John

---

6 E. Washburn Hopkins, *The Great Epic of India: Its Character and Origin* (Delhi: Motilal Banarsidass, 1994; 1st ed. 1901).

Brockington is an example of this line of scholarship.[7] Another good example is that of the work of James Fitzgerald, which has sought to establish some of the text's most important redactions.[8] There are, however, dissenting voices. Writing in 2001, Alf Hiltebeitel, one of the leading contemporary scholars of the *Mahābhārata*, wrote:

> ... since no one is close to proving anything let us be all the more cautious about what we are trying to disprove. ... I would only argue that even these axiomatically late portions must be looked at with an eye fresh to the possibility that they are not any later – or at least not much later: hours, weeks or months rather than centuries – than the rest, once the rest, and its principles of composition and design are better understood.[9]

Alf Hiltebeitel is of the opinion that the *Mahābhārata* was compiled in full by a team of scholars working under the direction of a single author over a relatively short period, some time between 150 bce and the year 0. Another dissenting voice was that of V. S. Sukthankar, the senior editor of the Critical Edition. Writing in 1942, Sukthankar launched a withering attack on Hopkins' ideas and those of

7 See, for example, John L. Brockington, *The Sanskrit Epics* (Leiden: Brill, 1998).

8 See, in particular, the introduction to Fitzgerald's partial translation of the *Śānti-parvan* (Book 12, The Book of Peace, cited in footnote 5), as well as his essay 'Negotiating the Shape of "Scripture": New Perspectives on the Development and Growth of the *Mahābhārata* between the Empires', in *Between the Empires: Society in India 300 BCE to 400 CE*, ed. P. Olivelle (Cambridge: Cambridge University Press, 2006).

9 Alf Hiltebeitel, *Rethinking the Mahabharata: A Reader's Guide to the Education of the Dharma King* (Chicago: University of Chicago Press, 2001), 29.

all who adhered to his'atomistic' approach.[10] For Sukthankar, Hopkins' work is 'as good as useless – as indeed it was bound to be'. It was not that Sukthankar was a precursor of Hiltebeitel in denying that the *Mahābhārata* contained different types of material from different eras, and indeed he does speak of early and late passages, but he was adamant that the Western preoccupation with dividing the epic text into chronological strata served only to obscure its true meaning. This was because he saw within the *Mahābhārata* clear lines of thematic continuity, which transcended the rigid lines of demarcation that most Western scholarship insisted on maintaining. He therefore concludes his criticism in a forceful manner:

> Let me emphasise with all the power at my command that it is only from this one point of view that you will be able to understand and interpret the *Mahābhārata*, and that all attempts to explain it merely as an evolute of some hypothetical epic nucleus are merely examples of wasted ingenuity.

For Sukthankar, the *Mahābhārata* is to be understood as possessing specific themes that are pursued in different ways and from different perspectives throughout its course. If we persist in dividing the text up into different units of pseudo-epic and epic proper, then we will lose sight of what the *Mahābhārata* as a whole and each of its passages is saying. More recently, even Fitzgerald, who has himself engaged in an extended scholarly debate with Hiltebeitel about the composition of the text, has reasserted Sukthankar's essential point, stating that 'most good scholarship now being done on

10 V. S. Sukthankar, *On the Meaning of the Mahābhārata* (Delhi: Motilal Banarsidass 2016; 1st ed. 1942). This book was originally delivered as a series of lectures.

the text undertakes to understand that text which the tradition itself finalized and appropriated at least fifteen hundred years ago.' He further speaks of 'clear lines of ideological continuity joining the mythic epic narrative of the *Great Bhārata* and the greater part of its didactic components'.

The reason I have rehearsed this debate quite fully is that it serves to support the understanding of the *Mahābhārata* that will be followed throughout this book. After this fairly brief discussion, we will not concern ourselves with hypotheses about chronological strata, but will focus primarily on the unifying themes representing the central teachings that the work as a whole is seeking to convey. It is usual to refer to the *Mahābhārata* as an epic, and perhaps compare it to the *Odyssey* or *Iliad*. I would not necessarily disagree with that designation, but at the same time I would strongly assert the identity of the work as a sacred text, a scripture that is revered and referred to by the contemporary Hindu community, who represent themselves as the true proprietors of the whole *Mahābhārata* tradition.

In relation to Christianity, Brevard Childs made similar points regarding critical scholarship and the Bible, arguing for a 'canonical approach' that insisted that we should understand a religious text in the form it is accepted by the tradition that reveres it, regardless of text-critical arguments.[11] In the same way, this line of thought can readily be applied to our understanding of the *Mahābhārata* in accepting its primary identity as a Hindu scripture and seeking to establish the main themes of religious thought that justify such a designation. At some risk of oversimplification, I would suggest that we can identify three principal themes that highlight the predominant religious dimension of the *Mahābhārata*'s discourse; it is around

11 Brevard Childs, *Biblical Theology in Crisis* (Philadelphia: Westminster Press, 1970).

these three elements of religious debate that the present work has been structured. They are as follows:

1. **Identity of Kṛṣṇa as a divine *avatāra*.** Throughout the *Mahābhārata*'s narrative, and in the *Bhagavad-gītā* in particular, it is made known that Kṛṣṇa, the cousin of the Pāṇḍavas who accepts the role of Arjuna's charioteer, is in fact a manifestation of Nārāyaṇa (Viṣṇu), the Supreme Deity, who has appeared in this world to restore the rule of *dharma* through the kingship of Yudhiṣṭhira. Today Kṛṣṇa is one of the main forms of the Supreme Deity who is worshipped by Hindus.
2. **Teachings on *dharma*.** The whole of the *Mahābhārata* narrative forms a reflection on the nature of *dharma*, considering how far it is possible to live in human society whilst adhering to the ideal of pure virtue. When must pragmatism come to the fore? Is telling a lie ever justified? These and other questions repeatedly resurface throughout the principal narrative and are frequently taken up in the didactic passages as well.
3. **Religious teachings.** Throughout the *Mahābhārata*, and in the later portions of the narrative in particular, we find extensive didactic passages that focus on virtually all aspects of religious thought. Particularly notable here is the *Mokṣa-dharma* section of Book Twelve, the *Śānti-parvan*, which contains extensive discussion of religious philosophy and some of the earliest passages of Yoga teachings that still exist today.

Each of these topics will be reviewed in some detail later on, but I think it would be useful to say a little more about them at this preliminary stage in order to give a fuller response to the question, 'What is the *Mahābhārata* about?'

KṚṢṆA, THE *AVATĀRA*

First, we will briefly consider the character of Kṛṣṇa as he is represented in the text. It is true to say that in some passages Kṛṣṇa appears to act like an ordinary human being, with all the limitations that this implies. Repeatedly, however, we are reminded that this display of humanity is nothing but a show, and the more sagacious characters recognise the divinity that moves amongst them in human guise.

Specific passages of the text reveal that Duryodhana and his party are in fact *asuras*, beings representing the forces of evil and chaos, who have appeared on Earth to disturb the equilibrium of the creation. For this reason, Nārāyaṇa, the Supreme Deity, appears in this world to assist the righteous Pāṇḍavas in their conflict with these forces of evil. Thus we learn that the outcome of the conflict will be a certain victory for the Pāṇḍavas because they are assisted by Nārāyaṇa himself, who has appeared on Earth as an *avatāra*, literally one who has descended. Kṛṣṇa is hence the aloof controller of all the events that occur, for despite his human appearance he retains his divine omnipotence. Unlike the Christian doctrine of incarnation, Kṛṣṇa's humanity is purely an illusion; he is wholly divine, a full manifestation of God, and therefore possessing and displaying the omniscience and omnipotence of the Supreme Deity.

We must therefore note that it is in the *Mahābhārata* that we have the earliest expression of the Hindu doctrine of *avatāra*, which is clearly enunciated in Chapter 4 of the *Bhagavad-gītā* and in other passages of the *Mahābhārata* as well. Later Indian scriptures such as the *Viṣṇu Purāṇa* and the *Bhāgavata Purāṇa* expand upon the idea of *avatāra* and include a number of stories of the different forms of Nārāyaṇa who have appeared on Earth to save the situation at times of universal crisis. It is in the *Mahābhārata*, however, that we encounter the first representation of this major theme of Indian religious thought. Others amongst the more well-known *avatāras* are occasionally mentioned in the *Mahābhārata,* but the narratives are not developed and the doctrine of *avatāra* relates overwhelmingly to the activities of Kṛṣṇa described in different parts of the text. In contrast to the position of Rāma within the *Rāmāyaṇa,* the main focus of the *Mahābhārata* narrative is always on the Pāṇḍavas and their struggle for justice against their vicious cousins, but still to some extent the whole of the *Mahābhārata* can be taken as an *avatāra* story similar to those encountered in Purāṇic literature.

One final point we must notice in the context of any consideration of the *avatāra* in the *Mahābhārata* is the revelation of the *Bhagavad-gītā,* which is located early on in Book Six, the *Bhīṣma-parvan.* There are some who would argue that the *Bhagavad-gītā* should be regarded as an independent work and not as an integral part of the *Mahābhārata,* but based on the reasoning presented above we shall bracket this point of view. The point here would be that the *Bhagavad-gītā* pursues the same themes as the *Mahābhārata* as a whole, most notably in terms of the need to adhere to one's dharmic duty. In relation to the ongoing discussion of the descent of the *avatāra,* the *Bhagavad-gītā* makes an important contribution. As well as outlining the doctrine of *avatāra,* the *Gītā* also has much to say about Kṛṣṇa's divine nature, emphasising the omnipotence of the Deity, the extent of God's love, and the importance of divine grace in achieving liberation from this world. This discussion of the nature of God culminates in Chapter 11 of the *Gītā* where we have the stupendous vision of the glory of God, as Kṛṣṇa is revealed not just as the creator of the world but also, the pervasive presence that sustains the universal order. We can thus say that the idea of *avatāra,* the activities of Kṛṣṇa as an *avatāra,* and the eternal presence of God in this world comprise one of the principal themes pursued throughout the *Mahābhārata*'s narrative and didactic passages.

WHAT IS *DHARMA*?

The next major theme I wish to consider relates to the concept of *dharma*, what it is and how the people of this world should live in accordance with the concept. I think the best equivalents for the word *dharma* would be 'proper action', 'right living', or perhaps 'duty'. The central narrative offers us the character of Yudhiṣṭhira, who is referred to consistently as the *dharma-rāja*, the king who adheres strictly to *dharma*, and at the end of the *Mahābhārata* we learn that he performed only one unrighteous act in his life, and even that was based on advice given by Kṛṣṇa. Yudhiṣṭhira's understanding of *dharma* is of pure virtue: compassion, kindness, forgiveness, and absolute benevolence towards all living beings. He abhors the warfare he has to take part in and even after the victory of the Pāṇḍavas he is overwhelmed by remorse for the suffering and loss of life he may have caused.

There is no doubt that the *Mahābhārata* has great admiration and sympathy for Yudhiṣṭhira's understanding of *dharma*, and the way he puts his principles into practice throughout his life, but at the same time it also has misgivings about its practicality, particularly for a man whose duty it is to administer justice and protect the kingdom through might of arms. It may well be that the character of Yudhiṣṭhira is based to some extent on Aśoka, the Mauryan emperor who ruled most of India in the third century bce, and vowed to renounce violence after witnessing the horrors of warfare. Whether or not this is the case, we can observe how the *Mahābhārata* reflects on the practicality of pure virtue in a world beset by violence and iniquity without presenting us with simplistic answers to complex questions. Where I think the greatness of the *Mahābhārata* lies is in the fact that it does not give us such unequivocal responses, but rather develops and illustrates both sides of the debate whilst leaving us to use our own integrity and intelligence to determine each issue as it arises.

We are clearly meant to admire Yudhiṣṭhira's kindness, compassion, honesty, and virtue, and similarly to reject Duryodhana's opposite characteristics as a man of war and aggression who sees greed and competition as proper stimuli for human endeavour. Hence we are shown Yudhiṣṭhira's treatment of Dhṛtarāṣṭra and Gāndhārī, the father and mother of Duryodhana, after all their sons have been slain in battle. Rather than condemning them for supporting their son, Yudhiṣṭhira shows them all the respect due to elders of the family, providing for their every want, and granting as much largesse as they require to give charity on behalf of their dead sons to assist them in their passage to the next world. Bhīma, the second of the five Pāṇḍava brothers, has a different perspective, however, and cannot forgive Dhṛtarāṣṭra for the wrong the old man has done them. He taunts him and his wife for their loss of status, and on one occasion shows his thigh to remind them of how he killed Duryodhana.

At this juncture, we are drawn to Yudhiṣṭhira's compassion and forgiveness, and somewhat repulsed by Bhīma's vindictiveness. Earlier in the narrative, however, we have another incident that occurs while the Pāṇḍavas are living in exile and have adopted disguises to conceal their identity. In the court of King Virāṭa, Draupadī, their beautiful wife, is harassed and almost raped by Kīcaka, the commander of Virāṭa's army. Draupadī approaches Yudhiṣṭhira to tell him of the problems she is facing but he advises her that they must learn to tolerate all the misfortunes that have befallen them. She then informs Bhīma of her plight and he immediately takes robust action against the sexual predator, luring him into an assembly hall on the pretext of meeting Draupadī and then doing him to death.

In this incident, we find Yudhiṣṭhira's 'virtuous' response to be weak and insipid, and our sympathy is drawn towards Bhīma's warrior ethos. In this way, and throughout its narrative, the *Mahābhārata* explores the contradictions and complexities involved in trying to properly appreciate what is *dharma*. Again, Karṇa is presented as a man separated at birth from his real parents but given shelter by Duryodhana, to whom he owes a debt of loyalty. When conflict arises, he knows that Duryodhana is in the wrong and he knows that, because Kṛṣṇa is the Supreme Deity, the Pāṇḍavas' triumph is inevitable, but so great is his sense of loyalty that he fights and dies for Duryodhana, shot down by Arjuna, the third of the Pāṇḍava brothers. Similarly, in Dhṛtarāṣṭra we are presented with a man who longs to adhere to *dharma*, but is drawn away from the righteous path because of his affection for his own sons.

Throughout the epic narrative we are shown incidents and characters that highlight the nature of *dharma* and also the difficulties involved in applying the precepts of *dharma* consistently throughout one's life. In the didactic passages as well, we find various statements that give direct indications of what is the truth about *dharma*. To illustrate this point, a few examples must suffice at this preliminary stage of our discussion:

> Never displaying malice towards any living being through thoughts, words, or deeds; acts of kindness; giving charity. This the eternal *dharma* adhered to by righteous persons.[12]

> Not harming (*ahiṁsā*); truthfulness; remaining free from anger; charity; these are the four principles you must adhere to, Yudhiṣṭhira. This is the eternal *dharma*.[13]

---

12 *Āraṇyaka-parvan*, 281.34.

13 *Anuśāsana-parvan*, 147.22.

> The wise say that *dharma* is whatever is based on love. This is the characteristic mark of *dharma* that distinguishes it from *adharma*, Yudhiṣṭhira.[14]

These quotations serve to illustrate the point that was made above in asserting that there is thematic unity between the narrative and didactic portions of the *Mahābhārata*. In the narrative, we have various characters illustrating the precepts of *dharma*, and indeed the problems inherent in attempting to implement those precepts in all situations of life, and here we have those precepts laid out before us. The wisdom of the *Mahābhārata* is in its refusal to accept a simplistic dichotomy between good and evil, between *dharma* and *adharma*, and it illustrates this point most aptly in the scenes from the narrative in which the different characters are placed in a variety of situations that challenge them to determine what course of action is most proper.

Passages of Religious Teachings

Let us now move on to the third of the points mentioned above regarding the position of the *Mahābhārata* as primarily a religious scripture. By the end of the *Strī-parvan*, Book 11 of the eighteen books of the *Mahābhārata*, the narrative is more or less complete. The battle is over and Yudhiṣṭhira is triumphant. All that remains to be told is a brief account of Yudhiṣṭhira's reign, a description of the great sacrifice he performs to atone for his sins, and then the departure of the Pāṇḍavas to the Himalayas and their elevation to the realm of the gods. Still, however, almost half of the text remains and most of this is given over to words of practical, ethical, and spiritual instruction, given firstly by the dying Bhīṣma to

14 *Śānti-parvan*, 251.24.

Yudhiṣṭhira and then, in Book 14, the *Aśvamedhika-parvan*, by Kṛṣṇa to Arjuna. It will not be possible for the present work to provide a full account of the topics covered in these passages, but they are certainly wide-ranging and provide invaluable source material for any inquiry into Hindu religious teachings. In summary, in Book 12, the *Śānti-parvan*, Yudhiṣṭhira is first instructed in the duties of a king, *rāja-dharma*, then how a king may act in times of emergency, *āpad-dharma*, and finally how a person may pursue the spiritual goal of attaining liberation from rebirth, *mokṣa-dharma*. This is followed by Book 13, which is known as the *Anuśāsana-parvan*, the Book of Instruction, in which Yudhiṣṭhira receives guidance on a range of subjects, some secular and some religious.

Previous to these lengthy expositions, we have a number of shorter but extremely significant passages of religious teaching interjected within the central narrative, the most notable of which is surely the *Bhagavad-gītā*, which has been mentioned several times already. It is probably not an overstatement to assert that the *Bhagavad-gītā* is the most widely studied passage of scripture within the Hindu religious tradition. As mentioned above, some scholars choose to regard the *Bhagavad-gītā* as a separate work that should not be regarded as an integral part of the *Mahābhārata*; there is some justification for this view, as several of the great Hindu teachers of the past presented detailed commentaries on the *Gītā* alone without giving the same prominence to other passages of the *Mahābhārata*, although they do frequently cite verses from these passages in their commentaries. Overall, however, I am strongly of the view that the *Bhagavad-gītā* is best understood within the wider context of the *Mahābhārata* as a whole, primarily on the grounds of the thematic unity of the entire *Mahābhārata*. Hence when we consider the position of the *Mahābhārata* as a text that includes lengthy and significant passages of instruction on the nature of God, on the relationship of God to the created world, and on the way that liberation from rebirth may be attained, then the *Bhagavad-gītā* must be assigned a salient position within that discussion.

If we return to the teachings presented in Books 12, 13, and 14, the *Śānti, Anuśāsana,* and *Aśvamedhika-parvans,* we can observe that apart from the practical and ethical guidance they contain, which is varied and manifold, the teachings on *mokṣa-dharma* that are presented there are of particular significance in the development of Indian religious thought. It is in the third section of the *Śānti-parvan* that we encounter ideas that form the basis of the Sāṁkhya system, and which have a major influence on Yoga teachings such as those found in Patañjali's *Yoga Sūtras*. The Upaniṣad portion of the Vedas presents a mystical doctrine of absolute unity, which asserts that there is no distinction to be drawn between the ultimate divine principle (Brahman), the eternal spiritual entity existing within, or identical with, every being (*ātman*), and the world of matter that we inhabit. This is succinctly stated in the words of the *Chāndogya Upaniṣad*: *sarvaṁ khalv idaṁ brahma,* 'All this world is Brahman alone.'[15] Within the *Mahābhārata,* however, we find a radically different strand of Indian thought that emphasises distinction rather than the unity of the soul with the world it is forced to inhabit.

Generally speaking, it is the Upaniṣadic philosophy of absolute unity that receives more prominence, particularly in the Western world, but in terms of Hindu belief and practice the Sāṁkhya ideas of the *Mahābhārata* are equally important, as these provide a basis for theistic and devotional forms of religion wherein the *ātman* and the Deity are distinct, at least to some degree. The Sāṁkhya teachings of our text are generally non-theistic, but there are important passages that represent devotional religion dedicated to both Śiva and Nārāyaṇa, including the *Viṣṇu-sahasra-*

15 *Chāndogya Upaniṣad,* 3.14.1.

nāma-stotra, the thousand names of Viṣṇu (Nārāyaṇa), and the *Śiva-sahasra-nāma-stotra,* the thousand names of Śiva, both of which are employed in Hindu temple ritual.

The expositions of Sāṁkhya thought are frequently followed immediately by teachings on the practice of Yoga, as the two are regarded as complementary, the former providing the theoretical basis and the latter the concomitant forms of practice. At this early stage, Yoga did not include the range of bodily postures and exercises that are so widely practised today, but focused almost exclusively on the technique of deep meditation. The ultimate goal of this meditation was to withdraw the mind and senses from external perception and thereby to turn the focus inwards, eventually to the point where the mind was so controlled that it could be fixed on the spiritual entity, the *ātman* that is our true transcendent identity.

The Sāṁkhya teachings discuss the elements of which matter is comprised and then insist that the *ātman* is of a different, spiritual nature and is therefore eternal and unchanging. In the Upaniṣads, it is asserted that realisation of the absolute unity of our own identity with the ultimate reality is the means by which liberation from the material domain may be achieved. The Sāṁkhya teachings are somewhat similar, but they reveal that it is realisation of distinction that is the gateway to liberation, that being the distinction between the true self and its physical and psychical embodiments. Here there is no idea of unity, only of distinctiveness and individuality. The Yoga teachings that are found in close proximity to those on Sāṁkhya offer techniques of meditation whereby this theoretical revelation becomes realisation, as the eternal self becomes known through direct perception.

Hence when we consider the overall purview of Hindu religious thought, and the sacred texts that reveal the main ideas, we must be aware of the importance of the *Mahābhārata* as the earliest work in which highly significant strands of

Indian religious thought are located. We have the Sāṁkhya ideas that form a parallel strand to the Vedāntic ideology of the Upaniṣads; we have the earliest extant teachings on the practice of Yoga; and we also have foundational passages expounding some of the earliest known expressions of monotheistic and devotional Hinduism, dedicated both to Nārāyaṇa and to Śiva. Moreover, there are numerous considerations of other areas of doctrine and belief, such as the tension between destiny and free will, the sacred nature of cows, the importance of charity, the possibility of fully implementing the ideal of non-violence (*ahiṁsā*), and many others as well.

Summary of the Eighteen *Parvans* of the *Mahābhārata*

As was mentioned earlier, the *Mahābhārata* contains a total of eighteen *parvans*, or sections, which are named according to the principal content. These *parvans* vary enormously in length from the *Mahā-prasthānika-parvan*, Book 17, which contains only three chapters, to the *Śānti-parvan*, Book 12, which contains over 300. Moreover, some of the longer *parvans* are further divided into sub-*parvans*; so, for example the *Bhagavad-gītā* appears in the *Bhīṣma-parvan*, Book 6 of the *Mahābhārata*, which thus has a sub-*parvan* that is named the *Bhagavad-gītā-parvan*. With this in mind, I want now to carry on to a consideration of the content of the *Mahābhārata* as it is set out in each of its eighteen books.[16] This is, of necessity, a wholesale abbreviation of the content, but nonetheless does provide a valuable insight into the progression of the narrative structure as well as the different types of material that are to be encountered within the vast scope of the work.

16 See the summary 'List of the Eighteen *Parvans* of the *Mahābhārata*'.

List of the Eighteen Parvans of the Mahābhārata

Book	Title	Translation	No. of chapters
1	*Ādi-parvan*	Beginning	225
2	*Sabhā-parvan*	Assembly Hall	72
3	*Vana- or Āraṇyaka-parvan*	Forest	299
4	*Virāṭa-parvan*	Realm of Virāṭa	67
5	*Udyoga-parvan*	Preparations	197
6	*Bhīṣma-parvan*	Bhīṣma	117
7	*Droṇa-parvan*	Droṇa	173
8	*Karṇa-parvan*	Karṇa	69
9	*Śalya-parvan*	Śalya	64
10	*Sauptika-parvan*	Night-time	18
11	*Strī-parvan*	Women's	27
12	*Śānti-parvan*	Peace	353
13	*Anuśāsana-parvan*	Instruction	154
14	*Aśvamedhika-parvan*	Horse Sacrifice	96
15	*Āśrama-vāsika-parvan*	Living in a Hermitage	47
16	*Mausala-parvan*	Club Fight	9
17	*Mahā-prasthānika-parvan*	Great Journey	3
18	*Svargārohaṇa-parvan*	Ascent to the World of the Gods	5

Book 1. The Ādi-parvan

The *Ādi* (Beginning) *Parvan* presents an introduction to the whole *Mahābhārata* and sets the scene for the events to follow, introducing us to all of the major characters. It opens with a glorification of the religious significance of the *Mahābhārata* before describing the circumstances of its first recitation by Vaiśaṁpāyana, a disciple of the author of the work, Vyāsa himself. We are then told of Viṣṇu's descent as Kṛṣṇa in order to assist the gods in maintaining the order of creation, before the story proper begins with an account of King Śaṁtanu's marriage to the goddess Gaṅgā and the birth of their son Devavrata, later known as Bhīṣma. After Śaṁtanu questions why Gaṅgā has drowned all her sons bar one, she renounces him and returns to the heavens. Śaṁtanu then marries Satyavatī, who has previously given birth to Vyāsa as the son of the *ṛṣi* Parāśara. Only when Devavrata agrees to renounce his claim to the throne and remain celibate for life will Satyavatī's father permit the marriage, and because of this great – indeed, dreadful (*bhīṣma*) – vow, Devavrata is henceforth known as Bhīṣma. He is blessed by his father to meet with death only when it is his desire to do so.

Śaṁtanu and Satyavatī have two sons, Vicitravīrya and Citrāṅgada, both of whom die young without offspring. Satyavatī then summons her other son, Vyāsa, to beget children by their widowed queens, but because of their unwillingness to accept him, Dhṛtarāṣṭra is born blind, Pāṇḍu is born very pale, and Vidura is born as the son of a maid sent by the queen in her place. Although he is the eldest, Dhṛtarāṣṭra cannot become king because of his blindness, so after Śaṁtanu's death Pāṇḍu is crowned instead and by his prowess he establishes a great kingdom. Whilst hunting, however, he kills a *ṛṣi* who has taken the form of a deer and is cursed to die if he ever indulges in a sexual act. Pāṇḍu then renounces his throne, but his first wife, Kuntī, reveals that she has the power, granted by the *ṛṣi* Durvāsas, to summon any of the gods and to beget a son by them. On Pāṇḍu's urging, she begets Yudhiṣṭhira as the son of Dharma, the god of justice, Bhīma as the son of Vāyu, the wind god, and Arjuna as the son of Indra, the lord of the gods. Pāṇḍu's other wife, Mādrī, makes use of Kuntī's gift to give birth to the twins Nakula and Sahadeva as sons of the Aśvins, twin deities. Just after the birth of Yudhiṣṭhira, Gāndhārī, the wife of Dhṛtarāṣṭra, gives birth to a hundred sons, the eldest of whom is Duryodhana. Some time later Pāṇḍu passes away due to the *ṛṣi*'s curse when he falls prey to sexual desires which he attempts to fulfil with Mādrī.

Returning from their forest abode to the city of Hastināpura, the sons of Pāṇḍu receive military training alongside the sons of Dhṛtarāṣṭra, firstly from Kṛpa and then from Droṇa. This culminates in the display of military prowess in which Arjuna first encounters Karṇa and Bhīma faces Duryodhana. As the rivalry between the two sets of brothers develops, the Pāṇḍavas are sent to live in a house of shellac, which is burned down on Duryodhana's instruction. The Pāṇḍavas escape from the fire and then live in hiding, while the world thinks that they are dead. During this time, Bhīma kills the *rākṣasas* Hiḍimba and Baka, both fierce beings, and Arjuna wins Draupadī as their joint wife at a competitive wedding ceremony. Thereby an alliance is forged with King Drupada, her father, who is the ruler of the Pañcāla kingdom. When the Pāṇḍavas then return home, the kingdom is divided between Yudhiṣṭhira and Duryodhana, with the Pāṇḍavas getting a deserted wilderness as their share. With Kṛṣṇa's aid they develop this desolate region into a flourishing domain. Whilst travelling abroad, Arjuna develops a relationship with his cousin Kṛṣṇa, marries Kṛṣṇa's sister Subhadrā, and assists Agni, the fire-god, in the burning of the Khāṇḍava forest.

Book 2. The Sabhā-parvan

As the title suggests the main action recounted in the *Sabhā* (Assembly Hall) *Parvan* takes place in the assembly halls of the kings. It opens with Yudhiṣṭhira, now firmly established as the ruler of half the kingdom, wishing to regain his father's predominance over all the other kings of India. This can be achieved when he performs a *rājasūya-yajña,* the ritual of kingship. The main obstacle to this goal is Jarāsaṁdha, King of Magadha, but with Kṛṣṇa's guidance Jarāsaṁdha is killed in single combat by Bhīma.

The *rājasūya-yajña* then goes ahead and at its completion Kṛṣṇa is proclaimed as the leading guest amongst all the kings present. When Śiśupāla, the King of Cedis, challenges this and insults Kṛṣṇa, he is killed by Kṛṣṇa, who is revealed as an *avatāra* of Viṣṇu, the Supreme Deity. Duryodhana is also present, but becomes envious of the splendour of the Pāṇḍava domain and is mocked by Draupadī and others when he falls into a pool of water. This envy leads to the dice match in which Yudhiṣṭhira is defeated by Duryodhana's uncle, Śakuni, and loses all their possessions including their kingdom and even Draupadī, who is viciously insulted before the assembly. These events lead to an undeviating sense of enmity between the two factions. As a result of their defeat in the gambling match, the Pāṇḍavas are exiled in the wilderness for twelve years with a further year to be spent in hiding without being recognised. If they are discovered in this final year they will have to repeat the full duration of their banishment.

Book 3. The Vana- or Āraṇyaka-parvan

The lengthy *Āraṇyaka* (Forest) *Parvan* describes the sequence of extraordinary events that befall the Pāṇḍavas whilst they are enduring their years of exile in the forest. At the outset, we find the pious Yudhiṣṭhira delighted by the peace and tranquillity of forest life, but Bhīma and Draupadī criticise him for his lack of warlike tendencies. They wish to return immediately and attack their enemies, but Yudhiṣṭhira insists that there can be no breach of truth (*satya*), for that is *dharma*. Arjuna then departs for the world of the gods to acquire the celestial weapons they will need for the upcoming conflict, which now seems inevitable. He first encounters Śiva in the form of a hunter and after fighting with him receives Śiva's blessing and the promise of the invincible Pāśupata weapon.

Ascending to the realm of the gods, Arjuna dwells with Indra, his true father, but when he spurns the advances of the beautiful Urvaśī he is cursed by her to lose his manhood for one year. Meanwhile the four other Pāṇḍavas hear the story of Nala and Damayantī from the *ṛṣi* Bṛhadaśva and then travel with the *ṛṣis* Pulastya and Lomaśa to all the sacred *tīrthas*, pilgrimage sites, in order to acquire the purity and strength of *dharma* that will assist them in their struggles. In the course of this journey, numerous stories are told to them relating to the places and persons they visit. In the foothills of the Himalayas, Bhīma meets his half-brother Hanumān and fights with the servants of Kubera in order to obtain celestial lotus flowers for Draupadī. Here also Arjuna descends from the abode of Indra and is reunited with his brothers. Yudhiṣṭhira then frees all four of his brothers from Nahuṣa, who is in the form of a serpent, by answering his questions on *dharma*.

The Pāṇḍavas then meet with the *ṛṣi* Mārkaṇḍeya who instructs them at length about the glories of Nārāyaṇa, who has appeared on Earth as Kṛṣṇa. Kṛṣṇa himself comes to visit the Pāṇḍavas in the forest and at this time Draupadī instructs Satyabhāmā, one of Kṛṣṇa's wives, on the conduct of the perfect wife. Desiring to see the Pāṇḍavas in their state of disgrace and to mock them, Duryodhana comes with his supporters to the forest where his cousins are residing. However, they are defeated by the *gandharvas* (celestial beings associated with music) and Duryodhana is made their prisoner. Arjuna rescues Duryodhana, who is humiliated by this act of grace and becomes even more inimical towards his rescuers. Draupadī is then kidnapped by King Jayadratha but is rescued by Bhīma; Jayadratha is forgiven by Yudhiṣṭhira but, as with Duryodhana, his hatred for the Pāṇḍavas is only increased as a result of this magnanimous act. Meeting again with Mārkaṇḍeya, the Pāṇḍavas first hear from him the story of Rāma and Sītā, and then learn about Sāvitrī's saving her husband from the clutches of death. Finally, the *Āraṇyaka-parvan* relates how Karṇa gave his celestial armour and earrings in charity to Indra and how Yudhiṣṭhira again saved his brothers by satisfying a *yakṣa,* a nature spirit, with a wonderful discourse on the subject of *dharma*.

Book 4. The Virāṭa-parvan

The *Virāṭa-parvan* tells of how the Pāṇḍavas passed the final year of their exile in disguise, living secretly in the realm of Virāṭa, the King of the Matsyas. After the twelve years of exile in the forest are over, the Pāṇḍavas travel to the land of the Matsyas. They first hide their weapons in a tree and then take up employment in the service of King Virāṭa. Yudhiṣṭhira becomes a brahmin advisor to the king, Bhīma becomes his chief cook, Arjuna (who has lost his manhood for a year due to Urvaśī's curse) becomes a dancing instructor to the princess, Draupadī becomes a lady-in-waiting to the queen, Nakula takes charge of the king's horses, and Sahadeva supervises his herds of cows.

The arrangement runs into trouble when Kīcaka, the king's brother-in-law and the commander of his army, begins to harass Draupadī. Yudhiṣṭhira tells her to tolerate his advances, but Bhīma takes assertive action and beats Kīcaka to death. When Duryodhana and his allies come to hear about this, they suspect that the Pāṇḍavas may be residing with King Virāṭa and decide on a cattle raid against the Matsyas. They steal away Virāṭa's cows but are defeated by Arjuna, who has now resumed his true identity. Recognising Arjuna, the Kauravas claim that the terms of the agreement have been breached, but Bhīṣma rules that a whole year has in fact passed and that the Pāṇḍavas have kept their side of the bargain intact.

Book 5. The Udyoga-parvan

The *Udyoga* (Preparations) *Parvan* tells of the negotiations and preparations that take place before battle is joined at Kurukṣetra. After the thirteen years of exile are complete, Duryodhana still refuses to return the Pāṇḍavas' kingdom to them. Even when Yudhiṣṭhira asks for just five villages to rule, Duryodhana refuses. Then the Pāṇḍavas begin to call upon their friends and allies, and to gather an army for war. Firstly, Śalya, the King of the Madras and the maternal uncle of Nakula and Sahadeva, comes to join the Pāṇḍava host but he is welcomed and flattered by Duryodhana and as a result joins his faction. However, King Drupada of the Pañcālas and King Virāṭa of the Matsyas bring armies to support the Pāṇḍavas. Dhṛtarāṣṭra sends his minister, Saṁjaya, to urge the Pāṇḍavas to give up their preparations on the grounds that making war is always evil, but Yudhiṣṭhira rejects this disingenuous embassy.

Within the Pāṇḍava camp, however, there are significant debates over the nature of *dharma* and righteous action, with Yudhiṣṭhira speaking out against warfare and *kṣatriya-dharma*, the duties of the warrior class. In these debates he is opposed by his brothers, by Draupadī, and by Kṛṣṇa, who has joined the Pāṇḍava side but only as an advisor and chariot driver. He will not bear arms, as he is related to both sides. After hearing the Pāṇḍavas' reply to Saṁjaya's embassy, Dhṛtarāṣṭra then receives instruction on moral conduct from Vidura (the *Vidura-nīti*) and on spiritual wisdom from the sage Sanatsujāta.

In the Kuru assembly, Bhīṣma, Kṛpa, Droṇa, Dhṛtarāṣṭra, and Gāndhārī all urge Duryodhana to make peace but he will not listen to their advice even when it is revealed to him that Kṛṣṇa is an *avatāra* of Nārāyaṇa. Saṁjaya then instructs Dhṛtarāṣṭra further about Kṛṣṇa's divine identity. Meanwhile, the Pāṇḍavas decide to send Kṛṣṇa as a peace emissary to the city of Hastināpura. Although he is graciously received by the Kauravas, Duryodhana rejects his words and then attempts to make him a prisoner. This attempt is rebuffed by Kṛṣṇa, who displays his *viśva-rūpa*, in which all the gods and all the warriors are seen as being present within his own person. Kṛṣṇa then reveals to Karṇa the secret of his birth as the first son of Kuntī; he is hence a brother of the Pāṇḍavas. But even when Kuntī herself begs him to do so, Karṇa will not give up his loyalty to Duryodhana. As the armies gather and move towards Kurukṣetra, it is clear that war cannot be avoided. Bhīṣma is an incomparable warrior but now we are told of his one weakness. He will not fight the Pañcāla prince Śikhaṇḍin, for he knows that in a previous birth the latter was the princess Ambā who gave up her life when she was kidnapped by Bhīṣma as a wife for Vicitravīrya, and in the present life was originally born as a woman before being transformed into a man, and a mighty warrior.

Book 6. The Bhīṣma-parvan

As the name suggests, this book of the *Mahābhārata* gives an account of the first ten days of the battle when Bhīṣma commanded Duryodhana's army. We first hear of how Vyāsa granted divine vision to Saṁjaya so that he could relate to Dhṛtarāṣṭra everything that takes place at Kurukṣetra. This power is first used by Saṁjaya to describe all the different regions of the world. As the fighting is about to commence, we hear of Arjuna's unwillingness to fight with his relatives and elders, which is followed by Kṛṣṇa's instruction in the *Bhagavad-gītā*.

Meanwhile Bhīṣma derides the prowess of the boastful Karṇa and the latter withdraws, saying that he will not fight under the command of Bhīṣma. The battle then begins with extensive descriptions of the fighting and individual encounters between the great warriors of both sides. We hear that Arjuna is still fighting mildly and will not encounter Bhīṣma. On the first day, the Kauravas prevail and Yudhiṣṭhira is dispirited, but thereafter the Pāṇḍavas gain the upper hand and on each day drive back the Kaurava host. After the fifth day's fighting, Duryodhana questions Bhīṣma as to why they are not victorious despite their mighty commanders and superior numbers. Bhīṣma then instructs Duryodhana about Kṛṣṇa's divine nature and his identity as an *avatāra* of Nārāyaṇa.

Bhīma kills several of Duryodhana's brothers, but Arjuna still will not fight against Bhīṣma to the full limit of his strength. On two occasions, Kṛṣṇa becomes so frustrated with Arjuna that he begins to attack Bhīṣma himself and has to be restrained by Arjuna in order to keep intact Kṛṣṇa's vow not to take up arms. Bhīṣma finally decides to give up the fight; he grants permission for the Pāṇḍavas to kill him and tells them that Śikhaṇḍin should be stationed in front of Arjuna. Bhīṣma will not shoot arrows at Śikhaṇḍin and from this position Arjuna is able to pierce Bhīṣma with innumerable arrows until the latter falls to the ground. Lying mortally wounded on the field, Bhīṣma urges Duryodhana to make peace, but his words are ignored. He is also finally reconciled with Karṇa.

Book 7. The Droṇa-parvan

The *Droṇa-parvan* gives an account of the events that take place in the five days of the battle during which Droṇa commands

Duryodhana's army.[17] After the fall of Bhīṣma, Karṇa rejoins the Kaurava host and Droṇa is installed as their commander. Under Droṇa's grim leadership the fighting of the Kaurava army becomes more intense and the commander himself inflicts terrible casualties upon the Pāṇḍava host. Kṛṣṇa and Arjuna travel by night to Mount Kailāsa, where they receive the blessing of Śiva. Whilst Arjuna is fighting elsewhere, his son Abhimanyu penetrates to the heart of the Kaurava army but is surrounded and slain by six mighty warriors including Droṇa and Karṇa. The other Pāṇḍavas cannot help him because they are checked by Jayadratha (husband of Duḥśalā, the only sister of the one hundred Kaurava brothers). When Arjuna learns of his son's death, he vows that he will either kill Jayadratha the next day or else enter a fire and kill himself. Learning of this from spies, the Kauravas position Jayadratha so that he is protected by the entire army, but with Kṛṣṇa's aid Arjuna is still able to kill him at the very end of the day.

Enraged by this setback, Droṇa orders his forces to continue fighting all through the night and a terrible slaughter takes place in the confused battle that follows. Fighting on behalf of the Pāṇḍavas, Ghaṭotkaca (the son of Bhīma and a *rākṣasa* woman named Hiḍimbā) appears to be virtually invincible. Eventually Karṇa kills Ghaṭotkaca with the weapon he received from Indra; but this invincible weapon can be used only once and Karṇa had been saving it for his fight with Arjuna. Seeing the destruction caused by Droṇa and realising that there is no one who can kill him in battle, Kṛṣṇa suggests a strategy to remove him. If Droṇa learns that his son Aśvatthāman is dead, he will put aside his weapons in a state of grief. Yudhiṣṭhira is known as a man of *dharma*

17 Incidentally, there is not a single instance of Droṇa being called Droṇa in the *Droṇa-parvan*.

who is always truthful, and when he says that Aśvatthāman is dead, Droṇa believes the falsehood to be true. He puts aside his weapons and sits down on the battlefield to meditate. Taking this opportunity, Dhṛṣṭadyumna, the son of Drupada and brother of Draupadī, cuts off Droṇa's head. On learning what has happened, Aśvatthāman launches a ferocious attack on the Pāṇḍava army. The *Droṇa-parvan* ends with a vision seen by Arjuna of the destructive form of Śiva, which precedes him wherever he goes on the battlefield.

Book 8. The Karṇa-parvan

The *Karṇa-parvan* recounts the events that take place over the two days during which Karṇa is the commander of Duryodhana's army. After the death of Droṇa, Karṇa is made general of the Kauravas and he takes a vow to kill Arjuna, his arch-rival. Somewhat against his will, King Śalya of Madras is persuaded to be Karṇa's charioteer and some harsh words are exchanged between them. Karṇa launches a destructive attack against the Pāṇḍava army but is unable to gain complete victory. Except for Arjuna, each of the Pāṇḍavas in turn is defeated by Karṇa, but he does not kill them because of a promise he had made earlier to his mother Kuntī. Whilst Arjuna is elsewhere, Karṇa afflicts Yudhiṣṭhira with many arrow wounds and forces him to flee from the field in a humiliating fashion. When Arjuna returns, insults and harsh words are exchanged with Yudhiṣṭhira and a quarrel ensues which is resolved by Kṛṣṇa's discourse on *dharma*.

Arjuna then goes to confront Karṇa directly. The two great archers are evenly matched but Karṇa forgets the *mantras* he needs to fight effectively because of a curse from his *guru*, Paraśurāma. Due to another curse received by Karṇa, his chariot wheel becomes stuck in the ground and disabled. Karṇa begs Arjuna to follow the correct warrior ethos, the *kṣatriya-dharma,* and pause whilst he repairs his chariot, but Kṛṣṇa reminds him of the absence of *dharma* when Karṇa and five others killed Arjuna's son Abhimanyu. On Kṛṣṇa's instruction, Arjuna strikes down Karṇa whilst the latter is thus disadvantaged.

Book 9. The Śalya-parvan

The *Śalya-parvan* describes events on the final day of the battle when Śalya is the commander of the Kaurava army. After the death of Karṇa, Śalya is installed as the new general and fights heroically against the Pāṇḍava captains. Yudhiṣṭhira then kills Śalya and the remnants of the Kaurava host begin to flee from the field of battle. Sahadeva kills Śakuni and the last of Duryodhana's surviving brothers are killed by Bhīma. When his army is thus vanquished and put to flight, Duryodhana uses magical powers and seeks his own safety by hiding in the depths of a nearby lake. Taunted by the Pāṇḍava chieftains, Duryodhana emerges and agrees to fight with Bhīma in single combat.

There is then a lengthy account of the tour of the holy *tīrthas* along the Sarasvatī River made by Baladeva, Kṛṣṇa's brother. He arrives at Kurukṣetra just in time to witness Bhīma's club fight with Duryodhana. They are evenly matched, but following the advice of Kṛṣṇa and Arjuna, Bhīma strikes down Duryodhana with a foul blow to the thighs. Baladeva's anger over this action is restrained by Kṛṣṇa. Only three of the leading Kauravas survive the battle: Kṛtavarman, Kṛpa, and Aśvatthāman.

Book 10. The Sauptika-parvan

The *Sauptika* (Night-time) *Parvan* records the events that take place during the night that follows the last day of the battle, when Aśvatthāman enters the Pāṇḍava encampment and massacres all the surviving warriors apart from Kṛṣṇa and the five Pāṇḍava brothers. Having met with the dying Duryodhana and been encouraged by him to act, Kṛpa, Kṛtavarman, and Aśvatthāman decide to gain vengeance on their victorious adversaries. Accompanied and empowered by a manifestation of Śiva, Aśvatthāman enters the camp of the Pāṇḍava army and slaughters the warriors who are sleeping therein. This includes the five sons of Draupadī, one begotten by each of the five Pāṇḍavas. When the Pāṇḍava brothers learn of this terrible event, Bhīma and Arjuna set out in pursuit of Aśvatthāman, who fires a mystic arrow to scorch the womb of Uttarā, the wife of Abhimanyu, and thereby destroy the embryo that is the last surviving heir of the Pāṇḍavas. Arjuna then captures Aśvatthāman, but his life is spared because he is a brahmin by birth and is the son of their teacher.

Book 11. The Strī-parvan

The *Strī* (Women's) *Parvan* describes the lamentations of wives and mothers as they gather on the battlefield to look upon the bodies of their loved ones. The *parvan* opens with words of wise instruction being given to Dhṛtarāṣṭra by Vidura and Vyāsa to comfort him in his grief. Dhṛtarāṣṭra then goes to visit the battlefield with Gāndhārī; Kṛṣṇa and the Pāṇḍavas meet them there. Gāndhārī then roams across the field accompanied by Kṛṣṇa, pointing out to him the corpses of the great men who lie there. In a mood of anger, she curses Kṛṣṇa to the effect that his family will die at his own hand, for she believes that Kṛṣṇa had the power to prevent the war but chose not to. All the women of the various royal families then grieve for those who have fallen and arrange for the funerals to be performed on the banks of the Gaṅgā.

Book 12. The Śānti-parvan

The extensive *Śānti* (Peace) *Parvan* does not carry the narrative forward to any great extent. It is mainly devoted to the teachings delivered by Bhīṣma to Yudhiṣṭhira and the other Pāṇḍavas. Following on from the lamentations of the *Strī-parvan,* Yudhiṣṭhira condemns himself for his wickedness in waging war. He wants to renounce the kingdom they have won but is dissuaded from doing so by Kṛṣṇa, Vyāsa, his brothers, and Draupadī. They then go to where the stricken Bhīṣma is still lying on the battlefield, his body shot through with arrows. Bhīṣma first glorifies Kṛṣṇa and praises him as Nārāyaṇa, the Supreme Deity. The first set of instructions follows on from Yudhiṣṭhira's questions as to how he should rule the kingdom. This passage is known as the *Rāja-dharma-parvan* and indicates the ideal conduct of a righteous king. This is followed by a passage known as the *Āpad-dharma-parvan* wherein Bhīṣma teaches that the rules of virtue may be broken in times of emergency. Yudhiṣṭhira is unhappy about this line of discourse and again criticises the *kṣatriya-dharma* for its wicked tendencies.

Yudhiṣṭhira then inquires from Bhīṣma about the means of gaining liberation from rebirth and is presented with the *Mokṣa-dharma-parvan,* a series of treatises spoken by Bhīṣma which deal with renunciation of the world, Sāṁkhya philosophy, the practice of Yoga, and devotion to Viṣṇu. He concludes with a passage known as the *Nara-nārāyaṇīya,* or more commonly simply *Nārāyaṇīya,* which praises Nārāyaṇa (Viṣṇu) as the Supreme Deity and emphasises the path of *bhakti.*

Book 13. The Anuśāsana-parvan

In the *Anuśāsana* (Instruction) *Parvan,* Bhīṣma continues to give religious instruction to Yudhiṣṭhira. There is little, if any, action taking place here, and the entire book is given over to teachings on a wide variety of subjects. Before Bhīṣma resumes his discourse, Kṛṣṇa describes his own personal devotion to Śiva, gives an account of his initiation into Śiva *bhakti*, and then reveals the *Śiva-sahasra-nāma* prayer. Bhīṣma's opening topic is the role of destiny in our lives, the law of *karma*, and the limits of free will, but he quickly moves on to speak on proper conduct, the subject at the core of *dharma-śāstra* literature. He glorifies the brahmins as the leaders and gods of humanity, he describes the duties of the four *varṇas*, the social classes, he discusses the role of women in society, and he outlines the laws of inheritance.

Bhīṣma then teaches Yudhiṣṭhira about the rituals for worshipping the gods and how the *śrāddha* rites should be performed for departed ancestors. He also discusses charity, the reasons for accepting a vegetarian diet, veneration of the cow, and those persons from whom food may be freely accepted. From a Śaivite perspective, he tells of Śiva's giving instruction to the Goddess Umā, and then reveals the *Viṣṇu-sahasra-nāma* prayer. The final instruction given here to Yudhiṣṭhira is that he must always respect the brahmins and regard them as his superiors. Finally, Bhīṣma glorifies Kṛṣṇa as the Supreme Deity, and then as the sun has now moved into its northern transit, the *uttarāyaṇa*, he gives up his life in the presence of Kṛṣṇa.

Book 14. The Aśvamedhika-parvan

The *Aśvamedhika* (Horse Sacrifice) *Parvan* is concerned with the *yajña* Yudhiṣṭhira performs to atone for his sins, but in fact much of the book is devoted to further teachings delivered by Kṛṣṇa to Arjuna. At the outset of the *parvan*, Yudhiṣṭhira is still grieving and again condemns his own wickedness in causing the frightful carnage at Kurukṣetra. He is advised by Vyāsa that a horse sacrifice can atone for any sins he may be guilty of. As they are preparing for the *yajña,* Arjuna asks Kṛṣṇa to repeat the *Bhagavad-gītā* to him, as he has now forgotten its teachings. Kṛṣṇa replies by giving a new pattern of instruction, beginning with a passage known as the *Anugītā*. The ideas presented here are similar in many ways to the teachings imparted by Bhīṣma in the *Mokṣa-dharma-parvan* of the *Śānti-parvan*.

As Kṛṣṇa is returning to his home in Dvārakā, he encounters the *ṛṣi* Uttaṅka, who threatens to curse him for not stopping the war even though he possessed the power to do so. Kṛṣṇa advises that such a curse would be futile and then once more manifests the *viśva-rūpa* before the *ṛṣi*'s eyes. In Hastināpura, Yudhiṣṭhira prepares for the *aśvamedha* (horse sacrifice) ritual; when Kṛṣṇa returns there he revives the stillborn son of Uttarā and Abhimanyu who was scorched in the womb by the weapon of Aśvatthāman. This heir to the Pāṇḍava dynasty is named Parīkṣit. Arjuna re-establishes the dominion of Yudhiṣṭhira over all the kings of the land and then the *aśvamedha* ritual is performed. At the end of the sacrifice, however, the god Dharma appears in the form of a golden mongoose and says that this ceremony was not equal in religious merit to an act of charity performed by a hungry brahmin couple who gave away their food.

Book 15. The Āśrama-vāsika-parvan

The *Āśrama-vāsika* (Living in an *Āśrama*) *Parvan* tells of how the surviving elders of the family departed from Hastināpura to live a life of religious simplicity. At the beginning of the *parvan,* Yudhiṣṭhira again shows his generosity of spirit by providing Dhṛtarāṣṭra with the means to perform *śrāddha* rites for his dead sons, though Bhīma argues against this and mocks the old king. After these rituals have been performed, Dhṛtarāṣṭra, Vidura, Kuntī, and Gāndhārī secretly depart for the Himalayas to practise religious austerity. Later the Pāṇḍavas and their followers go to visit the elders in their *āśrama* and meet with them again. By the grace of Vyāsa, the slain warriors are able to descend from the realm of the gods and meet with comrades and adversaries still living; the old enmities are gone and they greet each other as friends. At the end of the *parvan*, we learn that Dhṛtarāṣṭra, Vidura, Kuntī, and Gāndhārī have all perished in a forest fire that swept through their *āśrama*.

Book 16. The Mausala-parvan

The *Mausala* (Club Fight) *Parvan* describes the destruction of Kṛṣṇa's family, and the death of Kṛṣṇa and his departure from this world. When Kṛṣṇa's sons play a trick on some *ṛṣis* by dressing one of them as a pregnant woman, the *ṛṣis* curse the family to destroy itself. Some time later when they are drinking liquor, a quarrel breaks out between them and they begin to fight. The fight continues until all of Kṛṣṇa's clan is destroyed. A short time later Kṛṣṇa is shot and killed by a hunter who mistakes him for a black deer. Kṛṣṇa then returns to his original position, passing beyond the three worlds and entering the abode of Viṣṇu. Soon after the departure of Kṛṣṇa, the sea breaks through the city walls and Dvārakā is flooded. Arjuna comes to provide protection for the women of the city, but in the absence of Kṛṣṇa his might is spent and he is defeated by a mere band of robbers.

Book 17. The Mahā-prasthānika-parvan

In the *Mahā-prasthānika* (Great Journey) *Parvan*, the Pāṇḍavas and Draupadī renounce their kingdom and set out for the Himalayas. As they walk along the path into the mountains, they fall one by one as a result of a flaw in their character. Yudhiṣṭhira carries on alone, accompanied only by a dog that has joined them. Arriving at the summit, Yudhiṣṭhira is greeted by the charioteer of the gods who has come to take him to the celestial sphere. However, he refuses to go without the dog that has become dependent upon him; this is the final test of his unlimited virtue.

Book 18. The Svargārohaṇa-parvan

In the *Svargārohaṇa* (Ascent to *Svarga*) *Parvan*, we are shown the main characters of the *Mahābhārata* residing in *svarga* (a celestial world) in the company of the gods. Yudhiṣṭhira first sees his brothers and Draupadī in hell and Duryodhana and his faction enjoying the delights of this heaven. Due to his presence the others are released from hell, but still Yudhiṣṭhira will not accept that those who lived wickedly deserve a place amongst the gods just because they followed *kṣatriya-dharma* and died bravely in battle. At the very end of the *Mahābhārata* this tension over *dharma* is left without any conclusive resolution.

This all too brief summarisation of the content of the *Mahābhārata* does no sort of justice to the full richness of this great work, but it does at least provide an insight into the form and structure of its various component parts. I hope it has also served to highlight some of the more significant themes that run throughout the books, themes that are addressed directly in the numerous passages of instruction and illustrated in the principal events described in such detail in the central narrative and in the various subplots. With this basis now established, we can proceed to explore those themes more fully and, hopefully, begin to recognise the great lessons for life that the *Mahābhārata* has to offer us.

Discussion Topic: Scope of the Work

Here are some questions you might care to ponder after completing this chapter:

- What do you think is the best way to refer to the *Mahābhārata*, as an epic, as a book of wisdom, or as a sacred text?
- Why do you think the *Mahābhārata* contains so many stories and passages of instruction that are not directly related to the central narrative?
- Even at this early stage in our study, can we give any sort of answer to the question, 'What is *dharma*?'
- What reasons can we give to explain why the *Mahābhārata* is such a vast text?

II
THE MAIN CHARACTERS OF THE *MAHĀBHĀRATA*

In this chapter, I want to focus primarily on the main characters who dominate the central narrative of the *Mahābhārata*, for to a significant extent it is by means of its complex characterisations that it highlights the central truths of its exposition. Whatever else it may be, the *Mahābhārata* is a book of instruction that provides a perfectly rounded insight into human nature and human conduct, which range from the sublime to the most foul. As mentioned in the previous chapter, the *Mahābhārata* contains numerous passages of direct instruction on a range of different ethical, religious, and spiritual topics, most of which are presented through the mouth of an enlightened sage or a person of notable wisdom. This direct approach, however, is not the only way in which instruction is given, for the narrative itself can be regarded as an extended didactic treatise in which the conduct and attitudes of the different characters provide a crucial insight into the dilemmas facing everyone existing in the human condition, and offers some solutions as to how these dilemmas might be resolved. What the *Mahābhārata* does not do, however, is offer simplistic answers based on a straightforward dichotomy between good and evil. Human life is not like that.

Thus we are presented with a succession of characterisations, some of virtuous and admirable individuals and others of persons who seem bereft of most of the more elevated human instincts. It goes further than that, however. By placing each of its characters in a range of different situations, it shows the problems, the tensions, and the genuine dilemmas all of us face in seeking to attain the fullness of our humanity. It often seems to be saying to us, 'Look at this, what do you think about that?' before turning a page and saying, 'Ah, but now have a look at this, are you sure you were right the first time?' In this way it generally avoids creedal pronouncements, but rather draws our attention to the reality of our predicament in life, and helps us along the way as we try to find the most apt solution in any given situation. This, in many ways, is the real delight of the *Mahābhārata*.

If we were seeking out a simple dichotomy between good and evil, such as that which exists between Rāma and Rāvaṇa in the *Rāmāyaṇa*, then we might turn to look at Yudhiṣṭhira, the eldest of the Pāṇḍavas, and Duryodhana, who has been described as Yudhiṣṭhira's dark antithesis. And yet, as we shall see, Yudhiṣṭhira is by no means beyond reproach and even Duryodhana is praised for his honour, for his loyalty to friends, and for his courage in facing his enemies. The *Mahābhārata* does not deal in simplistic truths.

In pursuit of this line of discussion, I now want to focus primarily on three of the main characters: Yudhiṣṭhira, who is certainly righteous, Duryodhana, who is certainly unrighteous, and finally Dhṛtarāṣṭra, who in terms of virtue or iniquity falls somewhere between these two. My feeling is that a consideration along these lines will shed a good deal of light on the perspectives the *Mahābhārata* is seeking to bring to our attention. Before that, however, I want to offer a relatively brief discussion of the other main characters in order to highlight the particular role that each of them plays in the progression of the narrative. There are undoubtedly others that could be added, but I think those discussed here cover most of the main personalities who take the stage at various points in this vast exhibition of epic storytelling.[18]

You will probably notice that Kṛṣṇa and his brother Baladeva are both omitted from what follows, as are the female characters. The reason for this is that we will look in some detail at the divinity of Kṛṣṇa in a future chapter, and we will also devote a single chapter to a consideration of the manner in which the *Mahābhārata* provides instruction on the role of women, a part of which will be given over to a discussion of the principal female protagonists.

Arjuna

Arjuna is the son of Pāṇḍu and Kuntī, although begotten by Indra, the lord of the gods. Arjuna is the great hero of the *Mahābhārata,* the mightiest warrior, whose prowess ensures the Pāṇḍavas' victory. Despite his *kṣatriya* ardour, however, he lacks the blood lust sometimes displayed by his elder brother, Bhīma. He also shares Yudhiṣṭhira's qualities of compassion and forgiveness, as displayed in his lament at the start of the *Bhagavad-gītā*. He is reluctant to kill Droṇa and Bhīṣma and it is because of this reticence that the *Bhagavad-gītā* is revealed to him. However, we are also informed that he is proud of his preeminence as a warrior and his behaviour towards Ekalavya and Karṇa is dishonest, haughty, and contemptuous in a manner that we do not see in Yudhiṣṭhira. As the Pāṇḍavas proceed towards the Himalayas in the *Mahāprasthānika-parvan,* Arjuna falls and is forced to experience death because of his pride in his own martial prowess and his disregard for other warriors.

18 The Genealogical Tree in the Appendix summarises the relationships between the major characters.

Bhīma

Bhīma is the exemplar of the *kṣatriya-dharma* and through his character we are shown the need for this type of person in specific situations. When Draupadī is insulted after the gambling match, kidnapped by Jayadratha, and harassed by the lustful Kīcaka, we feel that Bhīma's resolute response might be more appropriate than Yudhiṣṭhira's constant call for tolerance. But his violence, greed, and vengefulness are *kṣatriya* qualities that are at times in conflict with notions of virtue. Bhīma is in many ways ideally suited for kingship, and his attitude and demeanour are very similar to those recommended by Bhīṣma to Yudhiṣṭhira in his teachings on kingship in the *Rāja-dharma* section of the *Śānti-parvan*. As an enforcer of the law and a chastiser of violent miscreants, Bhīma is a more effective person than Yudhiṣṭhira, and hence is closer to the ideals of the *kṣatriya-dharma*. The darker side of this tendency is displayed on the battlefield when Bhīma takes delight in slaying his enemies, and when he kills Duḥśāsana and drinks the blood of his adversary. On the final journey to the Himalayas, Bhīma falls from the path and this sad event is explained as being the result of his greed for food, his arrogance over his own strength, and his disregard for others whilst eating.

Karṇa

Karṇa is in many ways one of the most unfortunate characters in the whole drama of the *Mahābhārata*, as he was born as the elder brother of the Pāṇḍavas, fathered by the sun-god Sūrya, but was abandoned by his mother and forced to grow up in obscurity. He becomes a loyal comrade of Duryodhana and is then obliged to fight against his own brothers because of that oath of loyalty. He knows that he will not survive the battle, but regards it as a solemn duty to support Duryodhana and thus goes to his death at the hands of Arjuna. When, in the *Udyoga-parvan*, Kṛṣṇa tries to persuade him to join with his brothers, his honest response shows clearly that he knows right from wrong. He is also aware of Kṛṣṇa's divinity and of the inevitable defeat of the Kaurava army – at least in his more reflective moments.

Yet at other times his conduct is vile and immoral. His behaviour in the insulting of Draupadī is atrocious, his arrogance is sometimes unbearable, and we might also criticise him for his excessive loyalty to a wicked man. But here is the subtlety of the *Mahābhārata*, for we can surely make some allowances for one who has been dealt such a poor hand by destiny. Considering the manner in which he was abandoned by his mother and brought up in a demeaning position where he was subject to cruel insults from the Pāṇḍavas, we can perhaps understand why Karṇa was prone to these faults, although we cannot entirely excuse them.

The crucial debate raised by the life of Karṇa centres on the issue of *dharma* and loyalty. Karṇa's nature is that of a *kṣatriya* and his loyalty to Duryodhana is an expression of *kṣatriya-dharma*. In our own lives we would value a sense of loyalty to our family, our community, and our nation. But in its storytelling the *Mahābhārata* is also pointing out to us that loyalty and devotion of this kind can be problematic and misguided. What happens when one's family, community, or nation strays into the realm of wickedness and *adharma*? Should one continue to show loyalty to a family member, friend, or ally in a dispute in which he or she has acted in an immoral fashion? And at what point should one terminate that relationship? Is a commitment to *dharma* more binding than the loyalty one owes to family, friends, community, and nation? These are some of the issues explored by the *Mahābhārata* in its characterisation of Karṇa.

Nakula and Sahadeva

I have included these two youngest of the five Pāṇḍava brothers together partly because they are twins but also because they have a relatively minor role in the structure of the *Mahābhārata*'s narrative, and do not display character traits that are much dissimilar from one another. They are sons of Mādrī, Pāṇḍu's second wife, born of the Aśvins, who are themselves twin deities amongst the Vedic gods. In general, they do not take on the leading role played by their three elder brothers, but we do learn some things about them as events unfold. When the Pāṇḍavas are in hiding in the realm of King Virāṭa, Nakula worked in the royal stables because of his expertise in training horses, whilst Sahadeva tended the cows. In the battle at Kurukṣetra, both twins were successful in a number of encounters, the most notable being Nakula's killing of the three sons of Karṇa and Sahadeva's slaying of the hated Śakuni. On the final journey to the Himalayas, we learn that Sahadeva had great wisdom whilst Nakula was the most handsome of men; both of them fall and taste death because they had pride in these attributes.

Bhīṣma

In many ways, Bhīṣma is to be regarded as one of the most righteous and sagacious characters in the *Mahābhārata*, and yet there are some things about him that seem not quite right. These arise primarily from his absolute adherence to the *kṣatriya* code, an adherence that at times causes him to disregard the virtue exemplified by Yudhiṣṭhira. He is certainly a man of wisdom who can easily see through the wickedness of Duryodhana and the weakness of Dhṛtarāṣṭra. He fully understands the divine nature of Kṛṣṇa and expresses his devotion to him. He is also a great teacher who imparts religious instruction to Yudhiṣṭhira in a whole range of areas, including *dharma*, ethics, Yoga, *bhakti*, and the paths to *mokṣa*.

We are constantly aware of his wisdom and his absence of sensual desire, but at the same time the dedication he shows to his vows is sometimes cruel. Why does he side with Duryodhana? Why does he not intervene to stop the insulting of Draupadī? Why does he show such little regard for Ambā's misfortune? It is interesting to note that in his teachings to Yudhiṣṭhira, he emphasises the importance of *kṣatriya-dharma* and all that this entails. He even goes so far as to criticise Yudhiṣṭhira for his weakness, his tolerance, and his compassion, which in his view make the eldest of the Pāṇḍavas unsuitable to rule. Here perhaps we are seeing the tension between Yudhiṣṭhira's virtue and the harsher realism of the *kṣatriya* view. And despite the profundity of his vision, Bhīṣma consistently favours the latter perspective.

DROṆA

Like Bhīṣma, Droṇa is a man of great wisdom and a wise teacher who knows proper conduct and duty. In the debates that precede the conflict at Kurukṣetra, he shows that he understands perfectly well the vicious temperament of Duryodhana and his faction, and the purity and virtue of the Pāṇḍavas. And yet, as with Bhīṣma, there is something troubling about Droṇa's character. He is a brahmin and fulfils his social *dharma* by acting as a tutor to both the Pāṇḍavas and the Kauravas, training them in the disciplines of battle. However, when war breaks out he goes beyond this brahmanical role as a teacher, and fights vigorously on behalf of Duryodhana. This action raises significant questions about *dharma*, and whether it is appropriate for a brahmin to undertake acts of violence. Courage in battle is a part of the *kṣatriya-dharma* that Kṛṣṇa mentions in the *Bhagavad-gītā* (18.43), but it is not the *dharma* of a brahmin.

We might also note that it is whilst Droṇa is the commander of the Kaurava host that the fighting becomes even more vicious and all respect for the rules of righteous conflict is abandoned. He continues to lead the army forward even when night has fallen and he participates in the cruel killing of Abhimanyu. Whilst there is no doubt that Droṇa is a man of virtue and wisdom, there are significant doubts about his character. Pandering to Arjuna's vanity, he is cruel to Ekalavya; his attitude towards Drupada is patronising and superior; he silently tolerates the abuse of Draupadī in the assembly; he participates in warfare and violence; and because he accepts patronage from the Kauravas he feels obliged to fight for Duryodhana, thereby taking up the cause of *adharma*.

One gets the sense that in the character of Droṇa, and indeed his son Aśvatthāman, the *Mahābhārata* is showing the dangers of a brahmin taking to the duties of a *kṣatriya*. It is unnatural for one who is by nature a brahmin to engage in warfare, and when Droṇa takes up that role the result is that the fighting reaches an extremity of harshness and cruelty. As Kṛṣṇa says in the *Gītā*, *para-dharmo bhayāvahaḥ*, taking to another's *dharma* is a source of fear and danger (3.35).

Aśvatthāman

As the son of Droṇa, Aśvatthāman follows his father's path in developing expertise in the arts of war, and, along with Arjuna, receives private instruction from his father in the use of the most deadly weapons. It is on the battlefield that Aśvatthāman comes to the fore as a central character, first of all proving himself to be a powerful adversary for the Pāṇḍavas, including his role in the unrighteous killing of Abhimanyu, and then slaughtering the surviving warriors in the Pāṇḍava camp after the battle is over. In the prosecution of that slaughter it is said that Aśvatthāman became possessed by the destructive potency of Śiva, and later texts, though not the *Mahābhārata* itself, refer to him as an *avatāra* of Śiva.

Even after this dreadful act of violence is accomplished, Aśvatthāman's wrath is still not assuaged and he attempts to destroy the embryo of the last surviving heir of the Pāṇḍavas, Abhimanyu's son Parīkṣit, who is still unborn in the womb of his widowed wife Uttarā. The unborn child is protected by Kṛṣṇa and Aśvatthāman is captured by Arjuna, but is released on the order of Yudhiṣṭhira because he is a brahmin and the son of their teacher. As with his father Droṇa, the life and conduct of Aśvatthāman would appear to demonstrate the fearful consequences of a brahmin turning to the violent *dharma* of a *kṣatriya*. It is not appropriate and the consequences are frightful.

Duḥśāsana

Duḥśāsana is represented as being the most evil-minded of all the sons of Dhṛtarāṣṭra, more worthy of contempt than even his elder brother, Duryodhana. He is an eager participant in all the Kauravas' schemes against the Pāṇḍavas and he plays a central role in the humiliation of Draupadī, attempting to disrobe her and force her to stand naked in the assembly of the Kauravas. In line with his promise made at the time of this frightful act, Bhīma strikes down Duḥśāsana on the battlefield, tears out his heart, and drinks his blood. Duḥśāsana is probably the worst of all the characters we encounter within the *Mahābhārata*. He has none of Duryodhana's sophistication and engages in the worst type of action, albeit with the permission and approval of Duryodhana, and indeed Karṇa. When he meets his terrible death at the hands of Bhīma, we are left with the dilemma of deciding whether his brutal demise is the just desert warranted by such a vile individual, or whether the cruelty of his death represents an act of unacceptable violence.

Śakuni, Kīcaka, and Jayadratha

Although Śakuni, Kīcaka, and Jayadratha are relatively minor characters in the *Mahābhārata*'s narrative, they serve to demonstrate the darker side of *kṣatriya-dharma*. These are arrogant men driven by their desires who regard their position of power and kingship merely as an opportunity for gaining sensual pleasure. Hence they display an arrant disregard for virtue and have neither respect nor regard for others. Both Kīcaka and Jayadratha clearly regard women as objects to serve their selfish indulgence in sensual delights, and when they are rejected by women they resort to the use of brute force; these assaults on women surely demonstrate some of the most contemptible conduct we witness in the chapters of the *Mahābhārata*. Men such as these represent the forces of wickedness against which true *kṣatriyas* must contend. Hence we cannot but feel a degree of satisfaction when Kīcaka is killed by Bhīma and Jayadratha is humiliated by him. Śakuni's false conduct in the dice match reveals the iniquity of deceit, dishonesty, and cheating, and the *Mahābhārata* uses his character to demonstrate the negative results of this manner of dealing with others. In the hands of such a cunning malefactor, the innocent are exploited and deceived; the *kṣatriya-dharma* exists so that persons of this type can be punished and held in check.

Drupada

Drupada is the King of the Pañcālas, the father of Draupadī and Dhṛṣṭadyumna, who is a bitter foe of Droṇa. He is named in the *Gītā* as one of the leading warriors in the Pāṇḍava host and it is his son, Dhṛṣṭadyumna, who arranges their army and strikes the final blow that cuts off the head of Droṇa. Drupada himself dies in combat on the field of battle.

Virāṭa

Virāṭa is the King of the Matsyas in whose kingdom the five Pāṇḍava brothers live in disguise during the final year of their exile. With the aid of the Pāṇḍavas, he resists an attack on his kingdom by the Kauravas and he then gives his daughter Uttarā in marriage to Arjuna's son Abhimanyu. It is from this union that Parīkṣit is born as the sole surviving heir of the Pāṇḍava dynasty. Like Drupada, he loses his life in combat on the field of battle at Kurukṣetra.

Śalya

Śalya is the King of the Madras and the brother of Mādrī, Pāṇḍu's second wife. As such he is the uncle of Nakula and Sahadeva. Prior to the conflict at Kurukṣetra, he brings his army to fight alongside the Pāṇḍavas but is deceived by Duryodhana into taking the side of the Kauravas. After the death of Droṇa, he reluctantly agrees to act as the charioteer of Karṇa, whom he despises for his lower birth, and then, following the death of Karṇa, he is made commander of the much diminished Kaurava host for the final day of the eighteen-day conflict, but is struck down and killed by Yudhiṣṭhira.

Each of these character sketches could be continued at much greater length and it may be that your own opinions about some of them differ from the views expressed above. This is to be expected, for the *Mahābhārata* is rarely dogmatic in its vision. I want now to look in more detail at three of the central figures in the narrative, with a specific focus on exploring the manner in which the *Mahābhārata* uses its characterisations to reveal fundamental truths about human nature and about how we must seek to centre our lives on the ideals of *dharma*. We will begin with Yudhiṣṭhira, followed by Duryodhana and Dhṛtarāṣṭra.

Yudhiṣṭhira

I know well enough from discussions with Hindu friends that opinions will certainly vary about the character and qualities displayed by the eldest of the Pāṇḍavas. There can be no doubt that the *Mahābhārata* regards him in a very positive light, but his virtuous nature is not without blemish and on several occasions he is criticised for his unrealistic notions about *dharma*.

Throughout the *Mahābhārata*, there is a recurring tension between Yudhiṣṭhira's moral sense and the dharmic duties imposed upon him by his birth as a *kṣatriya*. Let us first consider the character and conduct of Yudhiṣṭhira from the perspective of his own view of *dharma* as virtue. Although they are never mere two-dimensional personalities, there is a clear sense in which Yudhiṣṭhira and Duryodhana are depicted as representing what is worthy and what is unworthy in humanity, and thereby present a moral treatise in narrative form. It is noteworthy that although we are constantly aware of the superiority of Yudhiṣṭhira's character over that of Duryodhana, this is based on virtue and not ritual or social ethics, as will be discussed more fully in a later chapter. In the execution of *kṣatriya-dharma*, Duryodhana may even be regarded as Yudhiṣṭhira's superior, for he is always keen to do battle and gives up his life in the ideal *kṣatriya* manner, while Yudhiṣṭhira is often timid and has no taste for warfare or punishment. Thus the *Mahābhārata*'s repeated stress on Yudhiṣṭhira's excellence is to be recognised as an emphasis on the importance of pure virtue.

The good character of Yudhiṣṭhira is repeatedly revealed throughout the narrative, with a number of passages specifically listing his qualities, and others demonstrating them by descriptions of his behaviour. When urging his son to make peace in the *Udyoga-parvan*, Dhṛtarāṣṭra describes Yudhiṣṭhira as true to his word, always diligent, devoted to the words of scripture, obedient to his family, loved by his subjects, kind to his friends, in control of his senses, and a protector of the righteous. Furthermore, he displays forbearance, tolerance, self-control, and honesty; he is always truthful, accepts good advice, and is compassionate to all beings.[19]

In the *Āraṇyaka-parvan*, we are given Kṛṣṇa's view of Yudhiṣṭhira's virtues and here it is notable how he emphasises his adherence to *kṣatriya-dharma* as well as his moral excellence. Kṛṣṇa praises Yudhiṣṭhira as follows:

> *Dharma* is greater than the winning of a kingdom and they describe the execution of *dharma* as an act of austerity. By executing the duties of your *dharma* with truth and honesty, you have conquered both this world and the next. In the beginning, you engaged in study, following various vows, and absorbed the complete science of warfare; having gained possessions and wealth through *kṣatriya-dharma*, you have executed all the traditional sacrifices. You take no delight in licentious pleasures and you do not strive in any way after the objects of enjoyment. You never abandon *dharma* because of greed, and thus, because of your nature, you are the *dharma-rāja*. Having won lands, riches, and objects of pleasure, your greatest delight is always in charity, truthfulness, austerity, faith, tranquillity, determination, and tolerance.[20]

These and other similar passages give some insight into the qualities that the *Mahābhārata* regards highly in its view of moral conduct. This understanding is one that is common to moralists of most cultures, emphasising truthfulness, honesty, loyalty,

19 *Udyoga-parvan*, 147.32–33.

20 *Āraṇyaka-parvan*, 180.16–19.

kindness, compassion, tolerance, self-control, and the restraint of lust, avarice, and anger. The teaching is presented far more effectively, however, by the portrayal of the life of Yudhiṣṭhira in which he is shown as the paragon of all the virtues that are universally admired. He is consistently portrayed as being of a gentle disposition with constant goodwill towards other living beings. He is kind and forgiving, tolerant and forbearing, and always anxious to avoid conflict of any kind. He is also notably non-competitive in his attitude towards others, transcending such worldly preoccupations by the strength of his virtue.

Following Jayadratha's assault on Draupadī, Bhīma argues that the offender should be slain for such a gross misdemeanour, but Yudhiṣṭhira exhibits the virtues of mercy, tolerance, and avoidance of anger in ordering that he be set free, punished only by humiliation and admonition.[21] His powers of forgiveness are similarly demonstrated by his attitude to Dhṛtarāṣṭra after the battle, again in marked contrast to that of Bhīma. Whilst the latter continues to bear a grudge against the old king for the wrongs he has done to them, Yudhiṣṭhira displays no ill will whatsoever and provides for his uncle's needs and wishes (Chapter 3 of the *Āśrama-vāsika-parvan*). Only on rare occasions in the heat of battle does Yudhiṣṭhira fall prey to anger and as a general rule he is able to withstand even the most extreme provocation, as at the conclusion of the dice match and in the kingdom of Virāṭa when Kīcaka harasses Draupadī. His truthfulness is likewise renowned; he will not deviate at all from the terms of their exile because he has given his word, and when he announces on the battlefield that Aśvatthāman is slain, Droṇa cannot doubt that it is so. This was the onlyuntruth that he ever spoke in his life and, according to the *Svargārohaṇa-parvan*, his only sinful act.[22]

21 *Āraṇyaka-parvan*, 256.7.

22 *Svargārohaṇa-parvan*, 3.14.

In the opening chapter of the *Āraṇyaka-parvan,* we are shown the quality of humility in Yudhiṣṭhira. As the Pāṇḍavas are departing for their exile, the citizens of Hastināpura glorify them with extravagant words of praise, but Yudhiṣṭhira disclaims these eulogies. Similarly, after the battle he repeatedly condemns himself as a great sinner for causing the suffering that has taken place and will not accept any of the speeches from his comrades which exonerate him from blame. As a king, he demonstrates his compassionate nature and his concern for others. After his victory at Kurukṣetra, he ensures that provision is made for the welfare of the women who have been widowed, as well as for the poor and the blind.[23] This characteristic is further demonstrated by his behaviour at the very end of his life when he refuses to enter the realm of the gods if that means he must abandon a dog that has followed him for many miles and looks to him for shelter.[24]

Though born a *kṣatriya,* Yudhiṣṭhira repeatedly expresses his loathing for violence and displays little of the desire for power that besets most kings and political leaders.[25] Though he wages war to regain the kingdom which has been stolen from him, he does so only because he is persuaded that it is a matter of principle and because Kṛṣṇa is the main advocate of conflict. He takes up arms not because of a desire for riches or vengeance, but because it is his duty;[26] for himself, he is shown as being delighted by the simple life in the forest

23 *Śānti-parvan,* 42.10–12.

24 *Mahā-prasthānika-parvan,* 17.3.7.

25 *Āraṇyaka-parvan,* 253.21.

26 Yudhiṣṭhira, nevertheless, says several times after the war that the slaughter was caused by the Pāṇḍavas desire for *artha* (wealth/power).

without any form of opulence. It seems therefore that he was a practitioner of *karma-yoga* even before instruction on that mode of action was given to Arjuna in the *Bhagavad-gītā*.

You will of course notice that the character of Yudhiṣṭhira has thus far been represented in a very positive light, and that the incidents referred to tend to show the very best side of his character. There are other passages in the *Mahābhārata*, however, that would appear to show the downside of his personality. In this regard, I would point to the gambling match where he loses his composure and as a result exposes his wife and brothers to humiliation and years of suffering. Moreover, on the battlefield, he is at times less than heroic in the way he confronts the enemy, and this timidity leads him to quarrel with Arjuna and to insult his brother. We will look at this issue in more detail and review these apparent shortcomings later on when we look at the *Mahābhārata*'s consideration of *dharma*, but I think we must accept that overall Yudhiṣṭhira is to be regarded as the most virtuous of all its characters. This quality of pure virtue is referred to frequently by many of the principal speakers and in the end it is Yudhiṣṭhira alone who is able to reach the realm of the gods without tasting the pain of death, for he was a man virtually without sin.

I want now to present three short extracts from the *Mahābhārata*, which give some insight into Yudhiṣṭhira's character and the way he is represented as the personification of *dharma*. These are my own summarisations of the relevant passages of the Sanskrit text.

Extract 1

> While the Pāṇḍavas were exiled in the forest, Jayadratha, the King of Sindhu, happened to pass by the *āśrama* where they were staying. At that time Draupadī was there alone. Struck by her beauty, Jayadratha began to praise her wonderful appearance, but he was immediately rebuffed

by the princess, who informed him that his manner of address was inappropriate as she was the wife of the five Pāṇḍavas. She then asked him to wait there for a while so that her husbands might receive him as a guest and show him due respect.

Smitten with attraction for her, however, Jayadratha continued to misbehave, urging her to abandon her husbands in their state of misfortune and become his queen instead so that she could once again enjoy the opulence of a regal position. Now becoming angry, Draupadī rebuked him once more, this time more sternly, and warned him of the consequences if he persisted, for her husbands are all great heroes. Jayadratha then laid hands upon her, forcing her into his chariot and departing from that place with her. When the Pāṇḍavas returned and learned from Draupadī's maid what had happened, they set off in pursuit of the kidnapper. Jayadratha's forces turned to face their pursuers but were quickly brushed aside by the mighty Pāṇḍavas. Seeing what was happening, Jayadratha was terrified. He set Draupadī down from his chariot and attempted to make his escape. When Draupadī was rescued, Yudhiṣṭhira asked Sahadeva to take her on his chariot. Arjuna then turned to Yudhiṣṭhira and said, 'Now that the army of Jayadratha is destroyed, you can take Draupadī back to the *āśrama* and comfort her. I will pursue Jayadratha to the ends of the Earth and through the heavens as well if necessary.'

Yudhiṣṭhira replied, 'Jayadratha is the husband of Duḥśalā, who is the daughter of our aunt, Gāndhārī, so he is not to be slain despite his wickedness. We must not make our sister a widow.' On hearing these words, Draupadī called out to Bhīma and Arjuna, 'If you wish to please me then kill that miserable wretch who is the King of Sindhu-Sauvīra. One who carries off another person's wife should never be spared even if he begs for mercy!'

Although Jayadratha was now two miles away, Arjuna still shot down his horses, and Bhīma, following in a chariot, caught him by the hair and gave him a sound beating before throwing him to the ground. Restrained by Arjuna, Bhīma said, 'This cruel wretch deserves to die for his treatment of Draupadī. But what can I do! The king is always so merciful and even you put obstacles in my path because of a childish sense of *dharma*!' Bhīma then shaved off Jayadratha's hair with a razor-sharp arrow and ordered him to travel throughout the land proclaiming himself to be the slave of the Pāṇḍavas. Terrified by his position, Jayadratha replied, 'It will be so.'

They then took Jayadratha back to the *āśrama*. Bhīma said to Yudhiṣṭhira, 'Please comfort Draupadī by telling her that this villain has become the slave of the Pāṇḍavas.' Feeling affection for his younger brother, Yudhiṣṭhira replied, 'If you have any regard for me, then set this wretched man free.' Understanding her eldest husband's mind, Draupadī then said, 'Let him go. He has become the king's slave and you have also disfigured him by cutting off his hair.' Jayadratha then grovelled at the feet of Yudhiṣṭhira and paid his respects to the holy men of the *āśrama* who lived with him. Seeing Jayadratha in that condition, having been so soundly beaten by Bhīma that he could only stand with Arjuna's support, Yudhiṣṭhira said to him, 'You are now at liberty, I set you free. Now go on your way and never do such a thing again. Shame on you! You intended to take a lady away by force even though you have no real strength. Who else would even think of acting in such a way?' But seeing Jayadratha's plight and his misery, Yudhiṣṭhira was then filled with pity and spoke to him again, 'May your heart now cleave towards *dharma*. Never again set your heart on immoral acts. Now you may depart in peace with those of your companions who have not been killed.'[27]

27 From Chapters 248 to 253 of the *Āraṇyaka-parvan*.

Extract 2

After the death of Duryodhana and his followers at Kurukṣetra, Yudhiṣṭhira became king at Hastināpura with the support and aid of his four brothers. Vidura, Saṁjaya, and Kṛpa continued to serve Dhṛtarāṣṭra, and Vyāsa, his actual father, used to recite stories from the Purāṇas to him. Dhṛtarāṣṭra would sometimes set prisoners free and pardon those who had been condemned to death as if he were still the king, but Yudhiṣṭhira never said anything about this. The son of Pāṇḍu used to supply him with costly robes and excellent foods, and all the kings who came there used to first offer their respects to Dhṛtarāṣṭra. Fearing that his blind uncle would grieve excessively over the death of his sons, Yudhiṣṭhira urged his brothers to ensure that all his needs and desires were met and they too always showed him respect. Bhīma, however, was the exception here, for his heart was still hard towards his uncle, understanding that all their woes, beginning from the dice match, had been caused by the wickedness of his heart.

In this way, Dhṛtarāṣṭra continued to live happily in Hastināpura. Devoid of malice as he was, Yudhiṣṭhira was always respectful to his uncle and ordered all the members of his household to act in the same way. When the days arrived on which *śrāddha* offerings were to be made on behalf of departed relatives, Yudhiṣṭhira ensured that Dhṛtarāṣṭra had money to give in charity to the brahmins on behalf of his dead sons. Thus did that foremost of righteous men, Yudhiṣṭhira the Just, who possessed great intelligence, show his respect to Dhṛtarāṣṭra along with his brothers. Seeing no ill will in Yudhiṣṭhira, and recognising that his conduct was always wise and virtuous, Dhṛtarāṣṭra gave up any sense of animosity towards the Pāṇḍavas. Gāndhārī, likewise, began to show affection for the Pāṇḍavas as if they were her own sons. Every morning, Dhṛtarāṣṭra offered prayers for the wellbeing of the Pāṇḍava brothers; he derived greater joy from their company than ever he had from the association of his own sons. Whatever wrongs had been done to him in the past, Yudhiṣṭhira forgot them all and showed constant respect for his uncle. He would never allow anyone to mention the evil deeds performed by Duryodhana and Duḥśāsana, lest Dhṛtarāṣṭra feel any sense of unhappiness.

Bhīma, however, became disturbed whenever he saw Dhṛtarāṣṭra, and was unable to tolerate his presence. He paid him respect only as an outward show with an unwilling heart. He secretly did acts that were disagreeable to the old king and through deceitful servants caused his commands to be disregarded. Recalling Dhṛtarāṣṭra's wicked counsels and the deeds of Duryodhana, Duḥśāsana, and Karṇa, he once slapped his arms in the presence of his uncle and exclaimed, 'These two mighty arms of mine are just like clubs. Coming within their grasp, the foolish sons of Dhṛtarāṣṭra have all been destroyed. These arms of mine deserve to be adorned now with sandal paste, for it was by them that Duryodhana and all his allies were despatched to the other world!' On hearing these and other words of Bhīma, Dhṛtarāṣṭra became very unhappy and at last expressed a desire to Gāndhārī to leave the city and to go far away to live in an *āśrama* in the mountains.[28]

Extract 3

After reigning in Hastināpura for many years, Yudhiṣṭhira and his brothers decided to renounce the world and depart for the mighty peaks of the Himalayas. So, along with Draupadī, the five of them left the city dressed in clothes made of tree bark accompanied by a dog that walked along with them. Thus there was a party of seven. They passed by the city of Dvārakā, now flooded by the sea, and Arjuna cast his bow, Gāṇḍīva, into the ocean. Now practising self-restraint and Yoga, they journeyed thence up into the mountains of the North. First of all, Draupadī fell by the

28 From Chapters 1 to 5 of the *Āśrama-vāsika-parvan*.

wayside; this was because she favoured Arjuna above her other husbands; then Sahadeva fell, this was because he was proud of his wisdom; then Nakula fell, this was because he was proud of his good looks; then Arjuna fell, this was because of his pride in his martial prowess; then Bhīma fell, this was because of his greed and his pride in the strength of his body.

So Yudhiṣṭhira went on alone with just the dog for company. Indra, the lord of the gods, then descended from the sky and invited Yudhiṣṭhira to accompany him in his chariot to the world of the gods. 'How can I go without Draupadī and my brothers?', asked Yudhiṣṭhira. 'They are even now in heaven waiting for you', Indra replied. 'They have cast off their human forms and departed from this world, but because of your virtue it is ordained that you may ascend to heaven without tasting death.'

Yudhiṣṭhira then said, 'This dog has become devoted to me, O lord. My heart is full of compassion for him; he must come with me.' Indra replied, 'You have gained a position equal to mine, with great prosperity and all the joys of the gods. Give up this dog; there will be no cruelty in such an act.' But Yudhiṣṭhira was unmoved. 'It is very difficult', he said, 'for a righteous person to perform a wicked act. I do not desire the prosperity you speak of if I have to cast off one who is devoted to me.'

'There is no place in our world for persons with dogs!' said Indra. 'Leave it behind! This is not a cruel deed.' But still Yudhiṣṭhira would not listen. 'I have vowed', he said, 'never to abandon one who is terrified, who is devoted to me, who seeks my protection, who is destitute, who is weak, or who wishes to save his life.' Again Indra said, 'Give up this dog, a filthy impure creature. You even gave up your brothers and Draupadī.'

'But they were already dead', Yudhiṣṭhira replied. 'I would never have abandoned them whilst they were still alive. To abandon a devoted follower is an evil act, O Indra.' As these

> words were spoken the dog vanished and in its place there was the god Dharma, Yudhiṣṭhira's true father. 'You have compassion for all beings', Dharma said, 'as this incident has demonstrated. You have given up the delights of heaven for the sake of a dog who was dependent on you and hence I say that there is no one in the celestial realm who can match you in terms of *dharma*.' Then Yudhiṣṭhira mounted the chariot of Indra and ascended to the world of the gods.[29]

What then are we to make of the character of Yudhiṣṭhira as revealed by these extracts from the *Mahābhārata* narrative? In the story of Jayadratha, we are shown a man who is free of anger and enmity, who is quick to forgive, has compassion even for those who have wronged him, and is generous, tolerant, and kind-hearted. He has a sense of pity for anyone who appears to be suffering, though some might feel that his forgiveness of Jayadratha is misplaced and could be regarded as weakness. We might also consider Jayadratha's response to Yudhiṣṭhira's forgiveness, in as much as the act of mercy makes him even more inimical towards the Pāṇḍavas and even more determined to get his revenge on them.

The account of Dhṛtarāṣṭra's last days in Hastināpura similarly shows Yudhiṣṭhira as a kind and gentle man who has no sense of malice, no desire for vengeance, and a genuine disposition towards mercy, kindness, and forgiveness. Bhīma's attitude might be more human, and is easily understood, but Yudhiṣṭhira stands above ordinary men and his virtue is extraordinary. We also see here another character trait of the Dharmarāja, his profound sense of respect for the elders of his family. I think it is also significant to note the lesson taught here by the *Mahābhārata* that forgiveness can often end quarrels and terminate a spiral of violence and hostility. Yudhiṣṭhira

29 From Chapters 1 to 3 of the *Mahā-prasthānika-parvan*.

forgives the injustices done to him by Dhṛtarāṣṭra and does not respond in kind. He thereby wins the old king over to him and the terrible conflicts that have taken place between family members are finally ended. Where one answers hostility in kind, the cycle of violence and hatred goes on without end.

The final account shows Yudhiṣṭhira's lack of desire for personal gain, his loyalty to those who come to him for protection, and his compassion for all living beings. Just for the sake of a dog he is willing to give up the rewards of his virtuous life. For Yudhiṣṭhira, *dharma* and virtue were never means to an end, they were his inherent nature. Some may feel that Yudhiṣṭhira is not a good role model because he is too weak and too tolerant of the misdeeds of others, and there are times when a more robust and aggressive attitude may be required in order to resist the forces of evil. And at times the *Mahābhārata* appears critical of Yudhiṣṭhira's position; Kṛṣṇa himself admires Yudhiṣṭhira but he does not always share his understanding of *dharma*.

We must be aware, however, that the *Mahābhārata* itself consistently shows Yudhiṣṭhira to be the most virtuous of all its characters; he is the Dharmarāja. He only committed one wicked act in all his life – and that at the urging of Kṛṣṇa himself. And it is Yudhiṣṭhira alone who does not fall on the final journey to the mountains because there is no blemish at all to be found in his character. Hence despite any misgivings we might have, it seems clear that for the *Mahābhārata* the character and disposition displayed by Yudhiṣṭhira represent an ideal towards which all human beings should aspire, however difficult it might be to attain.

Duryodhana

Let us now move across almost to the other extreme and explore the dark side of human life, exemplified by the character of Duryodhana. I say 'almost' because Duryodhana is not entirely without redeeming features and he certainly stands above the awful Duḥśāsana and perhaps his maternal uncle Śakuni as well. The characterisation of Duryodhana forms an important element in the *Mahābhārata*'s moral directives in indicating the traits and behaviour that are to be avoided by the righteous. He is never mild in his disposition, never gentle in his thoughts, words, or deeds, and never forgiving of any offence, real or imagined. He burns with envy over the success of the Pāṇḍavas, he is avaricious for power and opulence, and whenever his will is opposed he is consumed with unrestrained wrath. He has no misgivings about the suffering he will cause through waging war. He is vindictive rather than forgiving and has no remorse; he has no real sense of right and wrong, and in order to justify their misdeeds he and Karṇa construct specious arguments that convince no one.[30] Even after the humiliation of the Pāṇḍavas at the dice match, his vindictiveness is such that he wishes to further relish their discomfiture by seeing them suffering in exile in the forest.[31]

Unlike Yudhiṣṭhira, he shows scant respect for the elders of the family, rejecting the counsel of Gāndhārī, Vidura, and others, frequently with a haughty irreverence. He is untruthful and dishonest, as when he lies to his father about the purpose of their journey to Dvaitavana to mock the Pāṇḍavas, and his obstinacy is such that he is never seen to alter his resolve in light of superior advice. Whilst Yudhiṣṭhira is typically portrayed as contented with his lot, Duryodhana is beset by desires over which he exerts no self-restraint. He is a believer in the value of competitive endeavour and pursues

30 *Udyoga-parvan*, 21.9–15.

31 *Āraṇyaka-parvan*, Chapter 226.

this course with ruthless vigour. Yudhiṣṭhira is ready to compromise rather than fight, even if it means an inequitable division of the kingdom, but Duryodhana not only refuses this offer but states his belief in the value of competition as an impetus to success. In Chapter 50 of the *Sabhā-parvan*, he makes an interesting speech in which he presents himself as a true follower of *kṣatriya-dharma*, arguing that competition is inevitable, and that anyone striving for the same goal must be recognised as one's enemy.[32] He further urges that dissatisfaction with one's lot is a positive quality, for such a state of mind is the root of prosperity, *asaṁtoṣaḥ śriyo mūlam*.[33] From these passages in which Duryodhana plays a central role, we can get a fairly clear understanding of the ethical position advocated by the *Mahābhārata*. Of course, Duryodhana displays qualities that most people would find objectionable in terms of his violence, selfishness, and dishonesty, but it is also interesting to note the emphasis placed on tolerance and contentment in contrast to passion, desire, and thrusting competitiveness. One might suggest that Yudhiṣṭhira epitomises the quality of *sattva* discussed by the *Bhagavad-gītā*, while Duryodhana embodies the worst features of *rajas*. From Chapter 16 of the *Gītā*, indeed, it seems that the depiction of the *daivī sampad* in verses 1 to 3 and the subsequent account of the *āsurī sampad* are very much in line with the *Mahābhārata*'s representation of the characters of Yudhiṣṭhira and Duryodhana.

Let us now look at two extracts from the *Mahābhārata* in which the character of Duryodhana is revealed. As above, these are summaries of the text rather than direct translations.

---

32 *Sabhā-parvan*, 50.22.

33 *Sabhā-parvan*, 50.18.

Extract 4

Once, after the Pāṇḍavas had been exiled to the forest, Śakuni came to Duryodhana and spoke to him about the greatness he had achieved by this conquest, with all the kings of the world now paying homage to him. He spoke about the plight of the Pāṇḍavas. 'You are a sovereign and they are stripped of sovereignty; you live in prosperity whilst they have nothing; you live in a state of affluence whilst theirs is a life of poverty. You should go now and flaunt your prosperity in front of them. What happiness can be more complete than that enjoyed by one who lives in prosperity viewing the adversity of his enemies? Think of the joy you will gain when you see Arjuna in a state of poverty, clad in clothes made from the bark of trees, and Draupadī dressed in rags.'

Duryodhana was delighted by these words of his uncle, but he was frustrated because he thought that his father, Dhṛtarāṣṭra, would never give permission for them to go to Dvaitavana where the Pāṇḍavas were residing. He said to Karṇa, 'I shall certainly feel delight at seeing Bhīma, Arjuna, and Draupadī living in poverty in the woods. The joy I feel at possessing sovereignty over the world is less than I would derive from seeing the sons of Pāṇḍu clad in clothes made from the bark of trees and Draupadī dressed in rags. If King Yudhiṣṭhira and Bhīma look upon me in my state of affluence, only then will I feel that I have achieved the goal of my life. However, my father will never give his permission for this enterprise, so you must contrive some means by which we will be allowed to go there.'

Later Karṇa came to Duryodhana and suggested that they tell Dhṛtarāṣṭra that they wished to go to Dvaitavana to check on the number of cows in their possession. So they approached Dhṛtarāṣṭra with this request, taking with them a herdsman named Samāṅga who had been bribed to assist them in their scheme. Dhṛtarāṣṭra accepted their petition at face value but he was aware that the Pāṇḍavas were dwelling in that region and hence expressed some reluctance. 'After being defeated by deceitful means, the Pāṇḍavas are now living in the forest in a state of distress', he said. 'Yudhiṣṭhira will never allow his anger to be aroused, but Bhīma is passionate by nature and because of your pride and folly you are bound to cause them offence.' Śakuni then replied to the blind king, 'Do not worry, we are going on this journey just to hunt and to count the number of cows we possess; we will not go anywhere near the Pāṇḍavas' residence.'

Somewhat unwillingly, Dhṛtarāṣṭra granted them permission and the three of them set out on their journey accompanied by a large military force. Arriving at Dvaitavana they camped in a place four miles from the Pāṇḍavas' *āśrama* with splendid pavilions erected for Duryodhana, Karṇa, Śakuni, and each of Duryodhana's brothers. Rich foodstuffs were cooked for them and entertainment was provided by dancers, musicians, and storytellers. However, Citrasena, the King of the *Gandharvas*, was also sporting in that region and he ordered Duryodhana's men to depart from the place and not to disturb his pleasures. When they refused, the *gandharvas* launched an attack on the Kaurava host and routed the army, causing even Karṇa, Śakuni, Duḥśāsana, and Duryodhana to flee for their lives. Duryodhana was hauled down from his chariot and brought before Citrasena as a prisoner. In a state of terror, some of the Kaurava soldiers fled to the place where the Pāṇḍavas were residing and begged for protection. When he learned of what had happened, Bhīma was delighted and said, 'What we should have done, the *gandharvas* have achieved for us! Our enemies have got just what they deserved.'

But Yudhiṣṭhira said, 'This is no time for cruel words. These men are in a state of distress and have come to us for help and comfort. We may have had disagreements with Duryodhana and his allies, but they are still our relatives and the King of the Gandharvas shows us a lack of respect by behaving in this way when we are near at hand.

Arjuna should now go and set Duryodhana free and you should go as well to support him along with Sahadeva and Nakula.' Arjuna accepted his elder brother's instruction and the four of them armed themselves and set out to free their relatives. Opposed by the *gandharva* host, Arjuna then displayed his full prowess and quickly defeated the mightiest of their warriors. In fact, Arjuna and Citrasena were old friends and when they eventually met one another warm greetings were exchanged.

'I knew that these Kauravas had come here to deride you, Arjuna, and for this reason I acted against them just to please you and your brothers', Citrasena said. 'If you would please us', Arjuna replied, 'then set this Duryodhana free. This is the will of King Yudhiṣṭhira.' Citrasena said, 'But these Kauravas came here for evil purposes, they do not deserve to be released. Let us go to Yudhiṣṭhira and give him a full explanation of what has happened.'

But even when Yudhiṣṭhira learned the full truth of the situation, he still insisted on Duryodhana's being released. 'I am very pleased that you did not kill him', he said to Citrasena, 'and henceforth I regard you as my dear friend and ally.' He then spoke affectionately to Duryodhana, 'My dear brother, you have acted rashly and one can never gain satisfaction by thoughtless deeds. Be at peace with your brothers now. Return home and do not give way to unhappiness or grief.' Without saying a word, Duryodhana saluted Yudhiṣṭhira and began to walk mechanically back towards his home, his heart filled with shame, grief, and burning hatred for the Pāṇḍavas.[34]

Extract 5

After Yudhiṣṭhira had performed the great *rājasūya-yajña* in Indraprastha and received the worship and praise of all

34 From Chapters 226 to 235 of the *Āraṇyaka-parvan*.

the kings in the world, Duryodhana returned to his home in Hastināpura in a disconsolate state of mind. He came to his father, Dhṛtarāṣṭra, and told him of the opulence and prosperity the Pāṇḍavas were enjoying in their newly established kingdom. All the great rulers of the Earth had attended the ceremony and each one of them had brought wondrous gifts as offerings to Yudhiṣṭhira. Thus the Pāṇḍava king was enjoying wealth and sovereignty that had never been known by any previous king.

'Seeing such prosperity in the son of Kuntī, my lord, I no longer see any point in living!' he exclaimed. 'They are growing ever stronger whilst our power is in decline. Constantly thinking about this, my heart is never at peace. Hence I am plunged into a state of grief and am growing pale and emaciated.' 'You are my eldest son, my dear one', Dhṛtarāṣṭra replied, 'so do not be jealous. One who is jealous can never be happy. Yudhiṣṭhira is a righteous man and bears you no ill will. You are his equal both in wealth and in terms of friends and allies. Never striving to obtain the wealth of others, persevering in one's own affairs, and protecting what has been earned are the true marks of greatness. The sons of Pāṇḍu are like your own arms, so do not turn against them; to quarrel with friends is a great sin. Give gifts in charity, fulfil your desires, enjoy the company of beautiful women, and let your heart be at peace.'

Duryodhana then replied at length to his father: 'One who has heard many things but has no intelligence will never understand the true import of the scriptures. You know so much, but you are not speaking wisely. You and I are bound together, so are you unaware of your own interests? Or are you hostile towards me? Your sons and allies are doomed to defeat simply because they have you as their ruler. If a man has a guide who merely follows the advice of others, then he is likely to trip over. How can his followers find the right path? You possess mature wisdom, you have learned the ancient teachings, and your senses are under control, but you should not block those of us who are intent on

> pursuing our own interests. Bṛhaspati has taught that the *dharma* of kings is different from that of common men, and so kings must rigorously pursue their own interests.
>
> The only criterion that should guide the conduct of a *kṣatriya* is the attainment of success. So regardless of whether the means are virtuous or wicked, there must be no scruples. One who desires to snatch the prosperity of his enemy should bring all directions under his rule; a weapon is not just an instrument that cuts, but a means to defeat the foe. And anyone who causes a person distress, for whatever reason, is to be regarded as his enemy. To be discontented is in fact the root of prosperity, so I want to be discontented! A successful king is one who tries to gain the prosperity of others and any wealth that has been accumulated by another can be acquired by plunder. This is the custom of kings. Just as a snake will swallow frogs, so the Earth swallows kings who are peaceful.
>
> Anyone who pursues the same goal as oneself is an enemy and anybody who foolishly neglects an enemy will be destroyed, as if by an incurable disease. Never let the enemy's prosperity be acceptable to you, for such a policy will become a great burden. One who seeks to expand his prosperity grows to greatness amongst his relatives, just as the body grows from childhood to the adult form. I covet the Pāṇḍavas' prosperity but I have not yet made it my own, and I still have doubts about my ability to take it from them. I am determined to resolve these doubts. I will either take their prosperity from them or die in battle whilst attempting to do so. What do I care for life, when the Pāṇḍavas are growing in power and wealth whilst our possessions know no increase?'[35]

These are two very different passages, one being primarily in narrative form and the other a speech in which Duryodhana

---

35 From Chapter 50 of *the Sabhā-parvan.*

reveals his philosophy of life. I think we can take it that the *Mahābhārata* does not regard the second extract as one of its passages of proper religious discourse; it is not to be placed on the same level as the *Bhagavad-gītā*. But it is still significant inasmuch as one can understand from it the type of ideas one should learn to avoid.

Our first passage shows Duryodhana in a particularly unfavourable light. Admittedly, he is somewhat led astray by the ever-devious Śakuni, but here also there is a lesson: one should be cautious in making friendships and in seeking advice. In marked contrast to Yudhiṣṭhira's attitude towards Dhṛtarāṣṭra that we witnessed above, Duryodhana is certainly not a magnanimous victor and is never willing to put old enmities aside. Yudhiṣṭhira also displays a sense of compassion even towards those who have wronged him, as is apparent in his attitude towards Jayadratha and here again towards Duryodhana himself, whilst Duryodhana displays a completely contrasting attitude. The Pāṇḍavas have been defeated and stripped of all they possess. Duryodhana's actions in achieving this might be regarded as straightforward materialism, but his wish to enjoy the sight of their misery shows an even greater wickedness, a sense of malice that goes beyond the mere desire for gain and prosperity.

In his dealings with his father in both these passages, Duryodhana displays a lack of respect, and again this attitude towards his elders is in marked contrast to that of Yudhiṣṭhira. He is, moreover, thoroughly dishonest, lying to Dhṛtarāṣṭra about the purpose of their visit to Dvaitavana and concocting a devious subterfuge to cover his tracks. The idea that one might mock others and derive pleasure from their distress reveals an attitude that is utterly devoid of the quality of compassion, which is shown as being another feature of Yudhiṣṭhira's dharmic identity. Finally, we should also note Duryodhana's response to the kindness shown to him by

Yudhiṣṭhira. He displays no gratitude whatsoever towards one who has sacrificed his own interests to save him. Just the opposite, his malice and hatred towards his cousin grow ever more profound because of his indebtedness to him.

The vision of *dharma* presented by Duryodhana in our second passage is actually rather interesting, and in some ways corresponds to the type of *kṣatriya-dharma* Yudhiṣṭhira finds so repugnant. And, of course, we should not forget that after his death in battle Duryodhana gains a place amongst the gods by dint of his adherence to that *kṣatriya-dharma*. Essentially here, Duryodhana is arguing for intense competitive endeavour and the view that all those who are our rivals or are striving for the same goal are to be regarded as enemies and therefore undermined. It is a vision of the world based on ruthless individualism and the quest for personal gain in materialistic terms. Duryodhana suggests that this is the true *dharma* of kings, the *kṣatriya-dharma*, and to some extent this view is confirmed in Bhīṣma's teachings on *rāja-dharma* found in the first half of the *Śānti-parvan* and in the *Artha-śāstra* of Kauṭilya.

By placing these words in the mouth of Duryodhana, one of its least attractive characters, however, the *Mahābhārata* seems to be suggesting that such ideas are wholly unacceptable. This is not a valid interpretation of *dharma*, despite the views of certain teachers. To understand the true nature of *dharma* we should turn to the Dharmarāja himself, for it is Yudhiṣṭhira who exemplifies and personifies the actuality of *dharma*, whilst Duryodhana represents and propounds perverse and specious misrepresentations. The *Mahābhārata* is here showing that we should not be single-minded individualists rigorously pursuing our own selfish goals; rather we must always prioritise consideration for the interests of others. Yudhiṣṭhira is known as *ajāta-śatru*, his enemy was never born, for he is the well-wisher even of those who have wronged him. This, of course, is an almost impossible level of virtue to attain, but it is the *Mahābhārata*'s vision of *dharma*. As is often the case, we can here see again how the *Mahābhārata*'s narrative exemplifies the teachings of the *Bhagavad-gītā*:

> *adharmaṁ dharmam iti yā manyate tamasāvṛtā*
> *sarvārthān viparītāṁś ca buddhiḥ sā pārtha tāmasī*
>
> But that understanding which is covered by *tamas* [darkness or ignorance] and so thinks *adharma* to be *dharma*, and has wrong conceptions on all subjects, is intelligence under the influence of *tamas*.[36]

This verse perfectly sums up Duryodhana's misrepresentation of the nature of *dharma* in his speech to Dhṛtarāṣṭra.

Dhṛtarāṣṭra

Whilst Yudhiṣṭhira shows the very best of human nature and Duryodhana reveals some of our worst qualities, Dhṛtarāṣṭra stands somewhere in between. As we saw above from his conversation with his son, he understands the ideals of virtue, and he would like to follow them, but at times his weakness and his attachment to his family prevents him from doing so. In this sense, he shows another facet of the moral dilemma: it is not always enough to understand virtue and vice, we must also have the mental strength and self-mastery to put that understanding into practice.

He was, of course, born blind and for this reason the kingship is passed to his younger brother, Pāṇḍu, which may have had an effect on his later attitudes, for he often appears oppressed by a desire for sovereignty that dulls his sense

---

36 *Bhagavad-gītā*, 18.32.

of moral rectitude. He is no fool, however, and constantly seeks instruction on religious and moral matters from his brother, Vidura, and from his adviser, Saṁjaya. One of the most significant passages of ethical instruction found in the *Mahābhārata* is the *Vidura-nīti* which covers Chapters 33 to 41 of the *Udyoga-parvan*. The teaching here is delivered to Dhṛtarāṣṭra at his own request by his brother Vidura, and this is immediately followed by Sanatsujāta's discourse to him on the subject of religious philosophy.

Dhṛtarāṣṭra is a man who knows right from wrong and has a clear understanding of *dharma*, but his desires and attachments repeatedly pervert his adherence to the proper course. Hence at the beginning of the dispute between the Pāṇḍavas and their cousins over the sovereignty of the kingdom, he quite reasonably judges that there should be a division of land between the two factions, but then spoils this balanced judgement by giving his own sons the best share. He is worried about the dice match but he still gives permission for it to go ahead and celebrates when his own side is winning. He then has further misgivings, and decrees that the Pāṇḍavas and Draupadī should be given back their freedom and all that they have lost, but he still allows a further instalment of the dishonest gaming to go ahead and does nothing to intervene when Draupadī is being insulted and humiliated by his sons.

Perhaps the most telling indictment of Dhṛtarāṣṭra's character comes from his own advisor, Saṁjaya, who has been given the power to perceive all the events that take place on the battlefield at Kurukṣetra. As he informs his master about the catastrophes that befall his army, one after the other, he repeatedly inserts the view that this is the result of Dhṛtarāṣṭra's misguided policies in favouring his sons over the Pāṇḍavas. On some occasions, Dhṛtarāṣṭra tries to make the excuse of blaming destiny for the death and destruction that is taking place, but Saṁjaya will have none of it and says that this sort of philosophising is indulged in by the wicked and weak-minded who seek to excuse their own faults. Dhṛtarāṣṭra therefore epitomises the virtuous person whose moral shortcomings arise because of weakness. He longs for the sovereignty his blindness deprived him of, and he seeks to achieve it through the elevation of his own son. He knows that *dharma* should prevail, and that justice should always be paramount, but his selfishness prevents him from living up to his own standards, and it is this weakness that ultimately leads to the slaughter at Kurukṣetra.

Dhṛtarāṣṭra's character is clearly exposed before, during, and after the dice match when his sense of *dharma* and good policy is repeatedly undermined by his affection for his avaricious son, and by his own desire for gain. Here is a brief summary of Dhṛtarāṣṭra's role in these terrible events, which lead inevitably to the ruination of the Kauravas. The passage begins immediately after the conversation between Duryodhana and his father recorded above.

> Śakuni suggested to Dhṛtarāṣṭra that in a dice match he would be able to win from Yudhiṣṭhira all the wealth and prosperity he had acquired as the ruler of Indraprastha. When Duryodhana asked permission for the game to go ahead, Dhṛtarāṣṭra said that he would take advice from his brother, the wise Vidura. Duryodhana replied that Vidura was always against them and that no man should depend on the advice of another. When an opportunity for gain arises, one must grasp it. Dhṛtarāṣṭra then complained that he thought the policy of turning powerful men into enemies was a bad one, saying, 'This will lead to war with all the terrible consequences that brings with it.'
>
> Duryodhana then once again recommended the use of dice as a means to gain an advantage over their opponents, thereby opening the door to happiness. To this Dhṛtarāṣṭra replied, 'Your words are not approved of by me. You do what you like but you will repent for this ac-

tion; action so devoid of *dharma* never brings prosperity. Vidura has taught me this. Fate has brought this destiny, which will mean the deaths of so many *kṣatriyas*.' Having said this, the weak-minded Dhṛtarāṣṭra regarded fate as supreme and unavoidable. Deprived of his reason by fate, and obedient to the advice of his son, he gave the order for a gambling hall to be constructed. Vidura advised against this course of action, but now Dhṛtarāṣṭra seemed determined to allow it to take place. 'If fate is not against us', he said, 'then this gambling will not lead to conflict. The whole world moves under the control of the Creator and the control of destiny. We are never free.'

When the dice match begins and Yudhiṣṭhira is losing everything to Śakuni, Vidura again comes to Dhṛtarāṣṭra and begs him to call a halt to the proceedings. 'Do not be swayed by your desire for profit', he says, 'or else, blinded by folly, you will later have to repent for your deeds.' But Duryodhana interrupts Vidura, accusing him of partiality towards the Pāṇḍavas, and Dhṛtarāṣṭra remains silent, allowing the gaming to continue. Yudhiṣṭhira is defeated time and again by Śakuni, leading ultimately to the loss of his liberty and the abominable insult to Draupadī. After this has taken place, jackals howl and asses bray simultaneously, thereby presenting a fearful omen. Dhṛtarāṣṭra then says to his son, 'O wicked-minded Duryodhana! Destruction has already come upon you when you insult these noble men in this way, and even their wedded wife, Draupadī.' He then offered Draupadī any boon she might desire, and, at her request, the five Pāṇḍava brothers are released from the bondage they were to endure as a result of Yudhiṣṭhira's defeat in the gambling match.

As the Pāṇḍavas are about to depart, Yudhiṣṭhira speaks respectfully to his uncle. Dhṛtarāṣṭra in turn praises Yudhiṣṭhira's virtue and asks him not to retaliate for the insults they have received. After they have left, however, Duryodhana speaks to his father once again and persuades him that the Pāṇḍavas will never forgive them for what has taken place there. They should be summoned back and after being defeated again at dice banished to the forest for thirteen years. Dhṛtarāṣṭra then said, 'Bring back the Pāṇḍavas even if they have gone a good distance from here. Let them play at dice again.' Droṇa, Bhīṣma, Somadatta, Vidura, and other elders condemn this decision of the blind king. Gāndhārī comes forward and urges her husband to abandon their son who seems determined to bring about the destruction of their race. 'You could not do it before because of your parental affection', she says, 'but let your mind now be guided towards peace, *dharma*, and true policy. Be true to your own beliefs and instincts. Prosperity gained by wicked means is soon destroyed but that which is gained without hostility descends from generation to generation.'

Even when he is advised in this way by his wife, Dhṛtarāṣṭra will not relent. 'If the destruction of our race is about to come, then it must be so', he says, 'I cannot prevent it. Let it be as my sons wish it. Let the Pāṇḍavas return and the gambling resume.' So the gambling match continues, the Pāṇḍavas are defeated again, and are sent into exile. Dhṛtarāṣṭra is then once more wracked by anxiety. He explains his misery to Saṁjaya: 'Why should I not be miserable when we will have to face the mighty Pāṇḍavas in battle?' Saṁjaya replied, 'This hostility is now inevitable and it is all due to your mistaken action; it will inevitably bring the wholesale destruction of the kings of the world.'[37]

This outline of Dhṛtarāṣṭra's actions during the gambling match reveals his nature very clearly and shows how his instinct towards virtue is repeatedly subverted by his weakness and his selfish desire. In this sense, Dhṛtarāṣṭra is a very human character, whose actions reveal a significant insight into the basis of our own deviations from the path of pure virtue exemplified

---

37 From *Udyoga-parvan*, Chapters 33–41.

by Yudhiṣṭhira. The idea of virtue revealed in the *Mahābhārata*'s narrative is one that is widely accepted and one that most of us, I think, would subscribe to. Why then do we not all live after the manner of Yudhiṣṭhira? The answer to this question is surely revealed in the characterisation of Dhṛtarāṣṭra as a man who has a deep understanding of *dharma,* but is unable to consistently adhere to its central precepts because of his desires and his emotional attachments. Such desires and attachments subvert our ability to see the world as it actually is and give us a distorted appreciation of our own actions. The result is that we will frequently invent moral arguments that are nothing more than specious justifications for our own selfish actions and lifestyle; and what is more surprising is that we will often be able to convince ourselves of the validity of those arguments. Thus we see Dhṛtarāṣṭra attributing the evils that are about to occur to the force of destiny, so as to convince himself that he did nothing wrong.

In this connection, it is interesting to consider a question put by Arjuna in the *Bhagavad-gītā* and the answer he receives from Kṛṣṇa:

> *arjuna uvāca*
> *atha kena prayukto 'yaṁ pāpaṁ carati pūruṣaḥ*
> *anicchann api vārṣṇeya balād iva niyojitaḥ*
>
> Arjuna said: What is it that impels a person to act sinfully even though he has no desire to do so, Vārṣṇeya, compelling him to act in that way as if by force.
>
> *śrī bhagavān uvāca*
> *kāma eṣa krodha eṣa rajo-guṇa-samudbhavaḥ*
> *mahāśano mahā-pāpmā viddhy enam iha vairiṇam*
>
> The Lord said: It is desire, it is anger; this arises from the material quality, or *guṇa,* known as *rajas.* You should

know this as a mighty devouring force, a great source of sin; it is the enemy in this world.[38]

Here again we can see how the teachings of the *Gītā* are brought to life in the *Mahābhārata* narrative, in this case showing Dhṛtarāṣṭra as a man who understands *dharma* but is drawn towards *adharma* due to the strength of his desires and his attachments, which overwhelm his moral sensibilities.

Discussion Topic: Main Characters

Here are some questions you might care to ponder after completing this chapter:

- Of all the characters portrayed in the *Mahābhārata,* who do you regard as the most worthy of respect, and why?
- How do you see the role of female characters represented within the *Mahābhārata*?
- Is Karṇa a hero or a villain in the *Mahābhārata*?
- Should we regard Kṛṣṇa as one of the characters of the *Mahābhārata* and assess his conduct alongside that of all the others?
- How can we explain Bhīṣma's conduct in failing to protect Draupadī and fighting for Duryodhana?

38 *Bhagavad-gītā*, 3.36-37.

SUDESHNA AND DRAUPADI.

Sudeshna is inducing and persuading Draupadi to go to Kichaka's house with the jar of liquor.

III
WOMEN IN THE *MAHĀBHĀRATA*

In this chapter, I want to move on from the previous discussion of the male characters who play a significant role in the narrative, and focus instead on the main female characters who have a central role in the unfolding of the *Mahābhārata*'s narration of events. Alongside this discussion, and complementary to it, I also want to look at the direct teachings on gender roles, and specifically the *dharma* of women, *strī-dharma*, which are contained within the *Mahābhārata*. What I think that wider perspective will reveal is the notable dissonance between the text's direct teaching on female *dharma*, which tends to emphasise subservience and submission, and the behaviour displayed by the three principal female characters, Draupadī, Gāndhārī, and Kuntī. So as to end on something of a more positive note, let us take the teachings on *strī-dharma* first so that we can then review the conduct of these three women in relation to these ideas.

TEACHINGS ON THE *DHARMA* OF WOMEN LOCATED IN THE *MAHĀBHĀRATA*

For this discussion I want to focus on two passages from the *Mahābhārata*, though it is to be noted that these are by no means unique. Hence our study will be exemplary rather than exhaustive. It is to be noted that the ideas on a woman's role and duty are very similar to those to be found in the *Manu-smṛti* and other similar *śāstras*.[39]

The Draupadī-satyabhāmā-saṁvāda

Chapters 222 and 223 of the *Āraṇyaka-parvan*, Book 3 of the *Mahābhārata*, tell of a discussion between Draupadī, the co-wife of the five Pāṇḍavas, and Satyabhāmā, one the principal wives of Kṛṣṇa, which took place when Kṛṣṇa visited the Pāṇḍavas whilst they were living in exile in the forest. This conversation forms a distinct unit of the text and is named the *Draupadī-satyabhāmā-saṁvāda*, the conversation between Draupadī and Satyabhāmā. The conversation begins with Satyabhāmā asking how Draupadī conducts herself as the wife of five husbands, a most unusual arrangement in Indian society. How does she keep them submissive to her will without ever causing them to be angry with her? In reply, Draupadī presents her view of how a wife should behave in relation to her husband.

Draupadī claims that she devotedly serves her husbands and their other wives without pride, anger, or desire. With affection and restraint, she waits attentively on their wishes without any selfish thoughts. She works hard to manage the home, never speaks harshly, never laughs loudly, never causes offence, and is never idle. She never cooks food her husbands do not like, and she is dutiful in performing the offerings to the ancestors and in serving guests. Even though they are gentle by nature, she treats her husbands as if they were venomous

---

39 It should be noted, however, that the relative chronology of the *Mahābhārata* and the *Manu-smṛti* is still subject to debate. See, for example, Johaness Bronkhorst, 'Manu and Mahabhārata', in *Indologica*, T. Ya. Elizarenkova Memorial Volume, Book 2, edited by L. Kulikov and M. Rusanov, 135–156 (Moscow: Russian State University for the Humanities, 2012).

snakes, always prone to anger. The eternal *dharma* for a woman is to serve her husband in this way, for he is her god and she has no object in life other than his service. She never disregards the instruction of her husbands over her sleeping and eating, nor with regard to the ornaments she wears; she never speaks ill of her mother-in-law and always defers to her opinion.

When Yudhiṣṭhira was king in Indraprastha, he ruled with magnificent opulence, keeping a huge household retinue and feeding many brahmins and sages. All this was overseen with scrupulous care by Draupadī, including keeping an account of income and expenditure. She alone knew the extent of the kingdom's wealth, taking this burden away from her husbands. By relieving them of the anxiety of managing the royal exchequer, she made her husbands favourable towards her. For a woman there is no god other than her husband. When he is satisfied, she gets everything she desires – clothes, perfumes, bedding, furniture, and even rebirth amongst the gods – but if he is angered then all things will be lost to her. Only by overcoming difficulties can happiness be won; therefore, a woman must be prepared to suffer in the service of her husband so that her desires may be fulfilled. She must be attentive to his wishes and serve him dutifully, even accepting the role and demeanour of a serving maid. A wife should never gossip about matters her husband has disclosed to her; she should be amicable towards his friends and cold towards those who are inimical towards him. She should never talk privately with other men and should make friendships only with women who are respectable. Such behaviour leads a woman to rebirth in the realm of the gods, and Draupadī therefore advises Satyabhāmā that she should dress and perfume her body with care and then devote herself to the worship of her husband.

This passage focuses exclusively on the conjugal relations between husband and wife, and does not seek to discuss wider issues of gender identity. What is clearly apparent is that in Draupadī's view marriage is not a relationship of equal partners and that the wife must accept and embrace a position of inferiority and service. There can be no doubt that to the modern mind this vision of conjugal relationships is one that is oppressive and pernicious, for the successful and prosperous woman is depicted as one who accepts her subservience and proves herself to be diligent and faithful. In response to this behaviour, the contented patriarch will bestow upon her the things she hankers after. The view of a woman's trivial nature is demonstrated by the goals she is thought to aspire after: items like clothing, jewellery, and perfumes are seen as sufficient to satisfy the female mind.

Despite our instinctively negative response to these chapters, there are a number of redeeming features that may also be borne in mind. First of all, Draupadī does not see herself as being confined exclusively to the home, and states that in the past she held an important position in the governance of the state, albeit as an act of service to her husbands. This does suggest that the *Mahābhārata* accepts that women have equal competence to their male counterparts in the weightiest of political matters, and are entirely capable of undertaking important tasks outside of a purely domestic sphere. We must also be aware of the historical context in which this piece was composed, at a time when the idea of gender equality was almost unknown. The economic and cultural milieu of a particular time will almost inevitably shape the way in which the world and our position within it is viewed. This raises the question of whether we can judge the values and value of a treatise by the standards of our own time when we are so far removed from that cultural and economic environment.

This latter point inevitably gives rise to a wider debate about the status of the *Mahābhārata* as sacred text, the extent to which its words are to be taken as authoritative, and whether or not its ideas are subject to challenge. In my experience, it is a mistake to regard the words of the *Mahābhārata* as holding the same position for Hindus as does the Qur'an for Muslims or the Bible for Christians. When reading passages of this type with Hindu groups, the typical response has always been either outright rejection and condemnation, or else a slightly milder refutation that suggests that these passages might have held some relevance in the past but are of no value today. More than anything, the *Mahābhārata* is a book of complex ideas, which we must think about deeply and then decide for ourselves what is of value and what is pernicious. This is exactly the advice Kṛṣṇa gives to Arjuna at the conclusion of the *Bhagavad-gītā*: *vimṛśyaitad aśeṣeṇa yathecchasi tathā kuru*, 'After fully considering what you have heard, you should then act as you see fit.'[40]

Bhīṣma's Instruction in the Anuśāsana-parvan

The thirteenth book of the *Mahābhārata* is entitled the *Anuśāsana-parvan*, literally the 'Book of Instructions', and consists almost entirely of teachings delivered to Yudhiṣṭhira by Bhīṣma as he lies dying on the battlefield. These teachings cover a wide range of subjects but a significant portion of the *parvan* is given over to instruction about the nature of women, conjugal roles, and the social position and rights of women. It is very much the case that in these passages the *Mahābhārata* is taking on the role of *dharma-śāstra*, finding resonance with texts such as the *Manu-smṛti* and the *Yājñavalkya-smṛti*.

It is in Chapters 38 to 47 of the *Anuśāsana-parvan* that Bhīṣma focuses his attention on gender issues and the form of the instruction is consistently depressing in terms of both

---

40 *Bhagavad-gītā*, 18.63.

its misogynistic perspectives and oppressive injunctions. This lengthy passage begins with a question from Yudhiṣṭhira concerning the nature of women in general, whom he describes as being *laghu-citta*, petty-minded. The main theme of Bhīṣma's initial response is the inherent tendency of all women towards licentiousness and marital infidelity. Even if a woman is married to a man of noble character, he says, she will still be attracted towards any other man who courts her, even if he be ugly and low-minded. He insists that this despicable nature is an existential feature of the female gender, for it was instilled in womankind at the time of creation in order to limit the number of people who might otherwise gain elevation to the higher worlds. They are trivial by nature and instinctively drawn towards trivial matters such as bedding, seats, jewellery, misconduct, gossip, and sensuality.

The principal feature of the female nature emphasised throughout Chapters 38 to 40 is the tendency towards infidelity, which leads women to seek a succession of lovers. The stereotype of the feminine nature depicts women as both deceitful and trivial, interested only in petty adornments. They can never be expected to reform themselves or to be reformed by good instruction, but must be compelled by force to behave in a manner that accords with the proper *dharma* of women. The implication of such negative stereotyping is obvious, for it provides justification for repressive behaviour towards women on the grounds that if such steps are not taken their nature will inevitably impel them towards acts of wickedness.

In Chapters 40 to 43, Bhīṣma moves on to narrate the story of Vipula and his guarding of Rucī, the wife of his *guru*, a story that illustrates the tendency of women towards marital infidelity, though at the conclusion Bhīṣma does admit that there are two types of women, the righteous and the wicked, rather than condemning women as a whole. Then, from Chapter 44 to Chapter 47, the text switches its point of emphasis as it adopts a dharma-śāstric mode of discourse in establishing rules of life in relation to gender issues. With regard to marriage, Bhīṣma expresses the view that taking only one wife is superior to polygamy, but acknowledges that polygamy is allowed for brahmins, *kṣatriyas*, and *vaiśyas*. He also confirms the rule that girls should be married before they reach the age of puberty. Laws governing dowry and female inheritance are also established, which make some allowance for female rights, but at the same time are weighted heavily in favour of sons over daughters. He insists that when a young bride enters the household of her husband's family, she must always be treated with kindness and consideration, for the gods bring down curses on households where the women are mistreated. It is also asserted that there are no religious rites prescribed for women; their only duty is to serve and assist their husband and sons, who are properly able to enact such rituals. On a more positive note, Bhīṣma also states that when women are cherished in society, there is prosperity and good fortune for all.

These four chapters of the *Anuśāsana-parvan* (44–47) contain the *Mahābhārata*'s principal expression of *dharma-śāstra* in relation to women. Based on the stereotype of the feminine nature presented in Chapters 38 to 43, this passage demands that strict limits be placed on the freedom of women in society. In marriage, there is no question of equal partnership and undoubtedly such a concept was alien to the early composers of *dharma-śāstra*. For the three higher *varṇas*, polygamy was acceptable, reinforcing that unequal status, and the notion of a girl choosing her own husband is roundly condemned. The problem of a girl being forced to marry a man she dislikes is recognised, but still it is considered ideal if the father chooses a husband for his daughter and she is married whilst still a child of seven or ten years. It is interesting to note how the author of these passages was aware of examples found elsewhere in the *Mahābhārata* that contradict his views. Here the case of Sāvitrī is mentioned as a princess whose father allowed her to travel the world to choose her husband, and then external authority is cited to show that such practice is not in accordance with *dharma*.

Regarding wealth and inheritance, which constitutes the real basis of social independence, women are not completely disenfranchised though it is clear that primary inheritance passed from father to sons rather than to daughters. Almost certainly this reflects the view that women had less need of independent wealth because their husbands were the providers of maintenance. A woman could inherit up to 3,000 coins from her husband, and if the wife had any private property this went to her daughters. It is difficult to say how effective such injunctions would be in freeing a woman from a state of dependence, but with the primary inheritance passing through the male line and with women having no acceptable means of earning their own income, one suspects that their position of subordination was ensured by economic constraints as well as the notion that a woman must never be granted freedom at any stage of life.

The repressive nature of the ideas expressed in these chapters is tempered somewhat by the denunciation of harsh treatment of women by husbands and society as a whole. Despite the obvious disparity between the genders, within her prescribed station the woman is to be admired and treated with respect and kindness. Here one recognises a perspective that takes the subordination of women for granted and is able to be magnanimous in the implementation of that inferior status.

One further point that cannot be overlooked in our examination of the *Mahābhārata*'s teachings on gender roles is the indication that a woman's becoming a *satī* – the practice of forcing widows to commit suicide on their husbands' funeral pyres – is at least tacitly approved of. This was a major issue at the start of the nineteenth century when Hindu reformers tried with eventual success to persuade the British rulers to outlaw this practice. There is no specific injunction on this practice to be found in the *Anuśāsana-parvan*, but a number of references to becoming a *satī* are to be found within the *Mahābhārata* as whole. The best known of these is Mādrī, Pāṇḍu's second wife and the mother of Nakula and Sahadeva, who commits suicide on the funeral pyre of her dead husband; and in this she is envied by Kuntī, who remains alive only to care for her own and Mādrī's sons.

Just before this occurs, there is a story narrated by Kuntī (Chapter 112 of the *Ādi-parvan*) in which she speaks of Bhadrā, the wife of King Vyuṣitāśva, who stated that without her husband a woman's life is no life at all, and therefore a widow should follow her husband into the afterlife. Then in Chapter 41 of the *Āśrama-vāsika-parvan*, the widows of the slain warriors are urged by Vyāsa to drown themselves in the Gaṅgā, and after the death of Vasudeva, Kṛṣṇa's father, his widows commit suicide on his funeral pyre and thereby accompany their husband to the realm of the gods. There is no suggestion that social pressure was exerted upon widows to take their own lives, but the indication that such an act was pious and was rewarded in the afterlife is clearly open to abuse.

Before we move on to consider the role played by the three principal female characters in the *Mahābhārata* narrative, we might pause for a moment to consider a couple of verses from the *Bhagavad-gītā*, which is, of course, an integral part of the *Mahābhārata*, as these shed further light on the wider issue. Chapter 9 of the *Gītā* places a consistent emphasis on *bhakti*, devotion to Kṛṣṇa himself, who is the one Supreme Deity; at the end of the chapter Kṛṣṇa utters three lines that refer to the power of *bhakti* in granting liberation from rebirth to persons of any social background:

> *māṁ hi pārtha vyapāśritya ye 'pi syuḥ pāpa-yonayaḥ*
> *striyo vaiśyās tathā śūdrās te 'pi yānti parāṁ gatim*
> *kiṁ punar brāhmaṇāḥ puṇyā bhaktā rājarṣayas tathā*
>
> Having sought shelter with me, Pārtha, even those of evil births, as well as women, *vaiśyas*, and *śūdras*, go to the highest destination. How much more so then in the case of righteous brahmins, and those religious kings who show devotion.[41]

Clearly the intention behind these words is the democratisation of spiritual perfection, for the highest goals of our existence are said to be available to persons of all backgrounds and are not, as some have argued, the sole prerogative of brahmins and enlightened kings. A problem arises, however, from the words *pāpa-yonayaḥ*, meaning sinful or evil births: some commentators have suggested that this phrase is expanded upon in the next line so as to give the indication that these sinful births are as women, *vaiśyas*, and *śūdras*. Grammatically, there is no reason to accept that reading, and it is equally valid to accept the statement as being a list of four types of person beginning with those who are *pāpa-yoni* in the sense of being born in the most deprived families or into communities that generally have no tendency towards spiritual pursuits. The reason I mention these verses is that I think they reveal very clearly the manner in which a passage that at the time of its composition was intended as urging liberalisation of ideas can be taken as oppressive to modern eyes. I think we should always be aware of this when we consider passages of ancient texts from the perspective of modernity, although it is equally clear that some of the statements from the *Anuśāsana-parvan* have no such egalitarian intent.

41 *Bhagavad-gītā*, 9.32, 33.

Female Characters of the *Mahābhārata*

There is no doubt that within the central narrative Kuntī, Gāndhārī, and Draupadī all conduct themselves in a manner that is notably different from that prescribed in the *Anuśāsana-parvan* or in Draupadī's words of instruction to Satyabhāmā. It is always difficult to establish the message that lies behind characterisations within a narrative, but still we can, I think, be fairly certain that all three of these women are to be viewed in a favourable light. Their character and conduct can therefore be taken as exemplary, although there are occasional indications that each is to be understood as being prone to feminine weakness.

Gāndhārī

As the wife of Dhṛtarāṣṭra and the mother of Duryodhana, Gāndhārī holds a position of some prominence within the *Mahābhārata* narrative and is consistently portrayed as a woman of wisdom and intelligence, capable of giving advice to the less able male protagonists. We first hear of her in Chapter 103 of the *Ādi-parvan*, where she is mentioned as the virtuous daughter of Subala, the King of Gandhāra, who adhered strictly to the principles of *dharma*. On hearing that Gāndhārī had been blessed by Śiva to be mother of one hundred sons, Bhīṣma arranged with Subala for her marriage to Dhṛtarāṣṭra in order to ensure the continuation of the dynasty. When she learned that her parents wished her to marry a blind man, Gāndhārī made a covering for her eyes and accepted a similar state of blindness, not wishing to be superior to her husband in any way. She also made the vow, *nātyaśnīyāṁ patim aham*, 'I will never eat before my husband does.'

In Chapter 107 of the *Ādi-parvan*, we hear that Gāndhārī is pregnant and has received the same benediction from Vyāsa that she will have one hundred sons. The pregnancy, however, lasts for two years and before she gives birth she learns that Kuntī, wife of Pāṇḍu, has given birth to Yudhiṣṭhira. Frustrated by this news, she strikes her abdomen, causing a solid lump of flesh to emerge from her womb. Vyāsa then divides this into a hundred pieces and places each piece into a jar of ghee. From there they mature into embryos and eventually take birth as the hundred sons of Dhṛtarāṣṭra, headed by Duryodhana and Duḥśāsana. She is also granted the boon of a single daughter.

Although the covering of her eyes appears to be an act of utter subservience to her husband, at various points throughout the narrative Gāndhārī shows herself to be willing and able to offer sagacious advice, although this is too often ignored. After the first part of the gambling match, she comes forward and tells her husband that he must put a stop to it.[42] She says: 'Do not let your opinion be swayed into following the advice of immature fools. Do not become the cause of the terrible destruction of this family.'[43] Then again:

> You remember all this, O descendent of Ajamīḍha, but I will remind you again. For good or ill, the words of scripture cannot regulate the conduct of evil-minded people. Those who are foolish and immature, O king, can never be like a learned elder, so let your sons be guided by you once more, and do not allow them to separate themselves from you, regarding you as an object of ridicule. Let the proper intelligence appear within you, guided by equanimity, by *dharma*, and by higher understanding. Do not adhere to the opposite path. Prosperity acquired through vicious means is soon dispersed, but wealth acquired through gentle means passes on down to sons and grandsons.[44]

42 *Sabhā-parvan*, 66.28–35.

43 *Sabhā-parvan*, 66.31.

44 *Sabhā-parvan*, 66.33–34.

In response to these wise words of advice from his wife, Dhṛtarāṣṭra merely replies by saying that he is powerless to change the course of events.

Similarly, in Chapter 127 the *Udyoga-parvan*, when preparations are being made for war, we find Gāndhārī giving enlightening instructions to her son, Duryodhana, after first condemning her husband for granting him power over the kingdom. Before he can think of vanquishing rival kings, she tells Duryodhana, he must first defeat the greatest foes of all by gaining control of his own self, dispelling any influence of *kāma* and *krodha* (desire and wrath), and then gain mastery over his senses. He should develop mature wisdom and make peace with the Pāṇḍavas, for when allied together, their united dynasty will be irresistible and all-powerful. Again, however, her wise words fall on deaf ears, for Duryodhana is angered by what he has heard and stalks off to be with Karṇa, Śakuni, and Duḥśāsana, who share his disregard for virtue.

In the *Udyoga-parvan*, she proclaims to the assembled leaders of the Kauravas that Yudhiṣṭhira is the rightful king, because it is the custom of their family that the eldest should take the throne.[45] She condemns her own son as an evil-minded (*pāpa-buddhi*) performer of wicked deeds (*atinṛśaṁsa-karman*), and states that Yudhiṣṭhira should now become king and govern the kingdom, acting under the guidance of Dhṛtarāṣṭra. This is in many ways a remarkable speech, as it demonstrates the extent of Gāndhārī's wisdom and enlightenment, which enable her to set aside her natural bias towards her own offspring and advocate a course of action from which all will benefit.

It is in the *Strī-parvan*, after the battle is lost and won, that Gāndhārī comes once more to the forefront of the narrative. It is revealed here that when Duryodhana came to seek her

45 *Udyoga-parvan*, 146.27–35.

blessings for victory in the conflict, all she would say to him is *yato dharmas tato jayaḥ*, 'wherever there is *dharma*, there will also be victory',[46] giving a clear indication of the Pāṇḍavas' ultimate triumph. After her initial anger at the Pāṇḍavas subsides (as a result of which Yudhiṣṭhira's toe is scorched when she sees it below the bottom of her blindfold), she then comforts the Pāṇḍavas like a mother for their own tragic losses, *sāntvayām āsa mātṛvat*.[47] She tells Yudhiṣṭhira that despite the death of all her sons, she has no ill-will towards him, although she condemns Bhīma for his unrighteous killing of Duryodhana and for the fact that he did not leave a single one of her sons alive to give her some comfort.

Encountering Kṛṣṇa on the battlefield, she points out to him the bodies of each of the fallen warriors, and the wives and other relatives grieving over them.[48] She asserts that Kṛṣṇa had the capacity to prevent the battle, perhaps by using his own military might to enforce a peace treaty, but opted not to do so. Of course, the readers of the *Mahābhārata* are well aware that it was the mission of the *avatāra* to bring about the destruction of the royal order, but Gāndhārī does not mention anything about Kṛṣṇa's divine identity or purpose, and simply argues that as a mighty ruler he could have intervened and prevented all this suffering. As a result, she curses Kṛṣṇa, saying that he will be the cause of the deaths of all his own family members and will himself suffer an ignominious end to his life. Kṛṣṇa is quite unmoved by this, saying that he will need to bring about the end of his own people and so Gāndhārī's curse will be of assistance in bringing his mission to its ultimate conclusion.

---

46 *Strī-parvan*, 13.9, 17.6.

47 *Strī-parvan*, 11.15.8.

48 *Strī-parvan*, Chapters 17–25.

The *Āśrama-vāsika-parvan* tells us that after Yudhiṣṭhira assumes his position as the rightful king, he shows constant reverence for Gāndhārī and Dhṛtarāṣṭra, providing for all their personal needs and for the *śrāddha* rites to be performed for their dead sons. She develops great affection for Yudhiṣṭhira, regarding him as her own son, but eventually leaves her place in the royal palace and goes to the forest with her husband, Kuntī, and Saṁjaya to live the life of a renunciant. Later on, the sacred fire they keep constantly burning in the *āśrama* is fanned by a violent wind and she dies in the ensuing forest fire along with Dhṛtarāṣṭra and Kuntī. We are then told that she is elevated to the realm of the gods alongside her husband, *pati-lokam anuprāptam*.[49]

Kuntī

Another of the female characters who plays a central role in the *Mahābhārata* narrative is Kuntī; she is also often referred to by her real name, Pṛthā. Chapters 104 and 105 of the *Ādi-parvan* tell of how she was born as the daughter of Śūrasena, a lord of the Yadu dynasty who was also the father of Vasudeva and hence the grandfather of Kṛṣṇa. Śūrasena's cousin and dear friend was King Kuntibhoja; because he was childless Śūrasena gave Pṛthā to him as an adopted daughter, as a result of which she acquired the name or title of Kuntī. As the sister of Vasudeva, she was the aunt of Kṛṣṇa, hence her own sons, the Pāṇḍavas, were the cousins of Kṛṣṇa.

When a rather ill-tempered sage named Durvāsas stayed in the residence of Kuntibhoja, Kuntī delighted him by the care and attention she devoted to rendering him service. As a result, Durvāsas granted her the gift of being able to summon

49 *Āśrama-vāsika-parvan*, 15.46.6.

any of the gods and bear children by them. Intrigued by this blessing, she first calls for Sūrya, the sun-god, and becomes pregnant with his child. Because she is still unmarried and fears the damage a premarital pregnancy will do to her own and her family's good name, she abandons the child, which is found and raised by a *sūta* couple named Adhiratha and Rādhā; a *sūta* being one of mixed family background, born of a *kṣatriya* father and brahmin mother. This child was Karṇa; because of his being brought up in a *sūta* family, the Pāṇḍavas, Draupadī, and others dismissed him as a person of lower birth, never realising that he was in fact their own brother.

For her marriage, Kuntī's father arranges a *svayaṁvara* at which she is able to select a husband from amongst the kings and princes of the land, and out of all of them she selects Pāṇḍu of the Kaurava dynasty. Unfortunately, however, Pāṇḍu receives a curse to the effect that if he ever engages in sexual relations he will immediately die.[50] He then decides to give up his royal opulence and retire to an *āśrama* in the forest with his two wives, Kuntī and Mādrī. Whilst Pāṇḍu is lamenting over his inability to beget children, Kuntī informs him of the blessing she received from Durvāsas. At Pāṇḍu's insistence, she uses the *mantra* bestowed on her by that sage to invoke three of gods, Dharma, Vāyu, and Indra, by whom she begets Yudhiṣṭhira, Bhīma, and Arjuna respectively. Pāṇḍu is still desirous of more offspring to strengthen his dynasty and line of descent, but at this point Kuntī refuses and instructs her husband, stating that his wishes now contravene the principles of dharmic life.[51]

When further petitioned by Pāṇḍu and Mādrī, she allows Mādrī to use the *mantra,* as a result of which she begets twin sons, Nakula and Sahadeva, by the two Aśvins. Kuntī is not

50 *Ādi-parvan,* Chapter 109.

51 *Ādi-parvan,* 114.64–66.

at all pleased by this, feeling that her co-wife has deceived her by invoking the twin gods, thereby obtaining two sons rather than just one. She therefore refuses Pāṇḍu's request that she allows Mādrī further use of her *mantra,* fearing that she will be surpassed in terms of the number of offspring each of them has. After Pāṇḍu's untimely death, and Mādrī's self-immolation, Kuntī returns to Hastināpura with her five sons, facing the ongoing hostility of Duryodhana and his allies.

Staying in the company of her sons, she escapes with them from Duryodhana's attempt to kill them by burning their house and then travels with them during their first forest exile. It is Kuntī who indirectly brings about the marriage of all five brothers to Draupadī. After Arjuna has won the hand of the princess at the archery contest, the brothers return to their temporary place of residence with Draupadī. When they get near to that place, they call out to their mother that they have received a great gift that day, to which Kuntī replies *bhuṅkteti sametya sarve,* 'Share it equally amongst yourselves.' Unlike Duryodhana, for the Pāṇḍavas the order of their mother cannot be disobeyed, and so they feel bound to follow the highly unusual practice of accepting a polyandric marriage with Draupadī.[52]

After the exile of her sons following the gambling match, Kuntī wishes to again accompany them to the forest, but is persuaded by Vidura that this would be unwise because of her age and frail condition. Thus for the duration of the exile and during the period of conflict, she lives with Vidura, who has been a constant friend to her sons.[53] The *Udyoga-parvan* tells of the preparations for war, the debates over the righteous use of violent means, and of the ill-fated peace negotiations.

52 *Ādi-parvan,* Chapter 182.

53 *Sabhā-parvan,* Chapter 69.

When Kṛṣṇa is asked by the Pāṇḍavas to act as a peace envoy, he comes to meet Kuntī, his aunt, who is still living at the residence of Vidura. On learning of the overtures being made for peace, she asks Kṛṣṇa to take a message back to Yudhiṣṭhira instructing him on the true *dharma* of *kṣatriyas*. The duty of a king, she says, is to protect the citizens and to ensure their prosperity by all means possible. If a wrongdoer seeks to usurp the kingdom, as Duryodhana has done, then it is the sacred duty of the ruler to wage war and chastise all such miscreants. This is the *kṣatriya-dharma* that Yudhiṣṭhira must adhere to, giving up all thoughts of tolerance and surrender.[54]

A little while later, she goes to Karṇa and tells him the truth about his birth, urging him to side with the Pāṇḍavas, who are his own flesh and blood. When allied with Arjuna, she tells him, they will be invincible and he will then be able to enjoy royal prosperity in association with his younger brothers. Karṇa, however, refuses to abandon Duryodhana, feeling honour-bound to support a man to whom he has pledged his loyalty, but he does promise his mother that he will spare all her sons with the exception of Arjuna.[55] Kuntī does not, however, reveal Karṇa's true identity to the Pāṇḍavas until after the battle when they have left him dead on the field. This is a subject of great regret for Yudhiṣṭhira, who laments the death of his elder brother, a man whom he had previously regarded as one of his greatest enemies.

During the time of the Pāṇḍavas' exile and after the slaughter at Kurukṣetra, a firm friendship is formed between Kuntī and Gāndhārī, both of whom have suffered greatly due to the folly and avarice of the male protagonists of the Kaurava faction; they come to regard one another as sisters

---

54 *Udyoga-parvan*, Chapter 130.

55 *Udyoga-parvan*, Chapters 143–144.

in distress rather than adversaries. Kuntī accompanies Dhṛtarāṣṭra and Gāndhārī into the forest to live a life of religious renunciation, acting as the eyes of Gāndhārī and guiding her on the journey, *gāndhāryās tu pṛthā rājaṁś cakṣur āsīd*.[56] When the sacred fire they carry with them ignites a forest fire, Kuntī dies in that blaze alongside Dhṛtarāṣṭra and Gāndhārī. It is surely enlightening to observe that despite the extreme issues that divided them in their earlier lives, these elders of the dynasty lived the final days of their lives in a state of harmony, and died together in a state of absolute amity. After her death, Kuntī is elevated to the realm of the gods, and in the *Mahābhārata*'s final book she is seen there by Yudhiṣṭhira, united once more with Pāṇḍu and Mādrī.[57]

Draupadī

Let us now turn to Draupadī, whom we have encountered already giving instruction to Satyabhāmā on the ideal manner in which a woman should render service to her husband. Draupadī plays a more pivotal role in the *Mahābhārata*'s central narrative than any other female character, and as the incidents in her life unfold we get a clear insight into both her character and her view of life. I will try to summarise the main incidents in which Draupadī is at the heart of narrative, and on the basis of this discussion highlight what her characterisation reveals about the attitude towards women displayed by the text as a whole.

In Chapter 155 of the *Ādi-parvan*, we are told of the wondrous birth of Draupadī, who appeared from out of the sacred fire at the conclusion of the ritual. This *yajña* ritual had been performed by brahmins at the request of Drupada, the

56 *Āśrama-vāsika-parvan*, 45.17.

57 *Svargārohaṇa-parvan*, 4.16.

King of Pañcāla, with the aim of gaining a son who would kill Droṇa, who had earlier humiliated him and taken away half of his kingdom. A son, Dhṛṣṭadyumna, first of all appeared from the flames, followed by the emergence of a beautiful fully grown daughter named Draupadī after her father; she was also called Yājñasenī after the manner of her birth and Kṛṣṇā because of her dark complexion.

In his defeat at the hands of Droṇa and the Pāṇḍavas. King Drupada had conceived a wish for his daughter to marry Arjuna, the mightiest of his adversaries on that occasion. He therefore arranged for a *svayaṁvara* ceremony, featuring an archery contest, which demanded that contestants hit an almost impossible target. Whoever hit that target would become the husband of Draupadī – whose unrivalled beauty awakened the desires of all the kings of the land – and it was Drupada's hope that only Arjuna could perform this feat. Chapters 175 to 191 of *Ādi-parvan* tell of how it was that none of the kings and princes assembled for the *svayaṁvara* could hit the target, so the hand of Draupadī remained unclaimed until Arjuna, disguised as a brahmin, came forward and succeeded in the task. One version of the story recounts that Karṇa might also have been able to hit the target but that when he came forward to make the attempt, he was insulted by Draupadī, who said that she would never marry such a person because of his lower birth as the son of a charioteer. This version, however, is omitted from the Critical Edition of the text.

As the five Pāṇḍavas are returning to their lodgings with Draupadī, they call out to their mother that Arjuna has won a prize, to which Kuntī replies that whatever it is must be shared between all of them. Because the command of the mother cannot be contravened, as explained above, Draupadī thus became the wife of all five of the brothers, spending a year with each of them in turn. This was a most unusual arrangement, for although polygamy was commonly practised by members of the royal order, polyandry was virtually unheard of. There are extensive debates between all parties as to whether this marriage arrangement is in accordance with *dharma*, but Yudhiṣṭhira argues that his intuition tells him that it is not to be forbidden, and because he is himself a manifestation of the deity Dharma, his instincts on *dharma* are always sound. And so it is that Draupadī becomes the common wife of all five of the Pāṇḍavas, although her greatest love is always for Arjuna.

After Dhṛtarāṣṭra rules on a division of the country, the Pāṇḍavas make a flourishing kingdom for themselves centred on the new city of Indraprastha. The arrangement is that Draupadī will live as the wife of each of the brothers in turn for a period of one year, and during that time none of the other four can enter the apartments where Draupadī is residing. In this way, Draupadī becomes the mother of five boys, bearing a son to each of the five Pāṇḍavas.

As narrated in Chapter 205 of the *Ādi-parvan*, on one occasion Arjuna is forced to enter Yudhiṣṭhira's apartments whilst Draupadī is living there as the latter's wife. Although this entry was necessitated by the need to give protection to a brahmin, and although Yudhiṣṭhira insists that no breach of trust has been made, Arjuna still feels obliged to adhere to the rule they have all agreed by going into exile for a year; he feels that it is only in this way that his adherence to the *dharma* of truth can be sustained. The travels of Arjuna are narrated at some length, along with his various encounters and adventures, but the passages of particular interest for the present discussion are those which describe how he accepts three new wives in addition to Draupadī: Subhadrā, Citrāṅgadā, and Ulūpī, and begets a son by each of them. When Draupadī learns of Arjuna's taking three other wives, she certainly does not behave in the manner that she later advocates in her conversation with Satyabhāmā,[58] telling him that he should give up her company and go and spend time with Subhadrā, although she later behaves with courtesy and kindness towards her co-wife. Perhaps this is an example of female solidarity against their unfortunate plight.

Having established a preeminent kingdom from his newly built capital city at Indraprastha, Yudhiṣṭhira then prepares to perform a great ceremony, the *rājasūya-yajña* that would celebrate the extent of his sovereignty. All the other kings of the land are invited and when Duryodhana sees the wonderful palace of the Pāṇḍavas, he becomes both envious and confused by the intricacies of its construction. As a result, he slips and falls into one of the indoor ponds of water, an affront to his dignity that is compounded several times over when he sees that Draupadī is looking down at him and laughing at his misfortune.[59] The haughty Duryodhana feels deeply insulted by this mockery, which intensifies his hatred for the Pāṇḍavas and his animosity towards Draupadī, whom he had failed to win at the *svayaṁvara* when his ability as an archer was shown to be inferior to that of Arjuna. Here we get a further insight into the character of Draupadī, who may claim to be a humble and submissive wife, but at heart is a *kṣatriya* lady who will not hesitate to gain an advantage over those she perceives to be her adversaries.

These unfortunate events at the *rājasūya* ceremony lead on to what is surely the pivotal incident in Draupadī's life, and indeed in the *Mahābhārata* narrative as a whole. Burning with anger and envy, Duryodhana and his uncle Śakuni make a plan to lure Yudhiṣṭhira into a gambling match in which Śakuni could win from Yudhiṣṭhira everything he owns by dint of his mastery

---

58 See section on the *Draupadī-satyabhāmā-saṁvāda* above.

59 *Sabhā-parvan*, 46.30.

of deceitful means of gambling with dice. This plan is brought to fruition as Yudhiṣṭhira loses game after game and is gradually stripped of his kingdom and all that he owns. Losing his head, the eldest Pāṇḍava then stakes and loses each of his brothers, his own self, and finally their beloved wife Draupadī. It is at this point that the full depth of the iniquity of the Kauravas is revealed, as they decide that they will drag Draupadī into the gambling hall and strip her naked in front of the entire assembly, including Bhīṣma and Droṇa.

At that time, Draupadī was in her chambers clad in a single garment because of the arrival of the period of her menstrual cycle. Nevertheless, Duḥśāsana grabbed her by the hair and dragged her into the assembly hall, thereby humiliating her before all the elders of the Kaurava dynasty. Addressing Bhīṣma and Droṇa by name, Draupadī bitterly condemns these elders for their silence and inaction whilst these shocking events are unfolding before their eyes, and one does indeed feel that this silence leaves a stain on the character of these men of wisdom. Eventually, Bhīṣma weakly responds by saying he cannot determine whether or not she is now the property of the Kauravas, when again one feels that proper adherence to the eternal precepts of *dharma* would compel him to intervene on her behalf. Duḥśāsana then begins to pull off Draupadī's clothing while Duryodhana exposes his thighs to her as a mark of contempt for her enslaved condition; Karṇa refers to her as a whore (*bandhakī*) for being married to five men. In that assembly, only Duryodhana, Duḥśāsana, Karṇa, and Śakuni approve of these atrocious acts, but the only person who speaks on behalf of Draupadī is Vikarṇa, one of Duryodhana's younger brothers.

Urged on by Karṇa, Duḥśāsana begins to strip Draupadī of her meagre clothing, but by a miraculous event, more and more garments appear to cover her modesty, as described in Chapter 61 of the *Sabhā-parvan*. In some manuscripts additional verses appear between verses 40 and 41 stating that it is Kṛṣṇa who provides the limitless garments, responding to prayers uttered by Draupadī; the editors of the Critical Edition, however, judged these verses to be a later addition.

Eventually, Dhṛtarāṣṭra does intervene by calling a halt to this horrific series of events, although, as is often the case, he is torn between adherence to *dharma* and his attachment to his sons and his own faction. As a result, an end is called to the disgraceful assault on Draupadī, but still the Pāṇḍavas are stripped of their kingdom and forced to live in exile for a period of thirteen years after the loss of a second dicing match. Bhīma, however, has taken a solemn vow that he will avenge these insults to Draupadī by breaking the thighs of Duryodhana and ripping out the heart of Duḥśāsana before drinking his blood. Now the outcome of the entire narrative is certain, for the abuse of Draupadī has been so terrible, and the insults so deep, that conflict between the Pāṇḍavas and the other Kauravas is inevitable. Draupadī thinks only of revenge and repeatedly urges her husbands to never forget the treatment she received at the hands of Duryodhana and his associates. Thus we can see the pivotal position of Draupadī in the progression of the *Mahābhārata* as a whole, as the narrative moves inexorably towards its sanguinary conclusion.

At the start of their exile and their life as forest-dwellers, Draupadī bitterly resents their misfortune and blames Yudhiṣṭhira for the loss of their opulent lifestyle. In Chapters 28 to 33 of the *Āraṇyaka-parvan*, we find an intense debate between Draupadī and Yudhiṣṭhira in which she demonstrates yet again her intelligence and learning, as well as the manner in which she feels able to challenge her husbands' behaviour. In Chapters 28 and 29, she demands of Yudhiṣṭhira why he does not unleash his anger against those who have wronged them, as this is the proper conduct to be expected of all *kṣatriyas* who properly adhere to their social *dharma*. Forgiveness, *kṣamā*, is right and proper in some situations, she says, but not when universally applied, as Yudhiṣṭhira does. She cites an ancient discussion on this subject between Prahlāda and Bali in which the former indicates the particular circumstances in which *kṣamā* inspires the wrong course of action. Because the wicked deeds of their enemies have been so extreme, forgiveness is inappropriate, particularly for a man of *kṣatriya* birth.

Yudhiṣṭhira replies to his wife's criticisms not by telling her that a woman should never speak to her husband in this way, but by presenting the counter-argument that the force of anger is always to be resisted by a righteous person. Anger leads inevitably to wicked actions that cause harm to those who are innocent, whilst forgiveness is a great virtue, the very essence of true *dharma*. Uncowed by this rejection of her views, Draupadī replies by praising the wonderful acts of the 'Ordainer', the Deity who oversees the fate of all beings as a result of their previous acts, and who has covered her husband's mind with *moha*, delusion, so that he holds to such ridiculous views. She then switches her line of discussion by praising Yudhiṣṭhira's matchless virtue, and condemning the Deity who controls the world for allowing such a righteous person to be afflicted in this way, with his happy and virtuous life now ruined. The Deity should shower blessings on the righteous as a reward for their virtuous deeds, but it appears that the opposite is in fact the case.

Now Yudhiṣṭhira condemns Draupadī's speech as being that of a *nāstika*, a non-believer, because of the harsh words she has directed towards the Deity. He does not perform virtuous acts in the expectation of some future reward, but because they represent the proper way in which a person should live; such acts of virtue are the essence of *dharma*, and *dharma* stands above every other consideration. Draupadī then says she regrets her previous words of condemnation directed towards the Deity, but she still does not accept Yudhiṣṭhira's understanding of his own *dharma*. Again she speaks in favour of resolute action as the means by which the most favourable outcome is achieved. Those who are foolish and weak say that our fate is determined simply by the power of destiny, as shaped by previous *karma,* but a more realistic view shows that proper action does indeed shape the results we achieve.

Positive outcomes are achieved through skilful activities, otherwise why would we engage skilled craftsmen to achieve difficult tasks? If destiny controls all things, we could act in any way we choose, seek the help of any person regardless of his ability, and the outcome would be the same. Any observation of the ways of the world will reveal that this is obviously not the case. Destiny is certainly a factor, but relying solely on destiny without taking appropriate action is sheer folly. The teachings she is presenting to Yudhiṣṭhira came originally from the celestial *guru,* Bṛhaspati; she learned them from her brothers who passed on to her the good instruction they received, and she learned similar lessons seated on her father's lap when he was receiving instruction from a brahmin. At this point, Bhīma joins the debate, reasserting Draupadī's side of the argument, and at the end no clear resolution of the issue is arrived at, although Yudhiṣṭhira does not change his view that they must passively accept their fate.

Not only is Draupadī a woman of great intelligence and learning, she is also renowned for her celestial beauty, which causes problems both for herself and her husbands. Chapters 248 to 256 of the *Āraṇyaka-parvan* give an account of how further difficulties came upon the Pāṇḍavas and their wife due to her unparalleled beauty. Once while the five Pāṇḍavas are away from their dwelling-place, she is approached by Jayadratha, an inimical king who is allured by her beauty and wishes to take her for his own. He first tries to tempt her by offering to take her away from the poverty of forest life to live with him a life of luxury in his palaces. Draupadī responds angrily to these words, calling Jayadratha a fool and a child who is a feeble wretch compared to the might of her husbands. With his advances thus rejected, Jayadratha attempts to seize Draupadī by force but is thrown to the ground by the angry queen. Eventually he does manage to take her away on his chariot but is pursued and captured by Bhīma and Arjuna. They are of the view that Jayadratha should be executed for his crime of kidnapping the wife of another, but Yudhiṣṭhira shows mercy and releases him on condition that he proclaim to all other rulers that he is the servant of the Pāṇḍavas. This act of apparent kindness on Yudhiṣṭhira's part simply inflames the hatred of the humiliated Jayadratha, and leads to disastrous consequences at Kurukṣetra.

A somewhat similar incident is described in the *Virāṭa-parvan* when the Pāṇḍavas were concealing their true identity whilst remaining in hiding in the kingdom of the Matsyas. Kīcaka, the powerful commander of the army of the Matsyas, becomes infatuated with Draupadī's beauty and makes repeated advances towards her, each time with more of a threat of physical force. Eventually, when it appears that she is likely to become a victim of rape, she appeals for help from her husbands. In rather typical fashion, Yudhiṣṭhira advises that one must adopt a mood of tolerance in the face of adversity, but Bhīma takes forceful action, dressing as a woman to disguise himself as Draupadī, and then beating Kīcaka to death when an assignation is arranged. This action reveals the true identity of the Pāṇḍavas but, fortunately, the time of their exile has already been surpassed, and they are free to return and reclaim their kingdom in line with the terms of their agreement with the Kauravas.

The *Āraṇyaka-parvan* also shows us the love, respect, and devotion felt by Bhīma and the other Pāṇḍavas for Draupadī. Once when she became weary on their travels, her husbands all felt great distress at her plight, and Bhīma summoned his son Ghaṭotkaca, who was able to carry her as they journeyed on.[60] A little later on, they find a most beautiful, sweet-smelling lotus flower blown by the wind, and Draupadī expresses a desire to get a bunch of these celestial blossoms. The Pāṇḍavas respond immediately to this request, and Bhīma sets out into the mountains to find where those lotus flowers were growing. On the way, he has a number of encounters, including a meeting with Hanumān and a fight with celestial beings, *yakṣas* and *rākṣasas*, who were guardians of the sacred lake where the lotuses were to be found.

Some manuscripts of the *Mahābhārata* emphasise Draupadī's devotion to Kṛṣṇa, and the way in which she prays to him for help during times of adversity. We have already mentioned her calling out to Kṛṣṇa when she was being disrobed after the gambling match, and in the *Āraṇyaka-parvan*, we are told of an incident in which Kṛṣṇa again miraculously delivered her and her husbands from a curse by an angry *ṛṣi* named Durvāsas. The editors of the Critical Edition, however, judged that these references to Draupadī's devotion were later additions that are not found in most of the manuscript versions, although they are widely known and highly regarded amongst the people of India.

After the battle at Kurukṣetra has been won, Aśvatthāman, the son of Droṇa, enters the camp of the Pāṇḍavas and kills all the surviving kings and warriors, including the five sons that Draupadī has born to the Pāṇḍavas. The Pāṇḍavas themselves were absent at that time, and when Draupadī learns of the loss of her sons, she displays the martial spirit of a *kṣatriya* and demands that her husbands avenge the cruel slaying of these young princes by killing Aśvatthāman. In the end, Aśvatthāman is captured, stripped of a mystical protective

60 *Āraṇyaka-parvan*, Chapter 144.

jewel that he bears on his head, and cursed to roam the Earth for 3,000 years in a state of poverty and distress. Throughout all the previous discussions over the righteous use of violent means, Draupadī takes a leading role in urging the Pāṇḍavas to follow the *kṣatriya* usage and to punish those who have wronged them. Here again she displays that same aggressive spirit, though she accepts that the punishment dealt to Aśvatthāman is fitting, as he is a brahmin by birth, and hence not to be executed by *kṣatriyas*.

At the beginning of the *Śānti-parvan*, when the conflict is over, we find Yudhiṣṭhira lamenting and bitterly regretting the death and destruction he sees himself as having caused. He proposes to renounce the royal status he has now recovered, and to go to the forest to live as a religious mendicant. His four brothers speak against Yudhiṣṭhira's determination to renounce the kingdom they have won, and in Chapter 14 Draupadī joins the discussion, bitterly condemning his decision and challenging his idea of *dharma*. He is *kṣatriya*, she says, not a brahmin, and as such it is his religious duty to rule the kingdom and protect the citizens. Moreover, he owes a debt of gratitude to his brothers, who fought so valiantly on his behalf. Before their exile, they were rulers of the earth and he has promised both herself and his brothers that they would regain that regal splendour when the battle was won. Turning the full weight of her frustration against him, she says:

30. *anṛtaṁ mābravīc chvaśrūḥ sarva-jñā sarva-darśinī*
yudhiṣṭhiras tvāṁ pāñcāli sukhe dhāsyaty anuttame

My all-knowing, all-seeing mother-in-law, whose
speech is never false, spoke these words to me,
'Yudhiṣṭhira will keep you in a state of happiness,
O matchless Pāñcalī.

31. *hatvā rāja-sahasrāṇi bahūny āśu-parākramaḥ*
tad vyarthaṁ saṁprapaśyāmi mohāt tava janādhipa

After slaying many thousands of kings through his vigorous exertion.' But I see, O king, that because of your stupidity, this will have been for nothing.

32. *yeṣām unmattako jyeṣṭhaḥ sarve tasyopacāriṇaḥ*
tavonmādena rājendra sonmādāḥ sarva-pāṇḍavāḥ

Those whose eldest brother has become insane must now follow on in the same way. As a result of your insanity, O king of kings, all the Pāṇḍavas must now become insane.

33. *yadi hi syur anunmattā bhrātaras te janādhipa*
baddhvā tvāṁ nāstikaiḥ sārdhaṁ praśāseyur vasuṁdharām

If your brothers have not become insane, O king, then, having bound you along with other non-believers, they should rule the kingdom themselves.

34. *kurute mūḍham evaṁ hi yaḥ śreyo nādhigacchati*
dhūpair añjana-yogaiś ca nasya-karmabhir eva ca
bheṣajaiḥ sa cikitsyaḥ syād ya unmārgeṇa gacchati

One who acts like a fool never achieves anything beneficial. Anyone who goes astray like this should be treated with incense, by applying ointments, by inserting medicines through the nose, and by various other medications.[61]

---

61 *Śānti-parvan*, 14.31–34.

Yudhiṣṭhira is eventually persuaded to give up his intention of renouncing the world, though only after Kṛṣṇa and Vyāsa have spoken at length to convince him that ruling the kingdom with justice and concern for the citizens is the best way for him to adhere to the principles of *dharma*.

At the end of the *Mahābhārata*, Yudhiṣṭhira and his brothers do finally decide that the time has come to accept a life of renunciation and depart from Hastināpura, journeying northwards on foot towards the Himalayas. It is here that we encounter Draupadī for the last time as one by one she and four of the Pāṇḍava brothers fall from the path and meet with death. We learn that each of them had a particular fault that led to their falling short of a state of perfect purity; the fault attributed to Draupadī is that she favoured Arjuna over her other four husbands. Yudhiṣṭhira then journeys on alone and is finally elevated to the realm of the gods without having to taste death, this because of his adherence to *dharma* without ever once deviating from righteous conduct.

The eighteenth and final book of the *Mahābhārata*, the *Svargārohaṇa-parvan*, tells of Yudhiṣṭhira's elevation to *svarga-loka*, the realm of the gods, and his first passing through *naraka-loka*, where those who have been wicked in life suffer the negative *karma* of their actions. There he perceives the presence of Draupadī and his brothers existing in a state of torment, but this is just an illusory vision that he is forced to experience because of the deceptive means employed to kill Droṇa. When the vision is dispersed, he sees Draupadī and his brothers all present amongst the gods, with Draupadī having resumed her celestial identity as Śrī, the goddess who bestows wealth, good fortune, and prosperity.

Other Female Characters within the Mahābhārata

In addition to the three principal female characters, who play a pivotal role in the central narrative, there are a good number of others, most of whom are referred to in the numerous secondary passages that punctuate the progression of that central narrative.

Śakuntalā: The wife of King Duḥṣanta, an ancestor of the Kauravas. She begot a son named by Bharata by him, but Duḥṣanta then refused to acknowledge either Śakuntalā or her son as his own. Refusing to accept this rejection, Śakuntalā forces Duḥṣanta to accept herself as his lawful wife and Bharata as the heir to the throne.[62]

Satyavatī: The wife of King Śaṁtanu and the mother of three sons, Vyāsa (by the ṛṣi Parāśara), Citrāṅgada, and Vicitravīrya. After the death of Śaṁtanu and his two sons, Satyavatī, alongside Bhīṣma, becomes the de facto ruler of the kingdom and oversees the perpetuation of the line by arranging for Vyāsa to beget sons by the wives of Vicitravīrya.[63]

Sāvitrī: In the *Āraṇyaka-parvan*,[64] the *ṛṣi* Mārkaṇḍeya narrates to the Pāṇḍavas the story of Sāvitrī, a princess of great learning and intelligence, who delivers her husband Satyavān from the clutches of Yama, the God of Death, by delighting him with a wonderful discourse on the true understanding of *dharma*.

Damayantī: Also in the *Āraṇyaka-parvan*,[65] we have the story of Damayantī and Nala, narrated to the Pāṇḍavas by a *ṛṣi* named Bṛhadaśva. This is a story of love conquering over

---

62 *Ādi-parvan*, Chapters 63–69.

63 *Ādi-parvan*, Chapters 97–100.

64 Chapters 277–283.

65 Chapters 50–78.

all adversity. Despite separation and innumerable tribulations, the love of Nala for Damayantī, and Damayantī for Nala, remains constant and unwavering until they are eventually reunited to give us a longed-for happy ending.

Sulabhā: The *Śānti-parvan* provides us with a good number of passages of instruction on the path to spiritual enlightenment, known collectively as the *Mokṣa-dharma-parvan*. In Chapter 308 of the *Śānti-parvan,* we learn of an encounter between King Janaka of Mithilā and a female renunciant named Sulabhā. The discussion between them has a number of points of interest, but here we might notice Sulabhā's rejection of Janaka's claim ...that despite his opulent lifestyle he is free of attachment, and also her response to Janaka's criticism of the idea of a woman living as a *saṁnyāsin* (renunciant) and acting as a teacher. At one point Janaka asks her, *kasya tvaṁ kuto vā,* 'Whose are you? Where have you come from?'[66] In a blistering response, Sulabhā states that Janaka's claim to enlightenment is a false one, for a truly enlightened person would see her in relation to her true identity as *puruṣa,* the spiritual reality, and not be preoccupied with the mundane conception of gender. It is interesting to note in this regard that the *Bhagavad-gītā* confirms Janaka's idea that one can attain spiritual perfection without the need for physical renunciation, and cites Janaka as an example of this.[67] Clearly, Sulabhā does not share the *Gītā*'s view on this point.

King Bhaṅgāśvana: In Chapter 12 of the *Anuśāsana-parvan,* Bhīṣma tells Yudhiṣṭhira the remarkable story of Bhaṅgāśvana, who lived as both a man and a woman. Having displeased Indra, King Bhaṅgāśvana was transformed into a woman after begetting a hundred sons by his wives. As a female, he becomes the consort of a sage living in the forest and begets another hundred sons

---

66 *Śānti-parvan,* 308.20.

67 *Bhagavad-gītā,* 3.20.

by him, but the angry Indra then engineers the deaths of both of these two groups of offspring. After propitiating the lord of the gods, Bhaṅgāśvana is offered the choice of having one of the two groups of offspring brought back to life, and the possibility of recovering his masculine identity. The choices he makes are interesting, and perhaps surprising. He first chooses to have the princes he bore as a woman brought back to life, stating that a woman's love for her children is always greater than that of a man, and then opts to remain as a woman because, having experienced both, he is certain that the sexual pleasure enjoyed by a woman is greater than that of her male counterpart.

Discussion and Conclusion

What immediately strikes one from this review of the *Mahābhārata*'s representation of the female gender is the dissonance between the direct teachings on a woman's conjugal role and position in society, and the manner in which the character and conduct of the main female protagonists is portrayed. In her conversation with Satyabhāmā, Draupadī describes herself as having a position of constant inferiority in relation to her husbands, fearing to do anything that might displease them or cause them to become angry with her. Her role in the government of the realm shows that her intellect and ability are respected, in contrast to the view of women presented by Bhīṣma in the *Anuśāsana-parvan*, but even here she is cast in the role of a servant rather than an equal partner.

In the progression of the central narrative, however, we find Draupadī conducting herself in a manner that is clearly at odds with that which she advocates in speaking to Satyabhāmā. In debating the proper course of action with Yudhiṣṭhira, she shows herself to be learned in the subject of *dharma*, and assertive in setting forward her own views. And it is surely significant that in these debates never once is her right to express an opinion challenged on the basis of her gender. Rather, she is allowed to participate as an equal in all discussions. Then, after the battle is over, her reference to Yudhiṣṭhira as *unmattaka*, mad or insane, could not display a greater contrast to her earlier speech to Satyabhāmā.

We must also notice the derogatory manner in which the character and attributes of women are described in the *Anuśāsana-parvan*. According to that passage, women are petty-minded and preoccupied with desire for pretty things and trivial gifts. Draupadī may indeed have desires for the material prosperity that comes with royal status, but she is no trivial fool, besotted with such acquisitions. She has learned about *dharma* from a young age and has the intellectual acumen to challenge Yudhiṣṭhira, the ultimate authority on *dharma*. It is also clearly the case that rather than regarding Draupadī as their servant, her husbands are all very much in love with her and have a great admiration for her intellectual attributes. They aspire to serve her by responding to her wishes, as is demonstrated when Bhīma journeys into the mountains in pursuit of lotus flowers that have attracted her mind, as well as his violent response to Kīcaka's reprehensible behaviour. More than anything else, it is the Kauravas' abuse of Draupadī that makes war inevitable, because of the love and respect the Pāṇḍavas have for their wife.

Throughout the course of the narrative, Draupadī, Gāndhārī, and Kuntī are presented in a manner that clearly contrasts with the view of women as expressed in the *Anuśāsana-parvan*. They are wise, intelligent, and enlightened, and yet because of the imbalance of power between the genders, they are forced to endure numerous afflictions due to the less elevated dispositions of the male protagonists. They lack power to influence events, and though they speak out against the folly and iniquity of the male characters, they are effectively disenfranchised by the political and social systems of the age. One might also notice that whilst the dharma-śāstric passages of the *Mahābhārata* find an echo in the *Manu-smṛti* in advocating child marriage and a lack of choice for women over their marriage partners, this also is not reflected in the central narrative. The description of Draupadī's feminine beauty at the time of the archery contest demonstrates quite clearly that at this time she was a fully developed young woman, whilst Kuntī was allowed free choice of a husband by which she selected Pāṇḍu from amongst all the other princes of the land. We are also told the story of Sāvitrī, who was permitted to travel the length and breadth of her father's kingdom until she found the man she would choose as a husband. The exception here is with respect to Gāndhārī, whose marriage to Dhṛtarāṣṭra was arranged by her father to ensure a dynastic alliance, a common practice amongst almost all royal families of earlier centuries.

Gāndhārī's decision to accept voluntary blindness throughout her life certainly suggests an attitude of submission to the superiority of her husband, whom she does not wish to exceed in any way, but in later life she repeatedly shows herself to be willing to instruct Dhṛtarāṣṭra about proper conduct and at times criticise the course of conduct he is pursuing. Whilst her husband dithers and vacillates, it is Gāndhārī alone who comes forward and demands that the gambling match be stopped, and it is she alone who has the courage and moral capacity to demand that Yudhiṣṭhira should replace her own son as the ruler of the kingdom. Her husband is weak-minded and under the control of his attachment to worldly gain and familial prejudice; only Gāndhārī is able rise above such sentiments by displaying the elevated wisdom that places *dharma* above personal attachment.

Kuntī at times displays a single-minded focus on self-interest, but all three are women of intelligence and possess a level of wisdom that frequently appears to excel that of the male characters; the contrast between Gāndhārī and Dhṛtarāṣṭra is particularly noteworthy. Hence the reader of the *Mahābhārata* has a choice: either accept the type of thinking encountered within the *Manu-smṛti* and the *Anuśāsana-parvan,* or regard the representation of female characters as offering a more enlightened insight into gender roles. Ultimately, one is left to reflect on whether or not there would have been a more auspicious outcome to events if female wisdom had been allowed to prevail over the folly of the men. But then, of course, the counter-argument would be that it is the possession of power that acts as a corrupting influence on the human mind.

Finally, we must also be aware of the purely spiritual insights on issues of gender, which carry the discussion beyond any consideration of worldly *dharma*. As is emphasised by Sulabhā, one of the founders of the Sāṁkhya system, from the highest perspective there are no distinctions of male and female, for each individual living being is a spiritual entity moving from one bodily form to another. Designations such as man or woman, brahmin or *śūdra,* are temporary, pertaining only to one life and not to the enlightened perception of the highest reality. It is on this basis that Sulabhā criticises the gender-based questions put to her by Janaka, and, in more recent times, this exact same point was made by Swami Vivekananda when he called for a transformation of gender relations in nineteenth-century India.

Discussion Topic: Women

Here are some questions you might care to ponder after completing this chapter:

- How would you describe Bhīṣma's and Draupadī's instructions on the position and behaviour of women?
- As these teachings are a part of the *Mahābhārata,* should they be given any authoritative status by Hindus and others? If not, why not?
- Which of the female characters portrayed in the *Mahābhārata* do you most admire?
- What are the main differences you notice between the teachings on gender roles given by Bhīṣma and the conduct of the main female characters.

IV
The Divine Identity

As well as its recounting the story of a great conflict in ancient India, and the ethical dilemmas raised as a result of the events described, the *Mahābhārata* is also a deeply spiritual account of divine intervention in the world. In this chapter, I want to explore the way that the divine nature and the divine identity is presented within the *Mahābhārata*, with the primary emphasis on Kṛṣṇa as an *avatāra* of Viṣṇu, although he is never referred to by that term in the text itself. There can be little doubt that the *Mahābhārata* is one the earliest works of Vaiṣṇava theism that is still extant today, and this chapter explores the precise nature of the Vaiṣṇava doctrines it presents to its readers.

We will also have to notice, however, the role of Śiva in the progression of the narrative and the nature of the relationship between Viṣṇu and Śiva that we encounter within the eighteen *parvans* of the text as a whole. And, finally, I want to offer an overview of the theological perspectives located within the *Mahābhārata*, which draw our attention to the prevailing strands of monotheism, monism, and polytheism present within Indian religion as a whole, as well as the understanding that liberation from rebirth is attained not just through personal enlightenment, or yogic perfection, but also as a gift of divine grace granted by the Deity as an act of love. Although confining such a wide-ranging discussion within a single chapter is a daunting task, an attempt will be made to do justice to the complexities of the questions raised.

Vaiṣṇavism and the Mahābhārata

The earliest references we have to a Deity known as Viṣṇu are to be found within the hymns of the *Ṛgveda Saṁhitā*, although only five (or possibly six) of those hymns are dedicated exclusively to Viṣṇu, in comparison to the 250 or more dedicated to Indra. Vaiṣṇavism appears to have risen to prominence some time after the original Vedic era, and developed as a distinctive strand of Indian religious thought. Vaiṣṇavism elevated Viṣṇu, who is also often named as Nārāyaṇa, far beyond his Vedic status to the level of a monotheistic Deity, the creator and controller of the entire world, whose own existence is beyond this world in a domain that is purely spiritual. This spiritual domain is named as Vaikuṇṭha in the later Vaiṣṇava texts, although we only very rarely encounter this term in the *Mahābhārata*. The existence of the Vedic deities, including Indra, is not denied, but Vaiṣṇava teachings hold to the view that these are lesser gods who have power within this world but are themselves a part of the creation of Viṣṇu, and hence no more than the highest of mortal beings. On some occasions, we find the idea that the Vedic gods are in fact different manifestations of Viṣṇu, but more frequently they are shown to be servants of Viṣṇu who act as his agents in the supervision of the created world.

Although the idea is rarely encountered in the early texts, there is a widespread understanding that Brahmā, Viṣṇu, and Śiva are three aspects of the one inconceivable Supreme Deity who execute the three functions of creation, sustenance, and destruction in relation to this world. From the perspective of Vaiṣṇava teachings, however, Brahmā and Śiva are not to be regarded as equal divinities to Viṣṇu, but as his servants, or, at best, secondary expanded forms of Viṣṇu who act on his behalf. In later Vaiṣṇava thought, Viṣṇu is typically shown in association with the Śrī, or Lakṣmī, who is the eternal feminine principle of the divine, but this idea of dual divinity does not appear in the *Mahābhārata* and, although Śrī is quite frequently mentioned, it is never as the consort of Viṣṇu.

From a scriptural perspective, the full flowering of Vaiṣṇava theism is to be found in works such as the *Viṣṇu Purāṇa* and the *Bhāgavata Purāṇa*, and it is there that we find detailed descriptions of the form of Viṣṇu. He is said to be the colour of a dark monsoon cloud, with four arms bearing a conch shell, disc, lotus, and club, adorned with a garland, a crown, and various items of jewellery. His lower body is clad in a garment of yellow silk and his smiling face reflects the benign nature of the Deity, although he is sometimes shown as sleeping on a bed made up of the cosmic serpent Ananta, with Lakṣmī serving him by massaging his legs.

A significant feature of Vaiṣṇava religious teachings is the doctrine of *avatāra*, which asserts that when the order of creation is disturbed in some way, the Deity assumes a particular form and 'crosses down' (the literal meaning of *avatāra*) in order to resolve the problem. The best known and most widely revered of such *avatāras* are certainly Kṛṣṇa and Rāma, and therefore the widespread worship of both of these deities falls under the broad heading of Vaiṣṇavism. Śaivism also includes the idea of divine descents, but the doctrine of *avatāra* is a central feature of Vaiṣṇava teachings to an extent not encountered in Śaivite devotion, and much of the content of the *Viṣṇu Purāṇa* and *Bhāgavata Purāṇa* is devoted to accounts of the descents of the numerous and variegated forms adopted by Viṣṇu to fulfil specific functions in this world.

The earliest texts available to us today in which we can clearly detect the appearance of this monotheistic Vaiṣṇavism are the *Mahābhārata* and *Rāmāyaṇa*, both of which almost certainly predate the Vaiṣṇava Purāṇas; and of these two great epic works, it is only in the *Mahābhārata* that we find a clearly stated exposition of Vaiṣṇava theism. So let us now consider the features of Vaiṣṇavism outlined above that are present within the vast corpus of the *Mahābhārata,* and the manner in which they are presented therein.

Within the *Mahābhārata,* we find a good number of passages in which Viṣṇu, or Nārāyaṇa, is extolled as the one Supreme Deity. There are also frequent passing references to the absolute divine supremacy of Viṣṇu, but the main passages that discuss this topic in detail are as follows:

1. Within the *Āraṇyaka-parvan,* there is a substantial passage that describes the teachings delivered to the Pāṇḍavas by the *ṛṣi* Mārkaṇḍeya. This passage contains forty-one chapters in all (181–221), and covers a wide range of topics including an account of the *ṛṣi*'s encounter with Nārāyaṇa in the form of a child after the destruction of the world.[68] He perceives the entire world with all its varieties within the body of Viṣṇu, and he is then instructed by the Lord about the divine nature of this one Supreme Deity. His name is Nārāyaṇa, and the world and all living beings, including the gods, are his body. He is the creator and destroyer, he is formless, *arūpin,*[69] but bears the conch, disc, and club.[70]
2. In Chapter 192 of the *Āraṇyaka-parvan,* Mārkaṇḍeya speaks about the life of another *ṛṣi,* of the name of Uttaṅka. Seeking the blessings of the Deity, Uttaṅka undertook acts of severe austerity and offered prayers in which he glorified the divine nature of Viṣṇu. The

68 *Āraṇyaka-parvan,* Chapters 186–187.

69 *Āraṇyaka-parvan,* 187.34.

70 *Āraṇyaka-parvan,* 187.38.

glorification of Viṣṇu enunciated by Uttaṅka is then recited to the Pāṇḍavas by Mārkaṇḍeya.

3. In Chapters 61 and 62 of the *Bhīṣma-parvan*, we find Saṁjaya urging Duryodhana and Dhṛtarāṣṭra to make peace with the Pāṇḍavas, first of all by emphasising the insurmountable prowess of their adversaries. He then reveals that the triumph of the Pāṇḍavas is certain because of the descent of Nārāyaṇa in the form of Kṛṣṇa to ensure that outcome, and he gives an account of Brahmā's prayers to the Deity to invoke the appearance of the *avatāra*. These prayers include an extensive treatise on the divine nature of Viṣṇu and his identity as the one Supreme Deity, the creator, controller, and sustainer of the world.
4. After the battle at Kurukṣetra is over, the Pāṇḍavas approach Bhīṣma, who is still lying on the battlefield, his body shot through with arrows. From that prone position, he delivers a huge body of instruction on a wide range of subjects, but before beginning these teachings he first offers prayers to Kṛṣṇa, who is with the Pāṇḍavas, praising him in terms of his true identity as Nārāyaṇa. Bhīṣma's eulogy of the Deity, which refers to his pervasive presence within this world, is presented in Chapter 47 of the *Śānti-parvan*.
5. Within the vast body of Bhīṣma's teachings to the Pāṇḍavas is a passage named the *Keśava-māhātmya* (*Śānti-parvan*, Chapter 200), which focuses primarily on the creative acts by which Viṣṇu generates Brahmā from a lotus sprouting from his navel, and then on the progression of the creation under the supervision of the Deity. This is followed shortly afterwards (Ch 202) by an account of Viṣṇu's appearance as the Varāha (boar) *avatāra*.

6. Almost at the end of the *Śānti-parvan*, running through Chapters 321 to 339, we find the longest passage of overtly Vaiṣṇava teachings, a section of the *Śānti-parvan* named the *Nārāyaṇīya*. This lengthy passage tells of the sage Nārada's entry into the spiritual realm of Nārāyaṇa, which is named as Śvetadvīpa, the white island. There he perceives numerous devotees of the Deity, all possessing the same form as their Lord, and receives instructions from Nārāyaṇa about the divine identity. Also included here are a number of narrative accounts relating to the nature and activities of the Deity. It is interesting to notice that these chapters appear to represent the teachings of Pāñcarātra Vaiṣṇavism, one of the earliest branches of the tradition, which is still prominent today although it has undergone extensive tantric revision and is now primarily focused on the rituals performed in temples dedicated to Viṣṇu and his *avatāras*. This is not merely a speculative opinion, as the text itself names the Pāñcarātra as the basis for the teachings it presents.[71]
7. And, of course, we cannot ignore the importance of the *Bhagavad-gītā*, which forms an integral part of the *Mahābhārata*'s wider discourse. It has at times been suggested that the *Gītā* should not be taken as Vaiṣṇava because the Deity it reveres is Kṛṣṇa rather than Viṣṇu, and at no point does it assert that Kṛṣṇa is an *avatāra* of Viṣṇu. This view, however, appears to be unsustainable for a number of reasons. First of all, it overlooks the position of the *Bhagavad-gītā* within the *Mahābhārata*, even though the *Gītā* itself is very much aware of its context and makes extensive

71 As, for example, in *Śānti-parvan*, 326.100 and 337.67.

> use of it, and the *Mahābhārata* consistently identifies Kṛṣṇa as a manifestation of Nārāyaṇa. Secondly, the vocative terms by which Arjuna addresses Kṛṣṇa, names such as Keśava, Madhusūdana, Janārdana, are almost all well-attested epithets of Viṣṇu, whilst on two occasions Arjuna refers to Kṛṣṇa directly as Viṣṇu.[72] And perhaps most convincingly of all, Arjuna asks Kṛṣṇa to reveal to him his form that is *catur-bhuja*, having four arms, a clear reference to the iconography of Viṣṇu.[73] Hence my feeling is that the *Bhagavad-gītā* must be included in any meaningful discussion of the Vaiṣṇavism of the *Mahābhārata*.

Based on these principal passages, we can now begin our necessarily brief discussion of the nature of the Vaiṣṇavism that is to be encountered within the *Mahābhārata*. Perhaps the most obvious point at which to start is with the narrative accounts of how Viṣṇu brought about the creation of this world. It is said that after the vast period of time when the world is manifest, it is withdrawn again into a state of dissolution. Viṣṇu then lies down on a bed made up of his serpent form of Ananta; when the time for a new creation arrives, a lotus flower sprouts from the navel of the Deity and Brahmā, the first created being, appears from within the whorl of the lotus. Brahmā wishes to begin the process of creation, but at that point two evil beings, Madhu and Kaiṭabha, appear from two drops of water set by Nārāyaṇa within the lotus. These two *asuras* prevent Brahmā from performing his creative task by stealing away the Vedas and hiding that pure wisdom within the ocean. Responding to prayers offered by Brahmā, Nārāyaṇa then

72 *Bhagavad-gītā*, 11.24, 11.30.

73 *Bhagavad-gītā*, 11.46.

awakens and destroys the *asuras*, thereby acquiring the name of Madhusūdana (literally the destroyer of Madhu). With the Vedas restored to him, Brahmā is then able to embark on the creative action that is his inherent duty.

We find this creation narrative, with minor variants, at several points within the *Mahābhārata*, and it becomes a staple element of most of the Purāṇas that were almost certainly composed at a later date. Mārkaṇḍeya narrates an account of the story to the Pāṇḍavas in Chapter 194 of the *Āraṇyaka-parvan*, adding the detail that it was with his disc weapon that Viṣṇu slew the *asuras*, and Bhīṣma makes a brief reference to it as a part of his attempt to convince Duryodhana that the Pāṇḍavas cannot be defeated.[74] The main focus of the *Keśava-māhātmya* (*Śānti-parvan*, Chapter 200) is on the creative potency of Viṣṇu, and this passage also provides a version of the same story, but it is in the *Nara-nārāyaṇīya* that the fullest account is presented (*Śānti-parvan*, Chapter 335).

Most of the passages of teaching contained in the *Mokṣa-dharma* portion of the *Śānti-parvan* (Chapters 168–353) adhere to the doctrines of Sāṁkhya and as such explain the origins of this world in non-theistic terms. The idea is that primal *prakṛti*, the original undifferentiated material substance, evolves gradually into the different elements of which this variegated world is comprised. In most of these passages, this process is said to take place without any creative impulse from a Deity, and as such present something of a contrast to the Vaiṣṇava accounts of creation encountered elsewhere in the *Mahābhārata*. In certain passages, however, we find the narrative and Sāṁkhya accounts of creation combined together (as, for example, in Chapter 291 of *Śānti-parvan*), whilst in the *Keśava-māhātmya* and the *Bhagavad-gītā* (9.10), it

74 *Bhīṣma-parvan*, Chapter 63.

is said that the evolutionary transformation of primal matter into the variegated world is instigated by the Deity as an act of divine creation.

The Form of Viṣṇu

Each of the passages referred to above has its own unique features, but our task here must be to take a more general overview of the style of Vaiṣṇavism that is typically found within the *Mahābhārata*. First of all then, let us consider the iconographic descriptions and pictorial representations of Viṣṇu that are such a pervasive feature of Purāṇic accounts and the later Vaiṣṇava traditions as a whole. The *Mahābhārata* is certainly aware of Viṣṇu as a Deity with a form that has four arms, but it is accurate to state that a focus on the divine form is a less prominent feature of the prayers and descriptions of Viṣṇu contained within the *Mahābhārata*. As mentioned above, the idea of Lakṣmī as the consort of Viṣṇu does not appear, and neither does the understanding of Viṣṇu as being of a blackish bodily hue. On the small number of occasions where his form is referred to, he is described as being golden or white in colour.[75]

The understanding of Viṣṇu as having four arms which bear four symbolic objects is similarly mentioned only infrequently in the *Mahābhārata*, but it appears often enough for us to state that it is a feature of the Vaiṣṇavism encountered therein.[76] The Deity is referred to by the terms *catur-bāhu* or *catur-bhuja*, both meaning 'four-armed', but the best known of such references is to be found in the *Bhagavad-gītā*.[77] It is also the case that we find Viṣṇu described as bearing a conch shell,

75 As, for example in *Āraṇyaka-parvan*, 186.86 and *Śānti-parvan*, 330.3.

76 As, for example, in *Āraṇyaka-parvan*, 260.5 and *Udyoga-parvan*, 64.15.

77 *Bhagavad-gītā*, 11.46.

disc, and club,[78] but again this is not a major feature of the *Mahābhārata*'s descriptions of the Deity.

Hence it is accurate to assert that the well-known iconography of Viṣṇu is very much in the background in the *Mahābhārata*, whilst the main focus of the prayers and descriptive accounts is on the role Nārāyaṇa plays as the creator and controller of the world and, most especially, on his pervasive presence within his creation. We have noted the passage in the *Āraṇyaka-parvan* in which Mārkaṇḍeya enters the body of Viṣṇu and beholds the entire creation within the form of the Deity. When Nārāyaṇa reveals his own identity to the *ṛṣi*, he describes how each part of the world, the mountains, rivers, trees, and living beings, are a part of his body, although he also states that he possesses no bodily form (*arūpin*).[79] This understanding of the Deity being omnipresent throughout the created world as the pervasive force that maintains the created order clearly resonates with the revelation of the *viśva-rūpa* in Chapter 11 of the *Bhagavad-gītā*, and is confirmed on several occasions in the course of Kṛṣṇa's teachings to Arjuna. We have noticed the *Gītā*'s mention of the four-armed form of the Deity, but a far more prevalent feature of its revelation about the nature of God is this same idea of the pervasive divine presence within this world, expressed in words such as *mayi sarvam idaṁ protaṁ sūtre maṇi-gaṇā iva*, 'as jewels are strung on a thread, so this whole world is strung on me',[80] or *mayā tatam idaṁ sarvaṁ jagad avyakta-mūrtinā*, 'this whole world is pervaded by me in my non-manifest form'.[81] Thus we can observe how the theology of the *Bhagavad-gītā* is entirely congruent with the Vaiṣṇava theism of the *Mahābhārata* as a whole.

---

78 As, for example, in the *Āraṇyaka-parvan*, 187.38.

79 *Āraṇyaka-parvan*, 3.187.34.

80 *Bhagavad-gītā*, 7.7.

81 *Bhagavad-gītā*, 9.4.

It is not therefore wholly unreasonable to suggest that the Vaiṣṇavism encountered in the *Mahābhārata* is quite closely related to the Upaniṣadic idea of the formless Brahman that is the ultimate substance of all things. The *Chāndogya Upaniṣad* states, *sarvaṁ khalv idaṁ brahma,* 'everything is Brahman alone',[82] and it is not too much of a stretch to suggest that the *Mahābhārata* holds the same idea but expresses it as *sarvaṁ khalv idaṁ viṣṇuḥ,* 'everything is Viṣṇu alone'. In the *Viṣṇu Purāṇa* and *Bhāgavata Purāṇa,* much greater emphasis is placed on the four-armed form and on the various *avatāras* of Viṣṇu, many of whom are described at great length, and so one might suggest that the *Mahābhārata* represents something of a transitional stage in which a more personal identity is ascribed to the Upaniṣadic Brahman, beginning a theological trend that becomes more fully developed at a later stage in the progression of Vaiṣṇava teachings. The connection between Brahman of the Upaniṣads and the *Mahābhārata*'s representation of Nārāyaṇa finds further confirmation from several verses which assert the identity of the Deity with the individual *ātman* within each living being.[83] Again a comparison can be made with Upaniṣadic statements such as *ayam ātmā brahma,* 'this *ātman* is Brahman'.[84]

In conclusion, I would suggest that it is accurate to refer to the theology of the *Mahābhārata* as essentially monotheistic, though this is a monotheism that is integrated with the monism of the Upaniṣads, and is accepting of the polytheism that can be detected within the hymns of the most ancient portions of the Vedas (*saṁhitā*). On a number of occasions, it is stated that the Vedic deities are in fact different manifestations of

---

82 3.14.1.

83 As, for example, in the *Śānti-parvan,* 291.37 and 326.24.

84 *Māṇḍūkya Upaniṣad,* 2.

the one Supreme Deity, a point that is graphically illustrated when Kṛṣṇa expands all the gods from his own body in order to prevent the Kauravas from imprisoning him[85] and in the three other manifestations of the *viśva-rūpa,* to Arjuna in the *Gītā,* to Nārada in the *Nara-nārāyaṇīyam,*[86] and to the *ṛṣi* Uttaṅka as Kṛṣṇa is returning to Dvārakā.[87] It is also the case, however, that these deities such as Indra and Agni appear in the *Mahābhārata* as independent semi-divine beings who are a part of the creation, and act as servants on behalf of the Supreme Deity, Viṣṇu, thereby offering a reconciliation of monotheism and polytheism.

Viṣṇu himself is not a part of this world. He is the creator whose own existence is purely spiritual, beyond any contact with anything mundane. This point is clearly made by Bhīṣma in his glorification of Kṛṣṇa where he refers to the Deity as *pañcānāṁ parataḥ sthitaḥ,* existing in a state beyond the five elements.[88] He further offers respect to Kṛṣṇa by saying *namas te triṣu lokeṣu namas te paratas triṣu,* 'I offer you my respects when you are within the three worlds and I offer my respects to you who are beyond the three worlds.' Similarly, Nārada states that Nārāyaṇa is ever untouched by the three *guṇas* that pervade all aspects of the material domain.[89] Viṣṇu is a Deity both with and without form, but even when he appears in a specific form, still he remains wholly transcendent and, unlike the Vedic deities, he is untouched by anything material.

---

85 *Udyoga-parvan,* Chapter 129.

86 *Śānti-parvan,* Chapter 326.

87 *Aśvamedhika-parvan,* Chapter 54.

88 *Śānti-parvan,* 47.55.

89 *Śānti-parvan,* 326.21–22.

One final point that we might note here are the occasional references to Viṣṇu existing in four forms, named as Vāsudeva, Saṁkarṣaṇa, Pradyumna, and Aniruddha. This idea is particularly, though not exclusively, associated with the Pāñcarātra school of Vaiṣṇavism and hence it is not unreasonable to suggest a Pāñcarātric influence over certain passages of the *Mahābhārata*, most notably the *Nara-nārāyaṇīya*, where the four forms, the *catur-vyūha*, are referred to on a number of occasions.

The Doctrine of *Avatāra* in the *Mahābhārata*

The idea of *avatāra* is central to classical Vaiṣṇava teachings, which include and emphasise a fully developed doctrine of *avatāra*. This doctrine asserts that at various times Viṣṇu descends to this world in a particular form in order to achieve a specific goal. This goal may be to deliver teachings, to restore *dharma* when it is neglected, or, most frequently, to assist the gods in their perpetual struggle with the *asuras*, their wickedly disposed adversaries. The *Mahābhārata* presents the earliest notions of *avatāra* found anywhere in the Indian religious traditions, and this concept is central to the narrative, which describes how Viṣṇu appeared in this world to restore *dharma* by bringing victory to the Pāṇḍavas and annihilating the militaristic kings who display an asuric nature.

In fact, the word *avatāra* is not found in the *Mahābhārata*, which generally prefers to use the term *prādurbhāva*, which means an appearance or a manifestation, whilst *avatāra* literally means a descent. This distinction of terminology does not have any great significance and because *avatāra* is the more familiar of the two, I will continue to use it in the present context, despite its absence from the text itself. It is certainly the case that the idea of *avatāra* holds a preeminent position within the theism of the *Mahābhārata,* as it is through the divine presence of Kṛṣṇa that the Deity consistently appears. Unlike the *Rāmāyaṇa,* however, in which the Rāma *avatāra* is the central character, the *Mahābhārata* narrative focuses primarily on the lives and deeds of the Pāṇḍavas with Kṛṣṇa drifting in and out of the main storyline, although we are constantly made aware that the unfolding of events is dictated by the will and controlling power of the manifest Deity.

The *Mahābhārata* offers its readers two forms of the doctrine of *avatāra,* the best known of which undoubtedly appears in the fourth chapter of the *Bhagavad-gītā,* where Kṛṣṇa presents the following revelation:

> *yadā yadā hi dharmasya glānir bhavati bhārata*
> *abhyutthānam adharmasya tadātmānaṁ sṛjāmy aham*
>
> *paritrāṇāya sādhūnāṁ vināśāya ca duṣkṛtām*
> *dharma-saṁsthāpanārthāya saṁbhavāmi yuge yuge*
>
> Whenever there is a decline in *dharma,* O Bhārata, and whenever there is an increase in *adharma,* it is then that I manifest myself. For the protection of the righteous, for the destruction of wrongdoers, and for the purpose of establishing *dharma,* I appear age after age.[90]

Here it is clearly stated that the descent of Viṣṇu in an *avatāra* form is prompted by the specific circumstances of this world, and in particular the decline of *dharma,* which is both the righteous conduct of humanity and also the natural order of the world that is set in place at the time of creation.

This understanding of the reasons for the descent of *avatāras* is repeated on a number of occasions throughout the

90 *Bhagavad-gītā,* 4.7–8.

Mahābhārata, sometimes with additional details being added. In his teachings to the forest-dwelling Pāṇḍavas, for example, Mārkaṇḍeya tells of the instruction given to him by the Deity:

> When the *daityas*, who are devoted to violence, and cannot be slain even by the best of the gods, appear in this world, along with harsh *rākṣasas*, I will take birth in the houses of the righteous. Entering a human body, I will vanquish them all.
>
> In the time for action, having thought of a particular form, I manifest myself again, having entered a human body in order to preserve the regulations of religious principles.[91]

Similar interpretations of the appearance of the Deity in the world are also to be found in prayers offered by Bhīṣma,[92] and in the *Nara-nārāyaṇīya*, which provides us with the most extensive formulation of the doctrine of *avatāra*:

> All these living beings, great hosts of *daityas*, *dānavas*, *gandharvas* and *rākṣasas*, have been created by Brahmā, the leader of the gods. The overloaded Earth is now afflicted by this burden. Many powerful *daityas*, *dānavas*, and *rākṣasas* will appear on the Earth, performing acts of austerity and thereby achieving the greatest gifts. The gods and *ṛṣis*, whose wealth is austerity, will surely be oppressed by all these beings when they become arrogant because of the boons they are granted. At such times, it is proper that this burden should be removed by me. This is to be achieved by various manifestations on the Earth in due order, and by the destruction of the sinful and the protection of the righteous.[93]

---

91 *Āraṇyaka-parvan*, 187.27, 28, 30.

92 *Bhīṣma-parvan*, 61.68 and *Śānti-parvan*, 143.11.

93 *Śānti-parvan*, 337.29–32.

These renditions of the doctrine of *avatāra* are in close accordance with the appearance of Kṛṣṇa, whose divine mission is to remove the burden to the Earth presented by the vast armies of the kings of the world, and to restore the rule of *dharma* as executed by the righteous Pāṇḍavas.

The second of the two versions of the descent of *avatāras* refers to appearances of the Deity at scheduled times in the progression of the ages of the world, rather than the manifestation being brought forth whenever the need arises. This understanding of *avatāra* is referred to by Hanumān during his encounter with Bhīma[94] and is also mentioned by Mārkaṇḍeya when outlining the instructions given to him by Nārāyaṇa in the form of a child:

> *śvetaḥ kṛta-yuge varṇaḥ pītas tretā-yuge mama*
> *rakto dvāparam āsādya kṛṣṇaḥ kali-yuge tathā*
>
> In the *Kṛta-yuga* my bodily hue is white and in the *Tretā-yuga* it is yellow. It is red in the *Dvāpara-yuga*, and black in the *yuga* known as *Kali*.[95]

Indian cosmology teaches that each period of creation is divided into a rolling succession of four great ages, known of *yugas*, each of which lasts for vast eons of time. The idea expressed by Hanumān and by Mārkaṇḍeya is that in each *yuga* an *avatāra* of Viṣṇu appears, performing deeds and imparting teachings appropriate for the qualities of that age. It is sometimes suggested that the black *avatāra* who appears in *Kali-yuga* is Kṛṣṇa, although Kṛṣṇa appeared at the end of the *Dvāpara-yuga*, with the *Kali-yuga* beginning only after his departure from the

94 *Āraṇyaka-parvan*, 148.16–33.

95 *Āraṇyaka-parvan*, 187.31.

world. Despite these references, it is clear that for the most part the *Mahābhārata* follows the understanding of *avatāras* appearing whenever there is a need for *dharma* to be preserved and the order of the world to be sustained.

The Vaiṣṇava Purāṇas, and most notably the *Viṣṇu Purāṇa* and the *Bhāgavata Purāṇa,* include fairly extensive lists of *avatāras,* along with accounts of the deeds and teachings of these manifestations of the divine. As noted in relation to iconography, however, we can say that despite the frequent glorifications of Kṛṣṇa, the Vaiṣṇavism of the *Mahābhārata* is less focused on these appearances of the Deity than is the case for the Purāṇas and the later traditions. There are occasional references to other *avatāras* scattered throughout the text, but full accounts of their activities are only rarely encountered. The exception to this statement is with regard to the Varāha (boar) *avatāra,* whose raising of the Earth from the waters is described in a passage entitled the *Viṣṇor Varāha-rūpa* (*Śānti-parvan,* Chapter 202) and the Matsya (fish) *avatāra* as revealed by Mārkaṇḍeya in Chapter 185 of the *Āraṇyaka-parvan,* although in this latter case the divine being is referred to as a manifestation of Brahmā rather than Viṣṇu.

Apart from Kṛṣṇa, the most widely revered *avatāra* form of Viṣṇu is Rāma, whose divinity is proclaimed, though not emphasised, in the *Vālmīki Rāmāyaṇa.* As might be expected, Rāma is referred to by Hanumān during his encounter with Bhīma, and Hanumān is quite specific in stating that Rāma is *viṣṇur mānuṣa-rūpena,* Viṣṇu in a human form.[96] A lengthy account of the *Rāmāyaṇa* narrative is presented to the Pāṇḍavas by Mārkaṇḍeya as an element of the teachings he presents to them.[97] This narration begins immediately following Jayadratha's abuse of Draupadī, when Yudhiṣṭhira asks if there

96 *Āraṇyaka-parvan,* 147.28.

97 *Āraṇyaka-parvan,* Chapters 258–275.

was ever a person more unfortunate than himself. In response, Mārkaṇḍeya states that Rāma also experienced great suffering, and then, at Yudhiṣṭhira's request, narrates his version of the life and deeds of Rāma, the manifestation of Viṣṇu who appeared on Earth to aid the gods and *ṛṣis* by destroying the evil Rāvaṇa. Reassuring the gods that this problem will be resolved, Brahmā tells them, *tad-artham avatīrṇo 'sau man-niyogāc catur-bhujo viṣṇuḥ*, 'at my request, the four-armed Viṣṇu will descend to fulfil that purpose'.[98] Here it is interesting to note that although the word *avatāra* is not used, a similar term, *avatīrṇa*, is used to indicate that Viṣṇu will descend to Earth in the form of Rāma.

At various points throughout the *Mahābhārata*, other *avatāras* of Viṣṇu are mentioned in passing, but there are no other extended accounts of their activities. Bhīṣma, for example, mentions three *avatāra* forms in his attempt to convince Duryodhana to make peace: Vāmana (the dwarf), Narasiṁha (the man-lion), and Varāha (the boar). The assertively Vaiṣṇava *Nara-nārāyaṇīya* does provide a short list of *avatāras* in the following passage where Nārāyaṇa himself is the speaker:

> When the Earth is submerged in water, I shall take the form of Varāha [a boar] and exert my energy in returning her to her proper place. In that same form, I shall then slay the *daitya* Hiraṇyākṣa, who will be proud of his strength, and then, on behalf of the gods, taking the form of Narasiṁha [man-lion], I will slay the son of Diti named Hiraṇyakaśipu, who will be a destroyer of the *yajña* ritual.
>
> The mighty Bali, a great *asura*, will be born as the son Virocana and he will cast down Śakra [Indra] from his position as lord of the gods. When Bali then assumes the position

98 *Āraṇyaka-parvan*, 230.5.

of lord of the world, I will take birth as the twelfth son of Aditi and Kaśyapa. I will then restore sovereignty over the world to Śakra, and restore the other gods to their own positions, Nārada. Bali will then be condemned to dwell in Pātāla, the lowest level of the created world. In the *Tretā-yuga*, I will be born as Rāma [i.e. Paraśurāma] in the family of Bhṛgu and in this form I will destroy the *kṣatriyas* who will possess great might and chariots.

At the point of conjunction between the *Tretā-yuga* and the *Dvāpara-yuga*, I shall become Rāma, the son of Daśaratha, and be lord of the world. Because of their afflicting Trita, the two *ṛṣis*, Eka and Dvita, who are sons of Prajāpati, will take unsightly forms as monkeys. The offspring of those two will take the form of animals and will assist me in fulfilling the mission of the gods. I will then slay in battle the ferocious lord of the *rākṣasas*, who will bring disgrace to the family of Pulastya by bringing affliction to the world. I will also slay his followers. At the end of the *Dvāpara-yuga* at the conjunction with the *Kali-yuga*, I will become manifest in Mathurā because of the presence of Kaṁsa.[99]

Reference is also made in the *Nara-nārāyaṇīya* to Haṁsa (swan) and Hayaśiras (horse-headed) *avatāras*, but no details of their mission or activities are given.[100] There are also more detailed *avatāra* stories that appear in certain manuscripts, but these have been excluded from the Critical Edition on the grounds that they are almost certainly later additions, which do not appear in the manuscript versions deemed to be the most authentic.

99 *Śānti-parvan*, 326.72–82.

100 *Śānti-parvan*, 326.94.

It is hence reasonable to conclude that despite the fact that the predominant representation of the Deity within the *Mahābhārata* is as Kṛṣṇa, a descent of Viṣṇu to this world, it appears that in this earlier period, the doctrine of *avatāra* was far less central to Vaiṣṇava theology than it became in the later tradition. Viṣṇu is more usually glorified in relation to his being the creator and controller of the world, and to his pervasive presence within the world, which is regarded as an instrinsic part of the divine identity. The brief references to *avatāras* found in the text make it clear that the idea of *avatāra* is recognised and asserted by the *Mahābhārata*, but in comparison to the Vaiṣṇavism of the Purāṇas and other later works, it holds a far less salient position in the Vaiṣṇavism of the *Mahābhārata*.

The Role and Position of Kṛṣṇa in the Mahābhārata

When we consider the theistic orientation of the *Mahābhārata*, the most prominent feature of the discussion must be the role of Kṛṣṇa, who is consistently stated to be a manifestation of the Supreme Deity, Nārāyaṇa, appearing in this world to restore the dharmic order that has become unbalanced due to the aggressive militarism of the royal order. This we have already noticed in considering the doctrine of *avatāra* as established in the *Bhagavad-gītā* and other passages. In one sense, the entire *Mahābhārata* can be regarded as an extended *avatāra* narrative, although we must recognise that there are many other strands that are pursued apart from this theme of divine intervention. Right from the start, however, we are made aware of the fact that this is not just a story of factional rivalry and conflict between human beings, for the Supreme Deity will play a central role in the unfolding of events, and in so doing he will be accompanied and assisted by the lesser gods of the Vedic tradition. The following extract is a summary of Chapter 58 of the *Ādi-parvan*, the *Mahābhārata*'s opening book:

> And Viṣṇu himself, who is worshipped by all the worlds, was born as the son of Devakī through Vasudeva for the benefit of the world. He is birthless and deathless, the creator of the universe and the Lord of all. He is the invisible cause of all things, he knows no deterioration, he is the all-pervasive *ātman*, and the centre around which all things move. He is present in all things, he is the *praṇava oṁkāra* (primordial sound) of the Veda, he is infinite, and cannot be moved by anything except his own independent will. Thus that being who is the universe itself, without beginning, birth, or decay, became incarnate in the Andhaka-Vṛṣṇi race for the sustenance of *dharma*.
>
> When the *kṣatriyas* reappeared after the slaughter by Paraśurāma, the Earth was ruled properly and produced abundant food for all. The kings performed *yajñas* and all the brahmins were learned in the Upaniṣads and Vedic rituals. The *vaiśyas* tilled the Earth but never behaved cruelly towards the animals they tended; all persons were virtuous, and dishonesty was unknown. Then it happened that fierce *asuras* began to take birth in the royal dynasties on Earth; they had been defeated in their wars with the gods and so now they sought refuge by appearing in this world. They disturbed the *dharma* and prosperity of the Earth, killing many people, and innocent creatures as well, as they marched their armies here and there. Devoid of truth and virtue, and proud of their might, they even insulted the *ṛṣis* who dwelt in *āśramas*.
>
> Oppressed by the burden of these *asuras* in human form, Bhūdevī, the Earth Goddess, approached Brahmā and

> sought his protection. She explained to him about the problems being caused by these *asuras*, although everything was known to him already. Brahmā then requested all the gods and their followers to take birth in the royal dynasties on Earth so that they could oppose and destroy the *asuras* there. The gods accepted this request as beneficial for the time and place; Indra approached Nārāyaṇa in Vaikuṇṭha and requested that he also appear with them. And Nārāyaṇa replied to Indra, 'It shall be so!'

This passage is quite clearly in line with the understanding of *avatāra* taught to Arjuna in the fourth chapter of the *Gītā*, and from this point onwards the reader is aware that behind all the events presented in the *Mahābhārata* there is the controlling force of divine intervention. We might also note that as well as being sons of Dharma, Vāyu, Indra, and the twin Aśvins, the Pāṇḍavas are also expanded forms of these secondary deities.[101]

This revelation of the divine identity of one of the principal characters significantly shapes the development of the *Mahābhārata*'s narrative and places it very clearly into the category of religious literature. We know from the outset that the Pāṇḍavas will emerge successful from their difficulties because the all-powerful Nārāyaṇa is supporting their cause. And if we had any doubts about this, the point is reiterated at various points in the progression of the story. When the battle begins at Kurukṣetra and the Pāṇḍavas are victorious during the first five days of fighting, the distressed Duryodhana approaches Bhīṣma, who is commanding his army, and asks why they are being defeated despite the superior strength of their host. It is at this point that Bhīṣma repeats the story of

101 As stated in the *Ādi-parvan*, 61.84–85.

the gods' request for Nārāyaṇa to descend to Earth and tells Duryodhana very bluntly that he cannot win the battle under any circumstances because the Lord himself is present on the other side. As we have seen, he then describes the glories and divine attributes of the Deity, Kṛṣṇa, who is present on the battlefield alongside Duryodhana's principal adversary.[102]

Hence it is made apparent that all the events described in the *Mahābhārata* narrative are being directed by Kṛṣṇa and unfolding according to his will. This is revealed directly to Arjuna through his vision of the *viśva-rūpa,* described in Chapter 11 of the *Bhagavad-gītā*. Shocked and overwhelmed by Kṛṣṇa's display of his awesome, all-pervasive magnificence, Arjuna asks about his cousin's true identity. In reply, Kṛṣṇa states that he is all-devouring time; Droṇa, Bhīṣma, Karṇa, and Jayadratha are already slain by his will, *mayā hatān,* and Arjuna's role can be no more than that of an instrument of the divine will, *nimitta-mātraṁ bhava savyasācin.*[103] The point here is clearly made. Arjuna is wracked by grief due to thinking that he will be the cause of the death of his family members, but Kṛṣṇa asserts that Arjuna's decision to either fight or withdraw from the action will not affect the outcome. The warriors will die because it is the will of the Deity who controls all things, and Arjuna can only decide whether or not to act as the instrument of that absolute controller who is Kṛṣṇa.

Elsewhere in the *Mahābhārata,* there could be questions as to whether Kṛṣṇa himself is truly in control of the outcome of events, and at times it does seem that the human form he has assumed imposes limitations upon him. At one point in the battle, he is described as being exhausted and perspiring,[104]

---

102 *Bhīṣma-parvan,* Chapters 61–64.

103 *Bhagavad-gītā,* 11.33–34.

104 *Droṇa-parvan,* 18.21.

and when wounded by a lance passing through his arm he is temporarily incapacitated.[105] Then, at the end, the *Mausala-parvan* describes how Kṛṣṇa is killed when a hunter's arrow strikes him in the heel. However, the overall perspective of the *Mahābhārata* makes it very clear that these apparent limitations are simply a part of Kṛṣṇa's acting out of the role of a human being. The reality is that he is the absolute controller of all things, and if we look at the account of his death, it becomes quite apparent that this is not like the death of any human being. Here is a summary of that passage:

> After his family members had been killed in a fight amongst themselves, Kṛṣṇa told his father Vasudeva that he would leave Dvārakā and go to the forest to live a life of renunciation, taking with him only his brother Balarāma. The women of the palace wept as he departed, but he told them, 'Arjuna will come here soon and he will relieve your suffering.'
>
> On entering the forest, he saw Balarāma sitting in a solitary place engaged in *yoga* practice. A white serpent with red eyes then emerged from Balarāma's mouth. Abandoning the human body, it left that place and entered the ocean nearby where it was welcomed by the host of celestial *nāgas*. After his brother had departed in this way, Kṛṣṇa wandered for some time in the lonely forest, deeply absorbed in thought, and then sat down on the bare Earth. He recalled Gāndhārī's curse upon him, as well as the prophecy uttered by Durvāsas when the latter was a guest in his house, and decided that the hour for his departure from the world had arrived. Sitting there, he withdrew his senses and absorbed his mind in *yoga* practice.
>
> A fierce hunter named Jarā then arrived at that place. Mistaking Keśava [Kṛṣṇa] for a black deer, he shot him

105 *Karṇa-parvan*, 19.13.

> in the heel with an arrow and then came quickly to capture his prey. But when he arrived at the spot, he saw a man absorbed in *yoga*, dressed in yellow, and possessing numerous arms. Fearful of the crime he had committed, Jarā came forward and bowed down, touching Kṛṣṇa's feet with his head. Kṛṣṇa spoke comforting words to him and then ascended into the sky in an effulgent form. On reaching the heavens, he was greeted by all the gods and higher beings who reside in those worlds. Filling all the worlds with his brilliant lustre, Nārāyaṇa, who is the creator and destroyer of the world, then entered his own immeasurable domain.[106]

What is apparent from this account is that the *Mahābhārata* does not regard Kṛṣṇa's death as a misfortune that befell him through chance; he was not a victim of unwanted circumstances. He alone decided on the time and means of his departure from this world and immediately after being shot by the hunter he ascended upwards past all the regions of this creation, and once more assumed his true identity as Nārāyaṇa, the Supreme Deity. It is also interesting to note that Balarāma is here identified as the divine *nāga* serpent Ananta.

The question of the presence of humanity and divinity in a single individual is one that has taxed Christian theologians over the centuries, as they debated the simultaneous divine and human identities of Jesus. From the Indian perspective, and from the perspective of the *Mahābhārata*, the understanding of the identity of Kṛṣṇa is one that Christians would refer to as docetic, indicating that the humanity of Kṛṣṇa is no more than a guise that does nothing to inhibit the absolute nature of the Supreme Deity appearing in this form. In one passage of the *Vālmīki Rāmāyaṇa*, where the gods glorify Rāma

---

106 *Mausala-parvan*, Chapter 5.

as a manifestation of Viṣṇu, he refuses to accept their words and says that he knows himself only as the son of Daśaratha. Nothing similar, however, is to be found in the *Mahābhārata* in relation to Kṛṣṇa, who never denies his divine identity, and is absolutely uninhibited by his apparent humanity. In the *Bhagavad-gītā,* this point is explicitly made when Kṛṣṇa states, 'Fools despise me when I accept this human form. They do not understand my higher nature as the Supreme Lord of the living beings.'[107]

Hence, whilst there might conceivably be some suggestion of Kṛṣṇa's human frailties in the *Mahābhārata* narrative, the *Bhagavad-gītā* is absolutely clear with regard to his true nature. In the *Gītā,* Kṛṣṇa makes a number of statements with regard to his higher identity, statements such as *ahaṁ sarvasya prabhavaḥ,* 'I am the origin of all things',[108] *mattaḥ parataraṁ nānyat,* 'There is nothing that is superior to myself',[109] or *mayādhyakṣeṇa prakṛtiḥ sūyate sa-carācaram,* 'It is with myself as the controller that *prakṛti* brings forth moving and non-moving entities'.[110] And as we must regard the *Bhagavad-gītā* as a passage of instruction integral to the *Mahābhārata* as a whole, we are obliged to take significant note of the manner in which it discloses the divinity of Kṛṣṇa, and be aware that its teachings on this subject are entirely congruent with those we have considered from other passages of the *Mahābhārata.*

The clearest revelation of Kṛṣṇa's higher identity is to be found in the vision of the *viśva-rūpa,* described in the *Gītā*'s eleventh chapter. There are three other occasions in the *Mahābhārata* when this cosmic form of the Supreme Deity is

107 *Bhagavad-gītā,* 9.11.

108 *Bhagavad-gītā,* 10.8.

109 *Bhagavad-gītā,* 7.7.

110 *Bhagavad-gītā,* 9.10.

displayed, twice by Kṛṣṇa and once by Nārāyaṇa to Nārada in the *Nara-nārāyaṇīya*.[111] Of Kṛṣṇa's two other displays of the *viśva-rūpa,* one is in the court of the Kauravas when they attempt to make him a prisoner[112] and the other is to a *ṛṣi* named Uttaṅka during his return to Dvārakā. This encounter with Uttaṅka again reveals very clearly that the human form adopted by Kṛṣṇa is nothing but an appearance that cannot inhibit his divine potency. Again, here is a summary of the passage in question:

> As Kṛṣṇa was travelling on his chariot back to Dvārakā, he encountered a *ṛṣi* named Uttaṅka. They greeted one another respectfully and then Uttaṅka asked whether Kṛṣṇa had brought about a peaceful resolution of the quarrel between the Pāṇḍavas and Kauravas. To this Kṛṣṇa replied, 'I tried to the best of my ability to secure a peaceful solution, but when my efforts in this direction failed, the Pāṇḍavas and Kauravas made war with one another and now their mighty hosts have been destroyed and only the five Pāṇḍavas remain. You know only too well that one cannot defy destiny.'
>
> When he heard this speech, Uttaṅka's eyes turned red with anger and he said, 'Although you had the power to do so, you did not rescue those ones of the Kuru race who were very dear to me. Therefore I shall curse you. Although you could have prevented this war, you were indifferent to the plight of the Kauravas who have now been slain.'
>
> Kṛṣṇa then said to Uttaṅka, 'Now listen to what I say. You are a *sādhu* and I apologise to you, but you should know that no one can afflict me on the basis of the power he gains from *tapas* [asceticism]. You have undertaken harsh austerities, remained celibate throughout your life, and

111 *Śānti-parvan,* 326.1–10.

112 *Udyoga-parvan,* Chapter 129.

> shown respect to your elders, and I do not wish to see a diminution in the merit you have thereby accrued. You should know that all the gods and all other types of living being have come into existence from me alone. I am the soul of everything, living or inert, and there is nothing superior to me. I am the Veda, I am *yajña,* I am Soma, and I am Oṁ. *Dharma* is my firstborn son, who has appeared from my mind, and in order to protect this son of mine I appear in various forms at different times. I have now been born amongst human beings and so I act after the manner of men. I appealed to the Kauravas with reason and I frightened them with a display of power, but when I resumed my human form they were again overcome by illusion and refused to listen to me. And so now they have been slain in battle.'
>
> Uttanka then said, 'Now I understand that you are Janārdana, the creator of the world, and I no longer wish to curse you. Please show me the form that you have spoken of.' Being pleased with the *sādhu,* Kṛṣṇa then revealed the eternal Vaiṣṇava form that Arjuna had seen. Uttaṅka then saw Kṛṣṇa's *viśva-rūpa* with its numerous arms and blazing effulgence like that of one thousand suns filling the entire sky. When he saw that marvellous sight, Uttaṅka bowed down and offered prayers to Kṛṣṇa, asking him to withdraw the *viśva-rūpa* and appear again in his human form.[113]

The story of Uttaṅka has an unusual twist to it. Uttaṅka is offered a gift by Kṛṣṇa and asks that water will appear for him in that desert region whenever he is in need. So the next time he is suffering from thirst and is short of water he thinks of Kṛṣṇa as instructed. However, all that happens is that a filthy hunter appears before him and offers a palm full of his urine, which Uttaṅka, perhaps not surprisingly, refuses in disgust.

---

113 *Aśvamedhika-parvan,* Chapters 52–53.

He is again angry with Kṛṣṇa but the Lord appears before him and reveals that the hunter was actually Indra, the lord of the gods, offering him nectar (*amṛta*). In future, however, the water Uttaṅka craves will appear in the form of rain clouds and these will be known amongst human beings as Uttaṅka clouds.

Like Gāndhārī in an earlier passage, Uttaṅka here suggests that Kṛṣṇa had the power to prevent the slaughter at Kurukṣetra but chose not to do so. Both of them use the word 'indifferent' in their speeches of condemnation. Gāndhārī had stated that this ability was based on the strength of the armies Kṛṣṇa could command, as well as his powers of persuasion, whilst Uttaṅka is not so specific on this point. However, we are aware from the passage we looked at from *Ādi-parvan* that Nārāyaṇa has come to Earth with the clear intention of provoking a war so that the *asuras* who are a burden to the Earth can be removed and *dharma* restored. So in that sense both Gāndhārī and Uttaṅka are correct; Kṛṣṇa had no real intention of promoting peace, although, as he says, it is unlikely that Duryodhana would have listened to any advice in that direction.

The Morality of the Avatāra

In any discussion the *Mahābhārata*'s revelation of Kṛṣṇa's divine identity, there are a couple more points that are frequently raised. First of all, there is the question of the morality of the *avatāra*, and then there are the numerous stories relating to Kṛṣṇa's early life as a young cowherd living in hiding in the village of Vṛndāvana. Let us consider first the apparently devious plans that Kṛṣṇa devises in the conflict, which appear to be contrary to the precepts of *dharma*. There is a certain irony here in that Kṛṣṇa has given the preservation of *dharma* as the reason for his descent to this world, and yet he shows himself repeatedly to be willing to bend and break the strict principles of *dharma*. Here we will notice a clear contrast to the conduct of Rāma as described in the *Rāmāyaṇa*, for despite a few minor discrepancies, the Rāma *avatāra* conducts himself as a man of unimpeachable character. It is certainly the case that the same cannot be said of Kṛṣṇa either in the *Mahābhārata* or in the Purāṇic stories of his early life. The apparently adharmic acts of Kṛṣṇa are listed by Duryodhana as he lies dying on the field of conflict after he has been vanquished by Bhīma:

> O son of Kaṁsa's slave, you seem to have forgotten that I was struck down by an unfair blow. It was you who caused this unrighteous act by reminding Bhīma with a hint about my thighs. Did you think I did not notice your making this suggestion to Arjuna, who gave the signal to Bhīma? Using *adharma*, you have caused the deaths of thousands of kings who always adhered to *dharma* in their fighting. You caused our grandfather's death by instructing that Śikhaṇḍin be placed at the front of the army. Ordering the death of the elephant named Aśvatthāman, you caused our *guru* to abandon his weapons so that he could be brutally killed by Dhṛṣṭadyumna. Using Ghaṭotkaca as a victim, you caused Karṇa to release the infallible arrow he had obtained from Indra, and you urged Sātyaki to kill Bhūriśravas when one of his arms was cut off. When Karṇa's chariot wheel sank into the ground, you prevented Arjuna from acting according to *dharma*, and instructed him to kill his opponent whilst he was at a disadvantage. If you had fought with myself, Bhīṣma, Droṇa, and Karṇa according to the rules of *dharma*, you would never have triumphed. By adopting *adharma* you have brought about the deaths of many virtuous kings who never deviated from proper conduct.[114]

Here Duryodhana is more than a little disingenuous in his interpretation of events, for his faction had never shown particular regard for using dharmic means in their conflicts

---

114 *Śalya-parvan*, 60.27–38.

with the Pāṇḍavas, and in the passage that follows Kṛṣṇa is quick to point this out to him. There are, however, very real issues raised concerning the morality and conduct of Kṛṣṇa, and this issue can be taken even further if we include the narrations of Kṛṣṇa's early life presented in the *Harivaṁśa, Viṣṇu Purāṇa,* and the *Bhāgavata Purāṇa,* in which he consorts with married and unmarried women in the middle of the night.

So why does the *Mahābhārata* present a picture of its divine *avatāra* in this way and deviate from the mode of representation that is emphasised so strongly in the *Vālmīki Rāmāyaṇa*? The text itself does not pose or respond to this question at any point, although it does accept the essence of Duryodhana's criticism, and makes it very clear that Kṛṣṇa does not absolutely adhere to *dharma*. When he is urging Yudhiṣṭhira to tell the lie that will bring about the death of Droṇa, Kṛṣṇa says quite plainly, *dharmam utsṛjya pāṇḍava,* literally 'abandon *dharma,* O Pāṇḍava'.[115] And after the speech in which he justifies the killing of Duryodhana by means of a foul blow, the *Mahābhārata* itself refers to his words as *dharma-cchalam,*[116] meaning a deceitful version of *dharma.*

If we are to look for an answer here, I would suggest that there are two possible responses to the question posed above concerning the moral standing of the *avatāra*:

1. Throughout the *Mahābhārata,* Kṛṣṇa takes a robust view of the purpose of *dharma*. As we will see in the next chapter, Kṛṣṇa is clear that *dharma* is for the service of humanity rather than the other way round, and so when they become an obstacle to the wellbeing of humanity, the strict rules of *dharma* must be set

115 *Droṇa-parvan,* 164.68.

116 *Śalya-parvan,* 59.22.

aside. Moreover, when Bhīṣma instructs Yudhiṣṭhira about the duties of a king in the *Śānti-parvan,* he emphasises the point that in times of emergency a ruler may adopt the *āpad-dharma* and use dishonest means to preserve his position and to protect his people. Yudhiṣṭhira, typically, will not accept Bhīṣma's ideas on this point, but it seems that Kṛṣṇa shares the grandfather's perspective. Indeed, his response to any criticism of the way he has conducted himself is to say that if they had adhered strictly to all the rules of dharma they would have lost the war, and what good would that have done for anyone? In that scenario, adherence to *dharma* would have led to the triumph of *adharma* in the form of Duryodhana.

2. When the question of Kṛṣṇa's conduct in relation to the women of Vṛndāvana is raised in the *Bhāgavata Purāṇa,* the sage Śuka gives an interesting response. He replies to the question by saying that because Kṛṣṇa is the Supreme Deity his existence is always in a higher realm beyond this world. *Dharma* is a part of the fabric of this creation and therefore it does not apply to Kṛṣṇa; he cannot be judged by the standards that apply to human beings. Nowhere is this argument suggested within the *Mahābhārata,* but given the constant emphasis on Kṛṣṇa's divinity, it is still a relevant point to raise here. It might also be apposite to consider Kṛṣṇa's words in the *Bhagavad-gītā* where he talks about the process of engaging the mental faculties in Yoga practice and thereby elevating oneself beyond this realm of existence. He says, *buddhi-yukto jahātīha ubhe sukṛta-duṣkṛte,* 'by focusing the intellect in this way, one sets aside both

righteous and unrighteous deeds',[117] suggesting that within this world there is *dharma* and there is *adharma,* but when one transcends this world such dualities are also transcended. And, of course, Kṛṣṇa is never truly within this domain of existence.

The Early Life of Kṛṣṇa

Vaiṣṇava devotional traditions frequently point out two phases in the life of Kṛṣṇa: first his childhood and youth as a cowherd in Vṛndāvana, then his role as a ruler and military tactician. The *Mahābhārata* focuses overwhelmingly on the second part of his biography and seems almost unaware of his early life as described in great detail in a number of later works, most notably the *Bhāgavata Purāṇa*. It is not quite accurate, however, to say that the *Mahābhārata* is unaware of this cycle of stories, as Kṛṣṇa's early life is briefly mentioned on a number of occasions. Examples of this are to be found in Śiśupāla's insulting of Kṛṣṇa where he emphasises his early life in an agricultural community,[118] in Vidura's address to the Kaurava assembly,[119] and in one of the conversations between Dhṛtarāṣṭra and Saṁjaya.[120] Moreover, it is in a later appendix to the *Mahābhārata* known as the *Harivaṁśa* that we find the first accounts of Kṛṣṇa's early life. Hence, whilst it is true to say that the *Mahābhārata* offers very little by way of reference to Kṛṣṇa's youthful exploits, it is not accurate to say that this phase of his life is wholly unknown to our text.

---

117 *Bhagavad-gītā,* 2.50.

118 *Sabhā-parvan,* Chapter 38.

119 *Udyoga-parvan,* Chapter 128.

120 *Droṇa-parvan,* Chapter 10.

Śiva in the *Mahābhārata*

There is no doubt that the principal form of theism encountered in the chapters of the *Mahābhārata* is Vaiṣṇava in orientation, primarily because of the significant presence of Kṛṣṇa both as the divine administrator directing the course of the narrative and as a teacher of Vaiṣṇava doctrine. Nonetheless, we must also be aware of a significant parallel tendency towards Śiva and Śaivite teachings, appearing and reappearing in both the narrative and didactic passages, and it would be delinquent for any study of the central ideas of the *Mahābhārata* to fail to include some notice of the role played by Śiva in our text.

A widely encountered view is that Hindu ideas on the nature of God focus on the divine trinity of Brahmā, the creator, Viṣṇu, the sustainer, and Śiva, the destroyer of the world. In the *Mahābhārata*, however, we find only hints of that trinitarian perspective, as both Viṣṇu and Śiva are spoken of as being the one Supreme Deity, whilst Brahmā is consistently relegated to a secondary status, dependent on Viṣṇu or Śiva for his position as the creator. As has already been noted, the central narrative reveals that Nārāyaṇa appeared in this world in the form of Kṛṣṇa in order to sustain the prevalence of *dharma* and to support the gods in their conflict with the *asuras*. It appears that Śiva also has a role to play in the completion of this mission, although his promotion of this goal is not always quite so evident.

Within the progression of the narrative, Śiva's interventions play a rather more significant role than might initially be expected. Gāndhārī has one hundred sons due to a benediction granted by Śiva; Draupadī is married to five husbands because in her previous life she petitioned Śiva for a perfect husband five times over; it is due to a blessing from Śiva that Ambā takes birth as Śikhaṇḍin to bring about the death of Bhīṣma; it is due to a boon from Śiva that Jayadratha is able to hold back four of the Pāṇḍava brothers, which results in the death of Abhimanyu; Śiva also granted a blessing to Bhūriśravas that enabled him to defeat and humiliate Sātyaki; in the form of a hunter Śiva engaged in combat with Arjuna before granting him the use of the Pāśupata weapon (although Arjuna did not use it in the battle); before his killing of Jayadratha, Arjuna travelled mentally to Kailāsa with Kṛṣṇa and sought Śiva's blessing for the next day's encounter; at the end of the *Droṇa-parvan,* Arjuna reveals that he sees Śiva going ahead of him on the battlefield destroying those who are to die that day before Arjuna has fired an arrow; after the battle is over, Aśvatthāman becomes empowered by Śiva and is then able to kill the surviving warriors of the Pāṇḍava host.

It is thus apparent that Śiva also plays a significant role in the fulfilment of the mission of the *avatāra,* although his destructive force is directed as much at the Pāṇḍava faction as it is at the Kauravas. We will be aware, however, that the descent of the *avatāra* was intended to put an end to all the militaristic might of the rulers of the world, and so the killing of the surviving Pāṇḍava chieftains was not in opposition to that principal aim. It seems to be the case that Śiva's interventions are frequently for the destruction of those on the Pāṇḍava side, as it would be anomalous for Kṛṣṇa to take on that role when he is such an ardent supporter of the Pāṇḍava cause.

In the later traditions, Śiva is represented as being a somewhat fearsome Deity, an outsider to the mainstream Vedic tradition who is present in the cremation grounds and is often surrounded by a host of frightful beings of terrifying appearance. This aspect of Śiva's identity is very much apparent in the *Mahābhārata,* not least when he is seen by Arjuna going before him into battle, ending the lives of the opposing warriors, and when he inspires, or even possesses, Aśvatthāman as a final act of destruction.

Within the *Anuśāsana-parvan*, the thirteenth book of the *Mahābhārata* that consists almost entirely of passages of religious instruction, there are three passages that are clearly Śaivite in orientation, and it is in these chapters that we find the fearsome demeanour of Śiva most graphically described. In some ways, Śiva in the *Mahābhārata* is the terrifying destroyer who wreaks havoc on the battlefield, but he also displays a benign face to those who worship him, and it seems apparent that he shares with Viṣṇu the aim of restoring *dharma* to the world. One further point to note here is that it is in the *Anuśāsana-parvan* and the *Droṇa-parvan* that we find the earliest references to Śiva being worshipped in the aniconic *liṅga* form.

Where Śiva enters the stage of the *Mahābhārata* narrative, he is typically praised as the one Supreme Deity, above all others, in exactly the same way, and often with the same language, as Viṣṇu is praised in the passages referred to above. So what are we to make of this? Is the *Mahābhārata* teaching some form of bitheism, or could it be, as some writers have suggested, that the text is comprised of a series of discrete interpolated passages, some of which are Vaiṣṇava whilst others show a Śaivite orientation? As far as the main narrative is concerned, I do not think this is the case and although no direct explanation is ever given, it seems that the idea behind these divine interventions is that Viṣṇu and Śiva are both forms of the one inconceivable, absolute Deity who appears in different identities in different situations.

Hence I think it is reasonable to conclude that the narrative portions of the *Mahābhārata* offer a form of syncretism between Vaiṣṇavism and Śaivism, as is frequently depicted in the combined form of Hari-hara. This conclusion is largely based on surmise rather than the direct statement of the text, but something of an indication towards this view can be gleaned from the account of Kṛṣṇa and Arjuna's nocturnal journey to Kailāsa. Both of them offer prayers to Śiva and glorify him as the Supreme Deity, but Arjuna notices that the offerings he had earlier made to Kṛṣṇa are now present at the side of Śiva, *dadarśa tryambhakābhyāśe vāsudeva-niveditam.*[121]

The one passage of the Mahābhārata that directly declares the supremacy of Viṣṇu over Śiva is the *Nara-nārāyaṇīya,* but even here the syncretist perspective is not entirely absent. Within that passage, when Arjuna asks Kṛṣṇa why he feels obliged to worship Śiva even though he is himself the one Supreme Deity, Kṛṣṇa replies:

> *rudro nārāyaṇaś caiva sattvam ekaṁ dvidhā-kṛtam*
> *loke carati kaunteya vyakti-sthaṁ sarva-karmasu*
>
> Rudra and Nārāyaṇa are one being, manifest in two different ways, Kaunteya, manifest in the world and present in all actions performed.[122]

Whilst it is reasonable to regard this syncretistic perspective as the principal theistic view of the narrative portions of the *Mahābhārata,* we must also note that in the *Śānti-parvan* and *Anuśāsana-parvan* there are passages that are overtly sectarian in the sense that they show either Viṣṇu or Śiva as the one Supreme Deity, whilst the other is only a secondary deity. This tendency is only apparent from the Vaiṣṇava perspective within the *Nara-nārāyaṇīya,* but the three Śaivite passages of the *Anuśāsana-parvan* consistently elevate Śiva above and beyond any divine identity ascribed to Viṣṇu. These three Śaivite treatises are the *Upamanyu-upākhyāna* (*Anuśāsana-parvan,* Chapters 14–17), the *Umā-maheśvara-saṁvāda* (*Anuśāsana-parvan,* Chapters 126–134), and the *Īśvara-praśaṁsā* (*Anuśāsana-parvan,* Chapters 145–146),

121 *Droṇa-parvan,* 57.61.

122 *Śānti-parvan,* 328.24.

each of which offers the reader a significant insight into the development of early Śaivite monotheism.

These passages provide extensive description of both the benign and ferocious features of Śiva, express the emotional love for Śiva of his devotees, and clearly hold to the view that Śiva is superior to Viṣṇu. This latter point is made most apparent by the appearance of Viṣṇu amongst the host of celestial beings glorifying Śiva, and by the accounts of Kṛṣṇa being initiated as a devotee of Śiva by Upamanyu, a well-known figure in early Sanskrit texts who repeatedly expresses his unwavering devotion for Śiva. Hence I think it is reasonable to conclude that within the *Mahābhārata* we encounter both the syncretistic view of Viṣṇu and Śiva as different aspects of the same Supreme Deity as well as the sectarian tendencies that insist on elevating one Deity above the other.

THE GODDESS IN THE *MAHĀBHĀRATA*

Alongside Śaivism and Vaiṣṇavism, the Śākta tradition that venerates the great Goddess, Durgā, Pārvatī, or Kālī, is the other notable strand of Indian theism. Within the *Mahābhārata,* however, we can find little if anything that could be properly identified as displaying any tendency towards Śāktism. The Goddess appears only in the later *parvans,* when the narrative is virtually complete, and there only in her position as the consort of Śiva in passages that are Śaivite rather than Śākta in orientation.

Between Chapters 5 and 6 of the *Virāṭa-parvan,* however, some manuscripts contain an additional passage known as the *Durgā-stava,* consisting of prayers recited by Yudhiṣṭhira, after which the Goddess appears to him and offers him blessings for success and prosperity. Furthermore, inserted into Chapter 22 of the *Bhīṣma-parvan* is a passage named the *Durgā-stotra* in which Arjuna, on Kṛṣṇa's instruction, offers prayers to

Durgā and receives her blessing so that he will gain victory. By examining and comparing all the manuscript versions available to them, the editors of the Critical Edition determined that these two passages were later additions to the *Mahābhārata*, as a result of which they are contained only in appendices to their work. This is somewhat unfortunate as they are significant examples of early Śākta devotion, which now have no clear textual location.

The Theology of the *Mahābhārata*

If one attempts a succinct definition of the understanding of the nature of God offered by the *Mahābhārata*, one is immediately confronted by the problem posed by the diversity of the teachings encountered within this voluminous work. Quite clearly, there are varying and diverse strands of religious thought interacting with each other as the text progresses, but for all that I think it is possible to make general statements, whilst allowing for the fact that these will at times appear to be contradicted in certain passages. If pushed to attempt to define the theology of the *Mahābhārata*, I would say that it offers a form of monistic monotheism that is quite compatible with the polytheistic tendencies of the Vedic revelation.

By that I mean that the *Mahābhārata* holds to the view that there is one Supreme Deity, the creator and controller of the world, who exists in a domain that is wholly transcendent to this sphere of existence. This Deity is named as both Viṣṇu and as Śiva and the suggestion seems to be that these apparently distinct divinities are in fact facets of the same Supreme Deity. If this understanding represents the monotheistic perspective, we will also need to be aware of the monistic ideas that distinguish this form of monotheism from that of the traditions of Islam, Judaism, and Christianity. In a number of passages, we find the idea that the world is not merely a creation of the Deity but is an expansion of his existence, so that in one sense the creator and the creation are non-different. This idea is most graphically illustrated in the four revelations of the *viśva-rūpa* described within the *Mahābhārata*. This understanding of the created world as a form of the Deity hence sustains the monistic doctrines of the Upaniṣads, epitomised by the statement *sarvaṁ khalv idaṁ brahma*, all this world is Brahman.

The conventional understanding is that monotheism and polytheism are antithetical doctrines, but within the *Mahābhārata* and other Indian texts no such clear cut dichotomy exists. The gods glorified in the hymns of the *Ṛgveda Saṁhitā* also appear within the *Mahābhārata*, but they are shown to be a part of creation, superior to humanity in all ways, but far below the level of pure spiritual transcendence in which the one Supreme Deity exists. In this way, a form of polytheism is shown to be entirely compatible with the overriding monotheistic perspective of the text as a whole.

Wherever the theology of the *Mahābhārata* is discussed, the central position of the *Bhagavad-gītā* in establishing points of religious doctrine must be acknowledged. What is indicated by the divine interventions observed within the central narrative is confirmed and to a significant extent explained by the *Gītā*'s theistic exposition. So on this basis as well, I would insist that the *Bhagavad-gītā* is best understood when considered within the wider context of the *Mahābhārata* as a whole, whilst the theology of the *Mahābhārata* cannot be fully appreciated without reference to the *Gītā*'s revelation of the divine identity.

With this point in mind, we can also move on to refer briefly to *mokṣa-dharma*, the path to liberation that will be reviewed more fully in the next chapter. Within the *Śānti-parvan*, we have a series of treatises based on the Sāṁkhya and Yoga systems, which put forward the view that liberation from rebirth is achieved through realised knowledge of our own spiritual essence, the *ātman* or *puruṣa*. From the theistic perspective, however, we also find the idea that liberation is granted to one who follows the path of *bhakti* as a gift of grace based on the love that is expressed by the Deity, who reciprocates the mood of love and devotion of the worshipper. Again, this idea of liberation from rebirth being achieved through divine grace and divine love is presented most clearly within the verses of the *Bhagavad-gītā*, but it is also encountered within the *Nara-nārāyaṇīya* (as in the *Śānti-parvan*, Chapter 327).

An interesting point to note here is that in the Śaivite passages of the *Anuśāsana-parvan*, and the *Upamanyu-upākhyāna* in particular, we find the idea that devotion to Śiva is not to be regarded simply as a means of gaining release from the miseries of life in this world, but is in fact an end in itself. The Śaivite devotees experience such beatific joy from their mood of devotion that they do not seek liberation, for the problems are life are all transcended simply by the experience of reciprocated love for the Deity. This idea of *bhakti* as both a means and an end becomes widespread in later Indian religion, and in particular where the youthful Kṛṣṇa is the object of devotion, but in this early period it is virtually unique to the avowedly Śaivite passages located in the *Anuśāsana-parvan* of the *Mahābhārata*. Therein, the prayers of the devotees renounce any desire for liberation, as the mood of love for Śiva is sufficient to drive away all forms of distress.

A further point that we might conclude with relates to the type of devotion that is typically found in the *Mahābhārata*. In the later *bhakti* traditions, there is an elevation of the mood of intimacy with the Deity alongside descriptions of expressions of emotional love of God, such as the hairs on the body standing erect, the shedding of tears, and a choking of the voice that inhibits any vocalisation of devotional sentiments. Within the

Mahābhārata, however, it is the awesome supremacy of the Deity that is emphasised, his absolute control over the world, and his vast pervasive presence that is somewhat akin to the Upaniṣadic references to Brahman. In that context, there is little room for intimate expressions of emotional love, and in Chapter 11 of the *Bhagavad-gītā* we find Arjuna regretting his previous intimate relationship with Kṛṣṇa when confronted by the awesome vision of the *viśva-rūpa*. The sole exception to this general rule of intellectual or reverential devotion is again to be found in the Śaivite passages of the *Anuśāsana-parvan* where we find descriptions of the symptoms of emotional ecstasy appearing on the bodies of the devotees of Śiva in a form that exactly matches accounts found in certain Purāṇas and poetic writings. The presence of this form of emotional *bhakti* in this location is difficult to explain, but its presence there is certainly worthy of note.

Discussion Topic: Divine Identity

Here are some questions you might care to ponder after completing this chapter:

- Is it accurate to refer to the *Mahābhārata* as a Vaiṣṇava scripture?
- What explanations can be given for elements of Kṛṣṇa's conduct that might appear to be unrighteous?
- Is the Kṛṣṇa of the *Mahābhārata* different from the Kṛṣṇa of the *Bhagavad-gītā*?
- What is the overall significance of the presence of Śiva in the *Mahābhārata*'s narrative and in the teachings of the *Anuśāsana-parvan*?
- To what extent is the *Mahābhārata* a Vaiṣṇava *avatāra* narrative?

V
The Question of *Dharma*

In this chapter, I want to focus on the manner in which the *Mahābhārata* considers and highlights the question of *dharma,* which is arguably the principal theme of the central narrative and is also discussed at length in a number of didactic passages. Naturally enough, if we are to properly consider the subject of *dharma* then the first requirement must be for us to arrive at a clear definition of what is meant by the term *dharma*. This question is one that is far easier to pose than to answer, for there are a number of different meanings for *dharma* as a word, as well as different understandings of how to interpret *dharma*.

Let us start off with some brief definitions. In Indian philosophical works, the word *dharma* is often used in the sense of an object that can be established as real; for example, one of the principal tenets of Buddhist teachings is that there are no *dharmas* because every object is subject to a constant process of transformation. Connected to this usage is the idea that the *dharma* of an object is its essential nature, or defining characteristic, so that one might say that giving off heat and light is the *dharma* of the sun and the *dharma* of fire. This understanding can be applied to humanity as well, as in the *Bhagavad-gītā* where Kṛṣṇa tells Arjuna that he will have to fight because he has been born as a *kṣatriya,* a warrior, and hence his essential nature, his *dharma,* will compel him to act in that way.[123]

In the *Mahābhārata,* however, the word *dharma* is generally employed in its more usual sense of 'right action' or 'proper behaviour', although, as we shall see, the idea that *dharma* is a state of consciousness as much as righteous conduct is never entirely lost sight of. One might thus presume that *dharma* refers to a system of ethics that prescribes the ideal mode of living; this is certainly a part of it, but what the *Mahābhārata* explores so effectively are the different ways in which 'right action' can be understood, and especially the tensions that can arise when differing forms of 'right action' appear to be in conflict with one another. In this chapter, I want to consider each of the main ways in which *dharma* is understood in the *Mahābhārata* and then look at the tensions between these differing views on *dharma* that are explored within both the narrative and didactic sections. So let us begin with brief definitions of the different forms of *dharma* one encounters when going through all of the eighteen *parvans,* before going on to look at each in a little more detail.

1. ***Dharma* as Religious Ritual**. If we keep in mind our definition of *dharma* as 'right action', then we must be aware that this can be understood in terms of the various religious rituals and offerings that are outlined in the *Anuśāsana-parvan* in particular.

2. ***Sva-dharma, Dharma* as *Varṇa* Duties**. Teachings on *dharma* are not necessarily understood as being universally applicable to all persons. In the view of the *Mahābhārata,* each person has duties to fulfil in

123 *Bhagavad-gītā,* 18.59.

accordance with one's social status as a member of a particular *varṇa*.

3. ***Dharma* as the Rules of *Dharma-śāstra*.** In ancient India, there were a number of Sanskrit texts that provided strict codes of rules or religious law. These texts are referred to by the collective title of *dharma-śāstra*, and *dharma* is also understood as strict adherence to the injunctions they prescribe.

4. ***Dharma* as Pure Virtue.** In contrast to the idea of *sva-dharma*, which varies from one person to another, there is also an understanding of *dharma* as being a universal set of moral precepts to be accepted and adhered to by each and every individual, regardless of *varṇa* or gender.

5. ***Mokṣa-Dharma*.** Whereas other understandings of *dharma* relate to one's position or duties at a social level, we should also be aware of the extensive teachings contained in the *Mahābhārata* that relate to renunciation of the world and various forms of spiritual practice that are designed to lead the aspirant towards liberation from rebirth. Such practices are referred to as *mokṣa-dharma*.

It is important to note that these five forms of *dharma* are not delineated as such by the *Mahābhārata* itself, and are based entirely on my own reading of the text. Nonetheless, there are clear indications that the *Mahābhārata* is very much aware of such distinctions and of the tensions that may arise between them, and so I feel that an analysis of the ideas on *dharma* along these lines is of value in understanding the work as a whole. Having given the preliminary delineation above for the sake of initial clarity, I want now to go ahead and consider each of them in a little more detail.

Dharma as Religious Ritual

There is, I think, a distinction to be noted in most religions of the world between the performance of sacred rites and adopting the lifestyle insisted upon for adherents of that tradition, and the question inevitably arises as to which should take precedence. Within the *Mahābhārata*, the principal ritual referred to is the Vedic *yajña* in which priests make offerings of various kinds into the sacred fire. The *Anuśāsana-parvan* includes a number of chapters that prescribe ritual offerings of a different kind, more akin to the *pūjās* of modern Hindu worship, but the overwhelming emphasis is on the Vedic tradition of fire sacrifice.

Particularly noteworthy in this connection are the two grandiose *yajñas* performed by the priesthood on behalf of Yudhiṣṭhira, one to mark the establishment of his predominant kingship, the *rājasūya-yajña* described in the *Sabhā-parvan*, and the other as a form of atonement for the sins he perceived himself as having committed in waging war against his enemies at Kurukṣetra, the *aśvamedha-yajña* described in the *Aśvamedhika-parvan*. In many ways, however, the principal significance of dharmic ritual lies in the manner in which it is critiqued at various points in the *Mahābhārata*, both because of the violence inherent in the ritual sacrifice of animals and because the orientation of the ritual is primarily towards worldly gains. As we shall see, challenges to the spiritual validity of ritualised religion are a theme of discussion that recurs on a number of occasions throughout the *Mahābhārata*.

Sva-Dharma, *Dharma* as *Varṇa* Duties

It might well be said that a discussion of *dharma* in relation to the four *varṇas* could be included under the heading of ritual acts, as there is a very real sense in the *Mahābhārata* that fulfilling one's prescribed duties in relation to *varṇa* and gender is equivalent to the execution of the *yajña* ceremonies. This point is very evident from the third chapter of the *Bhagavad-gītā*. I think, however, that the distinctions between them are sufficiently apparent for them to be considered under different headings, particularly as adherence to *varṇa-dharma* is such a prominent theme of the text as a whole.

So what do we mean by *sva-dharma* or *varṇa-dharma*? As many will be aware, the society depicted in the *Mahābhārata* is structured around four distinct social classes, each of which has a specific way of life prescribed for it. Each of these social classes is given the name of *varṇa*, a word that literally means 'colour' but in this context probably means 'type'. The four *varṇas* are brahmins, *kṣatriyas*, *vaiśyas*, and *śūdras*, and it is frequently asserted that adherence to *dharma* means fulfilling the duties of one's own social class, one's *sva-dharma* or personal *dharma*, so that society as a whole functions in an ordered fashion that promotes the prosperity of each individual.

It is the brahmin and *kṣatriya varṇas* that are of particular significance in the *Mahābhārata* narrative, simply because most of the principal protagonists are born as either brahmins or *kṣatriyas*, and much of the discussion around what course of action should be followed relates to the duties incumbent on an individual in relation to his *varṇa*. Hence the dharmic duties of two of the *varṇas* are revealed quite clearly within the structure of the narrative, but for a more precise understanding of the *dharma* of all four *varṇas* we can turn to the speeches of some of the main characters and to didactic passages that focus on this system of social organisation.

The opening section of the *Śānti-parvan* consists of a sub-*parvan* named the *Rāja-dharma,* literally the *dharma* or duties of a king, which covers the first 128 chapters of the *Śānti-parvan.* As one of the main duties of a king is to ensure the stability of the social order, this includes quite detailed instructions on the specific duties of each of the four *varṇas,* as follows.

> A brahmin fulfils his duty by self-control, recitation of the Veda, and imparting instruction to others. If he gains wealth from these activities, he should not indulge in any forbidden action, but should remain peaceful and satisfied with wisdom alone. Any wealth he acquires should be used to raise children, give charity, and perform *yajñas.* Whether or not he does anything else, a brahmin fulfils his duty by studying the Vedas. A *kṣatriya* should give but never receive charity, and he should execute *yajñas,* though never as a priest. He should learn the Vedas but not teach them, protect his subjects, be active in suppressing robbers, and show heroism in battle. Learned rulers who have performed *yajñas* and conquered in battle are the best of those who reach the realm of the gods. Those with knowledge of the ancient traditions do not praise a *kṣatriya* who returns from battle without a wound on his body. His highest *dharma* is the affliction of other warriors, and there is no conduct for him superior to the destruction of miscreants. Suitable undertakings for a king are study of the Vedas, *yajñas,* and charity; therefore he seeks battle. He must ensure that all subjects follow the proper ways of life appropriate for them according to the prescribed rules. Even if he performs no other duty, a king is to be known as equal to Indra if he properly enacts the duty of protection.
>
> Charity, study of the Vedas, and making money by honest means comprise the *dharma* of a *vaiśya.* A *vaiśya* should

> protect all animals like a father and thereby become joyful; any other course of action is wrong for him. After creation, Prajāpati entrusted the animals to the *vaiśya* and entrusted all beings to the brahmin and *kṣatriya*. If a *vaiśya* tends six cows on behalf of their owner, he may take the milk of one, and if he tends one hundred cows, he may claim two as his own. When a cow dies, he may claim half a share of the horns and hoofs, and the same is his share of the crop from the seeds he sows. A *vaiśya* should never be averse to the protection of animals and no other person should take up this duty. Prajāpati created *śūdras* as the servants of the other *varṇas*, and by such service the *śūdra* gains great happiness. He should render this service without envy and never seek to accumulate riches, for with such wealth he might sinfully make those of the higher *varṇas* subject to him; only with the permission of the king may he satisfy his desires in accordance with *dharma*. The *śūdras* should be completely maintained by the other *varṇas*; old umbrellas, turbans, seats, shoes, and fans should be given to a *śūdra* who renders service. If a *śūdra* approaches anyone from the higher *varṇas* and offers his service, he should be engaged; *piṇḍa* should be offered on his behalf by his employer and he should be maintained when he grows old or frail.[124]

A more succinct delineation of the *dharma* of each *varṇa* is also found within the *Bhagavad-gītā* in one of the passages in which Kṛṣṇa teaches the idea of *karma-yoga*. This is how Kṛṣṇa defines the duties of the four *varṇas*:

> Tranquillity, restraint, austerity, purity, patience, honesty, theoretical knowledge, practical knowledge, and faith in

124 *Śānti-parvan*, 60.8–34.

> the Vedic revelation are the duties of a brahmin, born of his inherent nature. Heroism, energy, resolve, expertise, never fleeing from battle, charity, and displaying a lordly disposition are the duties of a *kṣatriya*, born of his inherent nature. Agriculture, tending cows, and trade are the duties of a *vaiśya*, born of his inherent nature, whilst work consisting of service to others is the duty of a *śūdra*, born of his inherent nature.[125]

Thus we can see that of the four *varṇas*, the brahmins are the priests and teachers, *kṣatriyas* are the rulers, enforcers of law, and military chiefs, *vaiśyas* are merchants and agriculturalists, and *śūdras* are the skilled artisans and labourers. Clearly, with the economic and cultural transformations that have taken place over the centuries, the *varṇa* system has little relevance today in the form that it is outlined in the above passages. Within the context of the *Mahābhārata* narrative, however, it is of central importance, as many of the decisions taken by the principal characters are based on the understanding that *varṇa* duties are an essential element of every individual's life. Hence a complete understanding of the structure and progression of that narrative must include a clear insight into the social structure based on *varṇas* that dominated the ways of life followed at that time.

Very often today, the idea of *varṇa* is taken as being identical to that of caste, with translators giving 'caste' as an equivalent term. Whilst there are clear similarities between the two, as both are precise social divisions pervading the whole of society, it is misleading to regard *varṇa* and caste as identical. The *varṇa* system is a fourfold division of labour for a predominantly agricultural society; whilst caste, which corresponds with

---

125 *Bhagavad-gītā*, 18.42–44.

the Sanskrit term *jāti*, does have occupational implications, the principal role of castes in India today is as supportive communities for individual members. Moreover, the large number of individual castes inevitably renders the caste system quite markedly distinct from the *varṇa* divisions presented within the *Mahābhārata*. There is much more that could be said on this point, but suffice to say that one should avoid making any overly simplistic equivalence between caste and *varṇa*.

There are a number of further points on the subject of *varṇa* that might also be noted, namely the nature of the social elite as designated by the *varṇa* system, whether or not one's *varṇa* status is determined by birth alone, and the extent to which *varṇa* identity is reflected in a person's inherent nature. To take the first of these first, the system of social stratification outlined in the *Śānti-parvan* appears hideously repressive to the modern mind, particularly with regard to the status of *śūdras*, but it is worth noting that those in the highest stratum, the brahmins, are not expected to be the most materially affluent. Their elite status is based on enlightened wisdom, learning, and moral standing, and it is constantly asserted that due to their spiritual awakening brahmins should be indifferent to the acquisition of wealth. This is surely to be regarded as a positive feature of the *varṇa* system, standing as it does in marked contrast to the contemporary demeanour of social elites.

With regard to the question of whether or not a person's *varṇa* status is determined solely by birth, we can detect differing views within the *Mahābhārata*. Within the central narrative, the principal characters are regarded as being *kṣatriyas* or brahmins solely on the basis of their birth, and indeed, despite his undoubted martial prowess, in some manuscripts we find that Karṇa is rejected by Draupadī because he is not regarded as having taken birth in a *kṣatriya* family. Yudhiṣṭhira, by contrast, displays many of the attributes of a brahmin but is always accepted as a *kṣatriya,* whilst the status of Droṇa and his son Aśvatthāman as brahmins is universally accepted despite their taking up arms and waging war with an unrivalled ferocity. This is not the whole picture, however, and when, in our final chapter, we come to review the *Anuśāsana-parvan*'s teachings on the position of the brahmins, we will see that authoritative voices within the *Mahābhārata* hold differing views over whether *varṇa* designation is based on birth or personal qualities. Bhīṣma, a constant advocate of *varṇa-dharma,* holds to the view that birth alone is the absolute criterion, whilst Yudhiṣṭhira, the exemplar of *dharma* as virtue, expresses the opposite view. But more of that later on.

We should also be aware that the *Mahābhārata* views its teachings on *varṇa-dharma* as descriptive as well as prescriptive. What I mean by that is that a person designated as a *kṣatriya* does not have to follow the *kṣatriya-dharma* purely as a matter of prescribed duty, but does so because the *kṣatriya* mode of action is a reflection of his nature and identity. So in one sense, a brahmin, *kṣatriya, vaiśya,* or *śūdra* adheres to a particular lifestyle and code of conduct that is in accord with the nature he is born with; to act in that way is what is natural for that person, reflecting his preordained character and identity. This is perhaps one of the main reasons why it is presumed that the son of a *śūdra* will have the nature of a *śūdra* and will find the lifestyle of a *śūdra* entirely aligned with that nature. Thus it is that in the final verses of the *Bhagavad-gītā,* Kṛṣṇa tells Arjuna that any decision he makes to avoid fighting will have no effect because his *kṣatriya* nature will compel him to act, *prakṛtis tvāṁ niyokṣyati.*[126] It is not only his duty, it is what he is.

I have already mentioned that there is some degree of overlap between *dharma* in the form of religious ritual and

---

126 *Bhagavad-gītā,* 18.59.

dharma as adherence to *varṇa* duties, but I think a word or two more on that would be appropriate. The Vedic *yajña* is typically advocated in terms of the this-worldly benefits accrued by the performer of the ritual, but it is also made clear that the propitiation of the gods through the sacred offerings is beneficial for the world as a whole, as these lesser deities reciprocate by ensuring that the Earth is blessed with adequate rainfall, general prosperity, and the fertility of the land. This view of ritual acts is set forth in the *Bhagavad-gītā*[127] and other passages in the *Mahābhārata*, but this understanding is extended to include actions based on *varṇa* duties. Hence the life of the individual is regarded as a ritual performance based on the universal *dharma* of human society that not only ensures social order, but also propitiates the gods and ensures wellbeing of the world in every sense. And just as one of the results sought from the execution of the *yajña* is elevation to the realm of the gods, the same elevated rebirth is shown to be acquired by persons who devotedly adhere to the ritual life of *varṇa-dharma*, as is revealed at the end of the *Mahābhārata* when we find Duryodhana and his iniquitous allies elevated to the heavenly domain of the gods.

I have already suggested that, in the strictest sense, the idea of *dharma* based on four discrete social classes is of little relevance today, but as a final point for this part of the discussion I would like to qualify that assertion somewhat. Certainly, any revival of the *varṇa* system would be both unrealistic and undesirable, but we might consider the fundamental principle on which the idea of rigid social classes was based. First of all, it is clear from some of the verses cited above that *varṇa* is not simply to do with social classes, but is also to be understood in terms of the varying character types and propensities

---

127 3.10–14.

observable throughout society. These character traits and dispositions can be identified in almost every human society, and so in that sense one might say that *varṇa* represents an existential feature of humanity.

Furthermore, we should also notice the understanding that the primary aim of the *varṇa* system was the promotion of social order and general prosperity. The idea is that we are not just individuals pursuing our own personal goals, but also have a responsibility towards our families, our communities, and wider society. In the time of the *Mahābhārata*, such responsibilities were fulfilled by adherence to *varṇa* duties, and although such duties are no longer relevant, the underlying principle of social responsibility and the pursuit of the common good remains. *Dharma* is thus to be interpreted as social responsibility, action that promotes the common good, rather than the prioritising of self-interest at the expense of the wellbeing of society as a whole.

Dharma as the Rules of *Dharma-śāstra*

In addition to the more general discussions of the precepts of *dharma*, the *Mahābhārata* also makes reference to what are often known as 'Hindu Law Books'. These are Sanskrit texts that translate the more general principles into codified systems of religious law. In this sense, *dharma-śāstra* can be regarded as somewhat equivalent to the Islamic Sharia or the Jewish codes of conduct. It must be said that the *Mahābhārata* does not place any great emphasis on *dharma-śāstra* in its extensive consideration of *dharma*, but it is certainly aware of *dharma-śāstra*, refers to itself as a *dharma-śāstra*, and at times includes passages that are equivalent to some of those found in well-known dharma-śāstric literature such as the *Manu-*

smṛti, the *Viṣṇu-smṛti*, and the *Yājñavalkya-smṛti*.[128] If we turn again to the *Anuśāsana-parvan*, we can observe that Chapters 44 to 49 set out codes of conduct relating to *varṇa* rules, marriage, inheritance, and gender roles.

Outside of the *Anuśāsana-parvan*, *dharma-śāstra* is only rarely drawn into the frequent discussions of *dharma*, but the wider issue here is the extent to which the idea of *dharma* can be confined within rigidly established rules of religious law, and this is certainly a question that has a significance far beyond the text of the *Mahābhārata*. On this specific point, we find an interesting passage in the *Karṇa-parvan* in which Kṛṣṇa is the principal speaker.

The *Karṇa-parvan* tells of the fighting that took place at Kurukṣetra after the fall of both Bhīṣma and Droṇa. Karṇa is then made the commander of the Kaurava host and we hear of the bitter fighting that took place as he led the army into battle against the Pāṇḍavas. Whilst Arjuna is distracted on another part of the field, Karṇa focuses his attention on Yudhiṣṭhira himself and severely wounds him with his sharp arrows. Without anyone to protect him, Yudhiṣṭhira is forced to run from the field before Karṇa, and is left in a state of mental and physical torment. When Arjuna eventually comes to assist his elder brother it is too late and Yudhiṣṭhira condemns Arjuna and says that he might as well give up the bow named Gāṇḍīva and let another, more valiant warrior bear it. These words of Yudhiṣṭhira are unjust to Arjuna, for he is speaking in a state of acute anguish, but the situation is made even worse when

128 As indicated above, the idea of the *Mahābhārata* directly quoting from the *Manu-smṛti* is, however, problematic. See Johaness Bronkhorst, 'Manu and Mahabhārata', in *Indologica*, T. Ya. Elizarenkova Memorial Volume, Book 2, edited by L. Kulikov and M. Rusanov M., 135-156 (Moscow: Russian State University for the Humanities, 2012).

Arjuna reveals that he has vowed to behead anyone who says that he should give up the Gāṇḍīva bow. For Arjuna a vow can never be broken, for it is said that truth and *dharma* are one and the same, and so he draws his sword to strike down Yudhiṣṭhira. At this point Kṛṣṇa intervenes. Here is a summary of his speech to Arjuna:

> Kṛṣṇa then said to Arjuna, 'Stop! Stop! No one who understands the distinctions of *dharma* would ever act in such a way. You do not know about the decisions made by learned men who teach disciples about matters of right conduct. It is never easy to determine what course of action should be followed and what should be avoided, but it is possible if one follows the guidance of scripture. You think that you know what *dharma* is, but by acting in this way as if it were *dharma* you are showing your ignorance of *dharma*, for the killing of a living being is forbidden by those who truly adhere to *dharma*. In my opinion, never killing any living being is the highest *dharma*; one may speak a falsehood but one should never kill another being. So how is it that you are prepared to kill the king, your elder brother, who is himself one who comprehends *dharma*? The vow you took was an act of folly and now as another act of folly you are preparing to embrace *adharma*. Why are you going to do this without thinking properly about *dharma*? The true end of *dharma* is certainly a subtle matter, which is hard to understand.'
>
> Now listen to a narration which reflects on the subtle and complex nature of *dharma*. One who speaks the truth adheres to *dharma*; there is no virtue higher than truthfulness. However, the practice of the essence of truth can be very difficult to comprehend. There are a number of occasions on which one may speak a lie: at a marriage, to woo

a woman, when one's life or property is threatened, and for the sake of a brahmin. On such occasions falsehood becomes truth and truth becomes falsehood. Anyone who adheres blindly to the principle of speaking the truth is no better than a fool.

There was a *sādhu* named Kauśika who was not well read in the teachings on *dharma*. He lived at a good distance from any village, at a place where a number of rivers met, and he had taken the following vow: 'I must always speak the truth.' He became famous for his adherence to this principle. Once some people came to the forest where he lived, attempting to escape with their possessions from a gang of ferocious robbers. The robbers then approached Kauśika and said, 'A host of people came by here a little while ago. Which way did they go?' Kauśika told the truth, 'They entered this wood here.' Acting on this information, the robbers pursued their victims and when they found them they killed them all. And because of the *adharma* of speaking the truth, Kauśika was reborn in a low state of life.

There has to be some way of distinguishing *dharma*. Some say the highest knowledge is gained through reason (*tarka*) but many others say one gains knowledge of *dharma* from the *śruti* (scriptures). I do not disagree with this, but the *śruti* does not refer to every individual case. *Dharma* was created for the welfare of living beings and hence whatever sustains living beings is *dharma*. So we must understand *dharma* as that which leads to the welfare of people in the world. Now that I have given you a clear definition of *dharma* you must decide whether Yudhiṣṭhira should be killed.[129]

129 *Karṇa-parvan*, Chapter 49.

Arjuna accepts Kṛṣṇa's sound advice, but asks if there is some way of getting out of this dilemma without breaking his sworn word. Kṛṣṇa then suggests that as an insult is often said to be equal to death he might 'kill' his elder brother with insulting words, thereby escaping from an impossible predicament. Arjuna accepts this guidance and the problem is resolved.

There are a number of points of interest to be taken from this passage, but what I want to particularly focus on at present is Kṛṣṇa's view of *dharma-śāstra* as a means of determining right action. Are we obliged to live in strict accordance with a preordained set of rules even where doing so seems useless or even harmful? The answer given here does not entirely deny the value of *dharma-śāstra,* but at the same time our integrity and intelligence should always take precedence over dogmatic adherence. *Dharma* is whatever is most beneficial for all living beings, and we must always strive to achieve that end, even when doing so entails ignoring the injunctions of ancient texts. It is a significant lesson that is taught here, and one that has implications far beyond a mere study of the *Mahābhārata.*

Sanātana-Dharma, the *Dharma* of Pure Virtue

Standing to some extent in contrast to the dharmic duties related to *varṇa,* the *Mahābhārata* also offers us a vision of *dharma* in a form that is applicable to all persons in all places at all times. This is typically referred to as *sanātana-dharma,* the eternal, or, better still, the universal *dharma.* It is also known as *sādhāraṇa-dharma,* which literally means '*dharma* applicable to all persons'. In considering the meaning and significance of this *sanātana-dharma,* it is probably best to think of it as being pure virtue, the highest state of morality that a human being can aspire towards, including all the great qualities that are universally admired in societies and cultures across the world. Such qualities rest on core precepts such as compassion, charity, kindness, honesty, benevolence, never causing harm, tolerance, and consideration. The *Mahābhārata* certainly represents one of India's greatest contributions to this vision of universal virtue, expressing it in both narrative and didactic forms.

As has already been discussed, at the very heart of the central narrative we have two characters who represent an absolute antithesis in relation to the *sanātana-dharma*, Yudhiṣṭhira and Duryodhana. At the same time, we have other characters who embrace the *dharma* of pure virtue, but only to a limited extent; here one would include Dhṛtarāṣṭra, who is certainly drawn towards *dharma* by his inherent nature, but dragged away from it by his attachment to his sons, his faction, power, and opulence. Karṇa is another character who fully comprehends the importance of *dharma* in this form, but is pulled away from it towards the *kṣatriya-dharma* that is expressed through his loyalty to Duryodhana and his longing for triumph in battle.

We have already noticed the ways in which Yudhiṣṭhira exemplifies the purest form of *dharma* when we looked at the principal characters, but in the context of the present discussion it is worth briefly reminding ourselves of the typical manner in which he conducts himself. Dhṛtarāṣṭra outlined those qualities in terms of his being true to his word, always diligent, devoted to the words of scripture, obedient to his family, loved by his subjects, kind to his friends, in control of his senses, and a protector of the righteous. He displays forbearance, tolerance, self-control, and honesty; he is always truthful, accepts good advice, is compassionate to all beings, and attentive to precept.[130] Whilst ruling over his kingdom, Yudhiṣṭhira further displays his

130 *Udyoga-parvan*, 147.32–33.

dharmic attributes by always working for the wellbeing of his people. His constant thought was *kiṁ hitaṁ sarva-lokānāṁ bhavet*, 'What would be beneficial for all people',[131] and he always ensured that widows, orphans, and those who were disabled or poverty-stricken were properly provided for.[132]

Throughout the *Mahābhārata*, Yudhiṣṭhira is portrayed as being of a gentle disposition, with constant goodwill towards other living beings. He is kind and forgiving, tolerant and forbearing, and always anxious to avoid conflict of any kind. He is also notably non-competitive in his attitude to others, transcending such worldly preoccupations by the strength of his virtue. His powers of mercy and forgiveness are demonstrated by his attitude towards Jayadratha and Dhṛtarāṣṭra despite the wrongs they have done him. His strict adherence to honesty and truthfulness is shown by the way in which he insists they must honour the terms of their agreement by remaining in exile, and by the fact that the only untruth he ever spoke was that which brought about the death of Droṇa. Despite his lofty station as supreme amongst all the kings of the land, he retains the quality of humility, and his character is pervaded by the quality of *ahiṁsā*, never harming, which is frequently said to be the very essence of *dharma*. He is a king and a warrior, but he is fully aware of the horrors implicit in warfare, and loathes the aggressive mentality of other *kṣatriyas*, which leads to repeated acts of violence.

For any consideration of the *Mahābhārata*'s ideas on *sanātana-dharma*, attention must also be paid to the words and deeds of Duryodhana, as these reveal quite starkly the bleak antithesis of pure virtue. Again, we have already considered

---

131 *Sabhā-parvan*, 12.6.

132 *Śānti-parvan*, 12.10–12.

the characterisation of this arch-villain of the story, but it is worth reminding ourselves of his consistent misconduct both because of the light it sheds on our understanding of *dharma*, and the relevance this has for the modern world, which is still beset by a plethora of mini-Duryodhanas. As we have seen, the qualities he displays are harshness, avarice, contempt, dishonesty, anger, and a complete lack of any sense of kindness or compassion. He shows no forgiveness, and he nurtures grudges against others who have done no more than achieve the goals he himself is constantly longing for. Within the *Bhagavad-gītā*, one finds a fairly extensive passage[133] in which the aims, attitudes, and qualities of persons of this type are set out, and there seems little doubt that Kṛṣṇa's words here are directly related to the conduct of Duryodhana and his coterie of close associates.

Beyond the behaviour of Duryodhana throughout the central narrative, Chapter 50 of the *Sabhā-parvan* gives us a highly significant insight into the ideas and world view of a person who stands against the purity of *sanātana-dharma*. As the *Gītā* says, *adharmaṁ dharmam iti yā manyate tamasāvṛtā*, those whose intellect is covered by *tamas* (darkness) regard *adharma* as *dharma*,[134] and again we can observe numerous examples of this both in the history of religion and in the present day. In this passage, we are given a clear insight into Duryodhana's view of *dharma*, which is indeed *adharma* masquerading as *dharma*, and this in turn sheds a good deal of light on the *dharma* of virtue to which it forms the direct antithesis. The following speech is delivered by Duryodhana after he has been advised by his father to seek a peaceful reconciliation with the Pāṇḍavas:

---

133 16.7–18.

134 *Bhagavad-gītā*, 18.32.

10 Duryodhana said: Just like one boat bound to another boat, you are confusing me even though you possess wisdom. Why are you not attentive to our own interests? Or is it just that you hate me?

11 These Dhārtarāṣṭras [descendants of Dhṛtarāṣṭra] cannot flourish whilst you are their ruler. You constantly speak of the benefits that may come in the future, when you could already have achieved them for yourself.

12 A leader who has to be guided by others is deluded away from his true path. So how can those who follow him adhere to the proper path?

13 O king, you are endowed with wisdom, you have served your elders, and gained mastery over your senses; do not cause such confusion to those of us who are dedicated to fulfilling our proper duties.

14 Bṛhaspati has stated that the conduct of a king is different to the conduct of other people. Therefore the endeavour of a king is always in pursuit his own interest.

15 O great king, the conduct of a *kṣatriya* is focused entirely on gaining victory, whether such conduct be *dharma* or *adharma*, O mightiest of the Bharatas.

16 He should therefore advance against all directions, like a charioteer using his whip, seeking to gain the lamp of his enemies' prosperity, O best of the Bharatas.

17 Whether it be kept hidden or exposed, it is said by those who have knowledge of weaponry that a weapon is whatever can be used to subdue the enemy. A weapon is not to be understood simply as a tool for cutting.

18 Dissatisfaction is the very root of prosperity, and therefore I long for such dissatisfaction. One who endeavours for personal aggrandisement, he, O king, is the supreme leader of men.

19 One should never develop a sense of ownership with regard to either opulence or wealth, for others will plunder what one has previously acquired. This indeed is what is understood as *rāja-dharma*, the *dharma* of the royal order.

20 Despite having made an agreement with Namuci in good faith, Śakra still cut off his head. Such was his understanding of the universal code of conduct with regard to an enemy.

21 Just as a serpent seizes creatures that live in holes, the Earth devours these two types of person: a king who does not wage war and a brahmin who never leaves his home.

22 There is no one who is born as a person's enemy, O lord of men. One who pursues the same course of life as oneself, he alone is one's enemy and no other person.

23 A person who, due to stupidity, disregards the rising strength of the enemy faction, which is like a progressive disease, is cut off at the very root.

24 Just like an anthill appearing at the root of tree, which may eventually consume that tree because of its proximity, so an enemy, even though insignificant at present, may increase in strength.

25 O descendent of Ajamīḍha, O Bhārata, do not take delight in the prosperity of the enemy. This principle I am speaking of is the burden carried on the head by those who are resolute and wise.

26 One who wishes to expand his status, as one's powers increase naturally from the point of birth, flourishes in alliance with his kinsfolk. An energetic course of action then brings immediate expansion of one's status.

27 As long as I do not acquire the opulence of the Pāṇḍavas, I will have a doubt over whether I will gain possession of their prosperity or whether I will lie down dead on the field of battle.

> 28 What is life to me now, O lord of your people, when I am in a position like this? They are constantly growing in strength, whilst our prosperity remains unchanged.[135]

It is certainly the case that the *Mahābhārata* frequently includes differing opinions on subtle matters of *dharma*, using authoritative voices on both sides to allow for the question to be explored in terms of its full complexity. Here, however, I am certain that this is not the case, for, as ever, the voice of Duryodhana is that representing a complete abnegation of the ideals of *dharma*. What we have here is an infamous intermingling of *kṣatriya-dharma* with the pure wickedness that is the antithesis of the *dharma* of virtue exemplified by Yudhiṣṭhira. There is no need to analyse the passage in any great detail, as it pretty much speaks for itself, but it demonstrates very well the manner in which the character of Duryodhana is presented in order to give us guidance as to the type of ideas and values we should always seek to avoid. And in this regard, I am sure most of us will identify Duryodhana's perspective on life with certain political and economic ideologies that flourish in the contemporary world. As a final note here, in reading this speech one is reminded of the insight into this perverse mentality provided by Kṛṣṇa in *Bhagavad-gītā*, where he parodies the speech or thoughts of low-minded persons:

> 'I have obtained this much today, and I will obtain more to satisfy my desire. This much wealth is mine now, and this much more will come to me in the future.
>
> I have slain this enemy, and I will kill the others as well. I am the Lord, I am the enjoyer, I am successful, powerful, and happy.

---

135 *Sabhā-parvan*, 50.10–28.

I am wealthy and born into a good family. Who is there who can be my equal? I will perform sacrifices, I will give charity, and thus I will rejoice.' Such are the ideas of those deluded by ignorance.[136]

Mokṣa-dharma and the *Dharma* of Pure Virtue

We will now move on to briefly consider the idea of *mokṣa-dharma*, the form of *dharma* adhered to by renunciants seeking absolute liberation from rebirth. First, however, it is important to be aware that in many ways there is an overlap between the *dharma* of pure virtue we have just been considering and the *mokṣa-dharma*, particularly in terms of the ideal forms of interaction with other living beings. So it is that in the latter half of the *Śānti-parvan*, where the emphasis is on the quest for liberation, we find succinct statements that seek to establish the *dharma* of virtue by means of definition rather than through the actions of the principal characters. To sum up this section of our discussion, here are a selection of verses that seek to define the dharmic path adhered to by Yudhiṣṭhira, designated here as the *sanātana-dharma*.

adrohaḥ sarva-bhūteṣu karmaṇā manasā girā
anugrahaś ca dānaṁ ca satāṁ dharmaḥ sanātanaḥ

Never displaying malice towards any living being through actions, thoughts, or words, acts of kindness, and giving in charity; this is the *sanātana-dharma* adhered to by righteous persons.[137]

---

136 *Bhagavad-gītā*, 16.13–15.

137 *Āraṇyaka-parvan*, 281.34.

ahiṁsā satyam akrodho dānam etac catuṣṭayam
ajāta-śatro sevasva dharma eṣa sanātanaḥ

Not harming, truthfulness, remaining free from anger, and charity are the four practices you must adhere to, Ajātaśatru. This is the *sanātana-dharma.*[138]

sarvam priyābhyupagataṁ dharmam āhur manīṣiṇaḥ
paśyaitaṁ lakṣaṇād deśaṁ dharmādharme yudhiṣṭhira

The wise say that *dharma* is whatever is based on love for all beings. This is the characteristic mark that distinguishes *dharma* from *adharma,* Yudhiṣṭhira.[139]

anukrośo hi sādhūnāṁ su-mahad-dharma-lakṣaṇam
anukrośaś ca sādhūnāṁ sadā prītiṁ prayacchati

Amongst righteous persons, compassion is the great characteristic mark of *dharma;* and compassion is always a source of delight for the righteous.[140]

ata ūrdhvaṁ pravakṣyāmi niyataṁ dharma-lakṣaṇam
ahiṁsā-lakṣaṇo dharmo hiṁsā cādharma-lakṣaṇā

Now then I will speak about what is established as the characteristic mark of *dharma. Ahiṁsā* [not harming] is the mark of *dharma,* whilst *hiṁsā* [harming] is the mark of *adharma.*[141]

---

138 *Anuśāsana-parvan,* 147.22.

139 *Śānti-parvan,* 251.24.

140 *Anuśāsana-parvan,* 5.23.

141 *Aśvamedhika-parvan,* 43.19.

In verses such as these taken from the didactic passages of the *Mahābhārata,* we can observe how the precepts of *dharma* demonstrated through the life of Yudhiṣṭhira are set out as definitions of the universal principle of *dharma,* and this again demonstrates how these passages of religious and ethical teaching complement and enhance the ideas presented elsewhere in narrative form.

Mokṣa-dharma: *Dharma* of the Renunciants

The *Mahābhārata* is naturally considered in terms of the great narrative that runs throughout this vast work and in relation to the characters so wonderfully portrayed by the author. The present work, however, focuses on the *Mahābhārata* in its entirety, and that includes the extensive passages of religious, ethical, spiritual, and philosophical discourse contained in its eighteen books. Within the *Śānti-parvan* and the *Aśvamedhika-parvan* in particular we find a huge range of teachings on the means by which the embodied *ātman* can be liberated from its state of bondage in this world. The philosophy taught there is generally that of the Sāṁkhya system, whilst the spiritual practices of *mokṣa-dharma* are mainly those of the Yoga system, similar to those taught by Patañjali in the *Yoga Sūtras*. Although such ideas and practices are categorised under the heading of *dharma,* they also involve a physical and emotional withdrawal from the world and severe restraint in terms of indulgence in any worldly pleasures.

There is a clear contrast here between the understanding of *dharma* we have reviewed up to this point, which relates overwhelmingly to the manner in which we live in this world, and the path of *dharma* that aims exclusively at liberation from the world. The *Mahābhārata* itself overtly recognises this distinction, referring to the two as *pravṛtti,* the way of ritual action, and *nivṛtti*, the path of renunciation of action, although it is clear that the ideal of *dharma* as pure virtue exists under both headings. Whilst the emphasis on the Vedic ritual, *varṇa-dharma*, the *dharma* of women, and *dharma-śāstra*, all fall under the heading of *pravṛtti*, we find that in the *Śānti-parvan*'s teachings on spiritual liberation, we repeatedly encounter a view that rejects *pravṛtti* to a greater or lesser degree, and asserts the superiority of *nivṛtti* as the means by which all the difficulties inherent in worldly existence can be overcome.

This is therefore an ascetic understanding of *dharma*. It is in many ways identical to the *dharma* of virtue, the *sanātana-dharma* previously discussed, but within the *nivṛtti-mārga*, the spiritual path based on renunciation of the world, there is a strong vein of the world-denying ethos of wholesale renunciation. There is a consistent emphasis on the power of destiny, which is regarded as shaping all outcomes regardless of human endeavour, and this view of our existence has a clear tendency towards non-involvement in the world, which is incongruent with Yudhiṣṭhira's constant striving for the welfare of others. So whilst we must recognise a high degree of complementarity between the *dharma* of virtue and the *mokṣa-dharma*, there are clear differences of emphasis with regard to the attitude towards life in the here and now. Are we simply to accept the fate allotted to others as unavoidable destiny? Or are we to take vigorous action to alleviate their suffering? Certainly, the *mokṣa-dharma* emphasises compassion and non-harming, but at the same time it inevitably shifts the focus of our engagement away from this world towards a higher domain of reality. In the next chapter, I will consider the teachings on *mokṣa-dharma* more fully and I do not want to pre-empt that discussion at this point, beyond noting that this form of intense spirituality represents a further understanding of *dharma* offered by the *Mahābhārata* to its readers and students.

Tensions between the Differing Concepts of *Dharma*

One of the most interesting features of the way in which the *Mahābhārata* explores the idea of *dharma* is its illustration of the tensions that inevitably arise from the differing ideals of *dharma* noted above. Yudhiṣṭhira's continuous attitude towards the world is that of a man of pure virtue, but at times this is in conflict with his duties as a *kṣatriya*, and as a result he is frequently subject to criticisms from his advisers and family members. In other passages, the dharmic duty of the brahmins to perform the ritual of *yajña* is condemned from the perspective of both *mokṣa-dharma* and the *dharma* of virtue, because of the cruelty involved in the offering of slaughtered animals, and the materialistic goals sought by the performers of the ritual.

We will consider both these forms of tension in more detail shortly, but first we must notice a couple of other points regarding differing views on the subject of *dharma* that the *Mahābhārata* focuses upon. First of all, with regard to the idea that *dharma* can be determined by reference to the strict rules of *dharma-śāstra*, we have already seen Kṛṣṇa's rejection of that perspective in his speech to Arjuna in which he points out that hard and fast rules are dysfunctional because each situation is different and may require a different approach in order to ensure that *dharma* prevails. He therefore states that the underlying principle is whatever brings the greatest benefit to all living beings, and our pursuit of *dharma* must always be guided by that precept even if that means we go against the rules of *dharma-śāstra*.

We can observe a similar line of thought in the debates over whether Draupadī's marriage to all five of the Pāṇḍavas is in accordance with the rules of *dharma*. Drupada and Dhṛṣṭadyumna, Draupadī's father and brother, both insist that a polyandric marriage represents a clear contravention of the rules of *dharma*, but Yudhiṣṭhira replies that he feels in his heart that this marriage arrangement is pure and righteous. Because his heart never inclines towards any form of *adharma*, he asserts that in this case the formal rules governing marriage can be overridden.[142] Here the idea seems to be that rather than compiling strict forms of *dharma-śāstra* that can never be contravened, one must endeavour to elevate one's state of consciousness so that it cleaves instinctively to that which is righteous.

A further point we might note here relates to manner in which *varṇa-dharma* is adhered to. We noted above that *varṇa* designation is descriptive as well as prescriptive, in the sense that one's *varṇa* is regarded as reflecting one's own personal nature so that members of a *varṇa* have a natural propensity for the duties they are obliged to fulfil. Within the narrative, however, we find examples of members of one *varṇa* taking up the duties of another, and thereby illustrating Kṛṣṇa's warning, *para-dharmo bhayāvahaḥ*, another's *dharma* is a source of danger.[143] The most obvious examples would be Droṇa and his son Aśvatthāman, who are brahmins by *varṇa* but accept the *kṣatriya-dharma* of waging war; here it is noteworthy that these are the two warriors who indulge in the most extreme and horrific acts of violence. A similar point could be made with regard to the story of Rāma Jāmadagnya, another brahmin who takes up the weapons of war and inflicts unjustifiable slaughter on those he perceives to be his enemies. The lesson would seem to be that brahmins should live as brahmins; otherwise *varṇa-dharma* is perniciously distorted.

142 *Ādi-parvan*, Chapter 188.

143 *Bhagavad-gītā*, 3.35.

Varṇa-dharma and Sanātana-dharma

Turning to the ongoing tensions between the *varṇa-dharma* of *kṣatriyas* and the *sanātana-dharma* of pure virtue, espoused and adhered to by Yudhiṣṭhira, the examples from the text are too numerous to mention. Just a few of these must suffice to make the point.

We might start by considering again the dice match and the role played by Yudhiṣṭhira. Initially, he is unwilling to take part, regarding such competitive gaming as a potential source of quarrels and enmity, but as a *kṣatriya* he is honour-bound to accept a challenge from a rival. As the competition progresses, Yudhiṣṭhira's shortcomings in terms of *kṣatriya-dharma* become increasingly apparent. He has no aptitude for such gambling matches, and eventually loses control of himself with disastrous consequences for the Pāṇḍavas and their wife. Yudhiṣṭhira's inherent nature is shaped by the *dharma* of virtue and problems inevitably arise when he is forced to abandon his true nature and act as a resolute *kṣatriya*. We might also note the response of Bhīṣma, Droṇa, and others to the assault on Draupadī that follows the dice match. As men of virtue, they should have immediately intervened to prevent such foul malpractice, but as adherents of *kṣatriya-dharma* they fail to intervene by taking action against their king to whom they have taken a vow of loyalty. Bhīma, the ardent *kṣatriya*, then wishes to take immediate vengeance by assaulting those who have humiliated Draupadī, but Yudhiṣṭhira insists that no such action should be undertaken because he gave his word that he would abide by the rules of the match, and as a man of virtue he cannot break his word.

In many ways, Yudhiṣṭhira and Bhīma both represent the perfection of *dharma*, but with Yudhiṣṭhira this is the *sanātana-dharma*, whilst Bhīma is the perfect exemplar of righteous *kṣatriya-dharma*, and this difference between them is highlighted on a number of occasions with no clear cut verdict being given as to the absolute superiority of one over the other. We looked previously at the debates between Draupadī and Yudhiṣṭhira over whether they should observe the terms of their exile, and Bhīma is clear in asserting his view that they should return and regain by force of arms what has been taken from them.

Then when the Kauravas are defeated and captured by the *gandharvas,* Bhīma is delighted by this turn of events whilst Yudhiṣṭhira feels compassion over the discomfiture of his relatives and asks Arjuna to go and set them free. Similarly, when Jayadratha is captured after his attempt to kidnap Draupadī, Bhīma is in favour of killing him for his atrocious conduct, but Yudhiṣṭhira reminds him of the suffering this will bring to Jayadratha's wife and other relatives, and then sets him free. And in the *Virāṭa-parvan,* when Draupadī is harassed by Kīcaka, Yudhiṣṭhira urges tolerance and restraint whilst Bhīma follows the *kṣatriya-dharma* by taking assertive action and beating the miscreant to death.

The *Udyoga-parvan* contains lengthy debates between the principal characters on both sides over whether they should make war or seek a peaceful solution. Despite advice to the contrary from Dhṛtarāṣṭra, Vidura, Gāndhārī, Bhīṣma, and Droṇa, Duryodhana is adamant that he will make no concessions to the Pāṇḍavas despite their having fulfilled all the terms of their exile. On learning of the Kauravas' failure to honour the agreement made, most of those on the Pāṇḍava side, including Kṛṣṇa, Bhīma, Arjuna, and Draupadī, argue in favour of making war against the wrongdoers. Yudhiṣṭhira alone stands against the weight of *kṣatriya* opinion, condemning the use of violent means, which he sees as being devoid of true virtue. And here we may recall the verse cited above, which clearly states that *ahiṁsā,* non-harming or non-violence, is the true essence of *dharma*. In the following passage, Yudhiṣṭhira expresses his views on war and peace:

When word reached Hastināpura that the Pāṇḍavas had assembled a mighty host in order to wage war against the Kauravas, Dhṛtarāṣṭra sent Saṁjaya as a peace emissary. Yudhiṣṭhira greeted Saṁjaya with courtesy and respect, knowing him to be a man of virtue and wisdom. However, the message sent by Dhṛtarāṣṭra was full of duplicitous words; he argued that peace is always better than war and therefore as a righteous man Yudhiṣṭhira should give up his warlike intentions. He made no mention of the wrongs the Pāṇḍavas had been forced to endure and did not offer to restore the Pāṇḍavas' kingdom to them, as was their right. Perhaps hoping that Yudhiṣṭhira's mild disposition would again prevail, he asked him for a peaceful resolution of their differences but offered nothing in return.

When Saṁjaya had rather shamefacedly delivered his message and departed, Yudhiṣṭhira turned to Kṛṣṇa and begged him to protect and support them now that the hour of their trial had arrived. To this Kṛṣṇa replied, 'Here I am, O mighty one. Tell me what you wish of me. I will do whatever you ask.' Yudhiṣṭhira then spoke to Kṛṣṇa about the misfortunes of poverty they had been forced to endure because of Duryodhana's vindictive nature, and the support given by Dhṛtarāṣṭra to his son. 'There is no distress equal to that which one feels as a result of poverty!' he exclaimed. 'You have seen all these events unfold, O Mādhava. We will try first to make peace with our enemies, but if that fails then we must take up arms in a righteous cause. However, the slaughter of kinsmen and elders will indeed be a sinful act, as Saṁjaya has said, so what is to be gained from battle? Alas, this *kṣatriya-dharma* is indeed sinful (*pāpaḥ kṣatriya-dharmo 'yam*) and we have taken birth amongst the *kṣatriyas*.

A *śūdra* renders service, a *vaiśya* lives by trade, and a brahmin lives by begging, but we must live by slaughtering others. A fish lives by killing fish, a dog lives by killing dogs, and a *kṣatriya* lives by killing other *kṣatriyas*. O Kṛṣṇa, *kali* [as in *Kali-yuga*] always dwells on the battlefield. Lives are lost everywhere around and the outcome is dependent

> on destiny rather than our desire or endeavour. A coward may slay a hero and an unknown person may slay a famous warrior. Both parties cannot win nor can both be defeated, but on both sides there will be death and tragedy. If a *kṣatriya* runs from the battlefield he loses both fame and prosperity, but in all circumstances war is wicked [*sarvathā vṛjinaṁ yuddham* (v 53)]. Who is not himself damaged when he hurts another? Even if a person wins victory, he will still suffer losses, as his friends, children, and relatives are struck down in battle. We see, O Janārdana, that those who are quiet, modest, virtuous, and compassionate are usually killed in warfare whilst the wicked escape with their lives. Even after killing enemies, still one's heart will be afflicted by remorse for this cruel deed.
>
> Once violence begins it progresses in an endless cycle. The friends and relatives of slain kings will regroup and counterattack, and so it continues without ever finding a resolution. It may be true, O Madhusūdana, that exterminating the foe completely may lead to enduring prosperity, but such an act is most cruel. We do not wish to give up our kingdom nor do we wish to annihilate our entire race. Therefore peace is the best course, even if it is obtained through our personal humiliation. When those who strive consistently for peace find reconciliation impossible, then only is the time for war and terrible events must ensue. In a quarrel between dogs first there is tale wagging, then barking, then showing teeth, then loud roars, and eventually there is a fight. In such a contest the strongest dog will triumph and take the meat away from his defeated antagonist. It is exactly the same with men; there is no difference. Those who are weak must bow down and show respect to those who are powerful.'[144]

Speaking from the perspective of *sanātana-dharma*, as outlined above, Yudhiṣṭhira here pronounces an excoriating

144 *Udyoga-parvan*, Chapter 70.

condemnation of *kṣatriya-dharma,* stating that it is nothing more than wickedness, *pāpa,* and comparing rival *kṣatriyas* to dogs competing for a piece of meat. And yet in the same debate, authoritative voices, including that of Kṛṣṇa, urge Yudhiṣṭhira to adhere to that same *kṣatriya-dharma* that he so bitterly condemns. So what are we to make of it all? Is Yudhiṣṭhira correct or is he a hopeless idealist in a world where wickedness prevails?

Before addressing those questions, I want to refer briefly to an incident that occurs right at the very end of the *Mahābhārata* in the *Svargārohaṇa-parvan*. When Yudhiṣṭhira reaches the realm of the gods, he is shocked to see his old adversaries there enjoying the delights of that celestial domain. Yudhiṣṭhira strongly objects to the idea that wicked-minded persons such as Duryodhana, Duḥśāsana, and Śakuni should achieve such an elevated rebirth, but is told that this is their reward for fulfilling their *kṣatriya-dharma* by fighting bravely and giving up their lives on the field of battle. Moreover, after they have enjoyed the reward for their adherence to *dharma,* they will have to suffer the consequences of their wickedness in a future life. Yudhiṣṭhira, however, is reluctant to accept this verdict, for, as we have seen, he regards *kṣatriya-dharma* as no *dharma* at all.

Returning to the question posed above, is it the case that the *Mahābhārata* is showing us the superiority of virtue over *varṇa* in its exposition of *dharma*? Possibly, but I do not think the view is as clear cut as that and what it is really doing is highlighting the tensions between the two and showing that it is often difficult to determine exactly how to live one's life in relation to *dharma*. There is no doubt that the *Mahābhārata* has intense respect and even reverence for Yudhiṣṭhira's constant adherence to pure virtue, but we are also shown incidents in which his refusal to embrace *kṣatriya-dharma* is not entirely beneficial. Kings must rule and to do so must at times take harsh action against wrongdoers in order to protect vulnerable people against the assaults of powerful persons who have no sense of justice or morality.

We are drawn towards the compassion shown by Yudhiṣṭhira towards Dhṛtarāṣṭra and Gāndhārī after the battle, but we also feel that he should have done more to protect Draupadī from Kīcaka, and that Bhīma's response to this incident is perhaps more appropriate. So what I think the *Mahābhārata* is doing is eulogising the ideal of *dharma* as pure virtue, but at the same time exposing the problems that can arise when rulers embrace this ideal in an absolute sense. It may even be the case that there is a historical context that shaped the characterisation of Yudhiṣṭhira, as we know that in the first millennium bce there were a number of kings drawn towards the mode of conduct he epitomises, the most notable example being the Mauryan emperor Aśoka.

Looking at the issue from a wider perspective, we can see that this tension between pure virtue and pragmatism still has implications for the present day. We are naturally drawn to the idea of non-violence, yet we may also feel that the use of violent means is sometimes essential for those who protect society and prevent the spread of criminality. Likewise, we may feel that the *varṇa* system is an overly rigid imposition that restricts individual freedom, but at the same time we can recognise the necessity of fulfilling social obligations and acting in a manner that is beneficial for society as a whole, even at the expense of the advancement of personal self-interest. This is the balance that has to be struck in all considerations of *dharma*, and we might say that the wisdom of the *Mahābhārata* lies in the manner in which it refrains from presenting overly simplistic answers to complex questions, but draws our attention to the crux of the issues in order to facilitate our own endeavours to establish a way of life that is in accordance with *dharma*.

The Vedic Ritual and Mokṣa-Dharma

Although there are occasional references to other forms of ritual practice, the principal religious rite referred to in the *Mahābhārata* is the Vedic *yajña* in which offerings to the Vedic gods are made into the sacred fire. This is the path of *pravṛtti* based on ritual acts that are designed to bring benefits in the here and now. Of particular note in this regard are the *rājasūya-yajña* performed by Yudhiṣṭhira in the *Sabhā-parvan* to demonstrate his supremacy over other rulers and the *aśvamedha-yajña* he performs after the battle to atone for the sin of causing such terrible loss of life. From the perspective of the *nivṛtti-mārga,* the way of renunciation followed by those who seek to wholly transcend this world, the enactment of such rituals is critiqued on the grounds that it involves acts of violence towards animals whose flesh forms part of the offerings, and also because the goals sought through the performance of *yajña* are based on a yearning for worldly pleasure and satisfaction, and are of no value in the spiritual quest for liberation.

Hence within the sub-*parvan* of the *Śānti-parvan* entitled the *Mokṣa-dharma-parvan,* we encounter a number of passages in which purveyors of spiritual wisdom vehemently condemn animal sacrifice because such acts are entirely antithetical to the core precept of *ahiṁsā*. It is well-known that Buddhists and Jains were highly condemnatory of ritual violence, but what we witness within these passages of the *Mahābhārata* is the voice of those who do not seek to deny the authority of the Vedas but insist that animal slaughter forms no part of the Vedic revelation when it is understood in its purest form. Here are the words spoken by King Vicakhnu on observing a ritual involving animal sacrifice:

> 2 After seeing the mutilated torso of a bull, that king became aware of the terrible screams of the cows in the animal stockade of the sacrificial arena.
>
> 3 He then made the following pronouncement, 'May there be good fortune for cows in all parts of the world.' This prayer was spoken when the slaughter of the animals commenced.
>
> 4 'Such violence is praised only by men who do not adhere to the proper rules, the fools, *nāstikas,* and doubting souls who keep themselves hidden.
>
> 5 Manu, who keeps *dharma* in his heart, has asserted that all ritual acts must be free of violence. It is due to desire and attachment that men afflict animals in the space around the sacrificial altar.
>
> 6 A wise man should therefore pursue the subtle science of *dharma* by performing his duty on the basis of authority. Not harming other beings, *ahiṁsā,* is certainly recognised as superior to all other forms of *dharma.*'[145]

It is interesting to note here that Vicakhnu refers to those who indulge in animal sacrifice as *nāstikas,* a word that means 'non-believers' and is usually applied to Buddhists, Jains, and others who deny the authoritative status of the Vedas.

For Vicakhnu, rituals based on violence represent a similar deviation from Vedic orthodoxy, although his words should probably be regarded as polemical rather than offering a true representation of Vedic ritualism.

This pattern of instruction, challenging the violence of the *yajña,* is by no means confined to the *Vicakhnu-gītā,* and can be observed in a good number of passages located within

145 *Śāntiparvan,* 257.2–6.

the *Mahābhārata*'s *Śānti-parvan*. What is taking place here is the elevation of the precept of *ahiṁsā* to its status as the preeminent principle in adherence to *dharma* in its highest state. It is this emphasis on non-harming and nurturing other living beings through acts of service and compassion that underlies Yudhiṣṭhira's rejection of the *kṣatriya-dharma* and also leads sages and those who possess wisdom to vilify any form of ritual act that involves the slaughter of animals. Within this tendency, we can witness again the clear interaction between the *dharma* of virtue, the *sanātana-dharma*, and the *mokṣa-dharma* based on the teachings of Sāṁkhya and Yoga, and from both perspectives we can readily observe how tensions arise in relation both to *varṇa-dharma* and the *dharma* of Vedic ritualism.

And, finally, we might also notice another interesting debate located in the *Śānti-parvan* (Chapter 259), which focuses on whether or not imposing the death sentence on criminals is truly in accordance with *dharma*. King Dyumatsena is of the opinion that such executions are an essential part of his duty in protecting the citizens from violent wrongdoers, but his son, Satyavān, contends that less extreme forms of punishment should be imposed in the form of fines or imprisonment, and states that he bases his views on *sanātana-dharma*. We might regard this as another example of the tension between *kṣatriya-dharma* and *sanātana-dharma*, but the issue is not quite that clear cut, as Dyumatsena argues that his imposition of the death penalty is based entirely on compassion, but this compassion is directed towards the innocent citizens rather than towards criminals. There is no clear resolution to the debate given in this passage, and again the *Mahābhārata* is highlighting issues for our consideration, before leaving us to make up our own minds as to which view is more directly aligned with our notion of *dharma*.

DHARMA AND THE *BHAGAVAD-GĪTĀ*

I have already expressed the view that the *Bhagavad-gītā* should properly be regarded as a passage of instruction that is integral to the *Mahābhārata* as a whole, and this understanding is particularly applicable when we come to consider the concept of *dharma* and the tensions arising from differing interpretations of *dharma*. There can be no doubt that the *Gītā* is primarily a *mokṣa-śāstra* that shares the view of passages located in the *Śānti-parvan* that the highest form of *dharma* is that which forms the path to liberation from rebirth. This is the *dharma* of the renunciants, who have a natural tendency towards world-indifference because their goal is absolute transcendence of the world. The *Bhagavad-gītā* is somewhat different, however, as its emphasis on *mokṣa-dharma* rarely entails any form of world-indifference; just the contrary, it is deeply concerned with the wellbeing of human society and it is for this reason that Kṛṣṇa insists that Arjuna must adhere to his *kṣatriya-dharma* by suppressing wrongdoers.

In order to provide a reconciliation of *varṇa-dharma* with *mokṣa-dharma*, the *Gītā* introduces its idea of a *karma-yoga* whereby the duties of *varṇa-dharma* are undertaken solely to ensure the wellbeing of the world, without any intrusion of selfish desire for the results of action. When dharmic duties are performed in this desireless manner, they fulfil all the functions of the *varṇa-dharma*, but simultaneously form a part of the *mokṣa-dharma* that brings transcendence of the world and liberation from rebirth.

It is interesting to note, however, that once again this apparent reconciliation does not go unchallenged. In Chapter 308 of the *Śānti-parvan*, we learn of a meeting between a female ascetic named Sulabhā and King Janaka, whom the *Gītā* (3.20) refers to as a perfect exemplar of *karma-yoga*. In their discussion, Sulabhā completely rejects Janaka's claim that he can achieve the highest spiritual state whilst still living as a king with all the trappings of royalty. In Sulabhā's view, the idea that one can live the lifestyle of a king and yet remain wholly unattached is implausible, and hence she rejects Janaka's claims and in so doing casts aspersions on the *Gītā*'s idea of a *karma-yoga*.

Setting to one side Sulabhā's quite reasonable objections, we can also see that the *Bhagavad-gītā* seeks a similar pattern of reconciliation when considering the *dharma* of Vedic ritualism and the *mokṣa-dharma*. As is the case with the performance of *kṣatriya-dharma*, the rituals can be performed either to guarantee the welfare of all beings or else on the basis of selfish motivations. Kṛṣṇa explains that the performance of the Vedic *yajña* ensures that sufficient rain falls and that the Earth thereby remains fertile and bountiful.[146] The performance of the *yajña* on the basis of a mood of universal benevolence is another element of *karma-yoga* because it is devoid of selfish motive, and is therefore a form of both ritual *dharma* and *mokṣa-dharma*. Where the ritual is performed with a selfish desire for worldly acquisitions, this is just a form of materialism and it is roundly condemned by Kṛṣṇa.[147]

Turning our attention to the *Bhagavad-gītā*'s perspective on the *sanātana-dharma* of pure virtue, verses 2 and 3 of Chapter 2 can be taken as a criticism of Arjuna's emotional response to his situation, which is based entirely on worldly attachments.[148] I have already mentioned that there is a good degree of overlap

---

146 *Bhagavad-gītā*, 3.10–16,

147 *Bhagavad-gītā*, 2.42–44.

148 This differs from my previous interpretation, published in *Religious Doctrines in the Mahābhārata* some years ago, that Yudhiṣṭhira's idea of *dharma* was rejected in a peremptory manner in these verses; I now believe this to be erroneous.

between the *sanātana-dharma* and the *mokṣa-dharma* as both entail a withdrawal from self-centred aspirations for worldly success. With its overt concerns for the wellbeing of the world, the *Gītā* does in fact carry that ideological congruence to a further degree than is found anywhere else in the *Mahābhārata*.

The point is made that the *dharma* of pure virtue is in fact an essential element of *mokṣa-dharma*, for unless one develops a sense of compassion for all beings and embraces the ideal of *ahiṁsā*, renouncing any tendency towards greed, malice, or anger, there is no possibility of aspiring for the highest spiritual goals. From the *Gītā*'s perspective, transcendence of the world must be pursued alongside ardent concern for the welfare of all beings. This point is made very apparent in verse 28 of Chapter 7 where the two paths of knowledge and of devotion are both said to be contingent on the renunciation of all wrongdoing and the performance of righteous action. Furthermore, if we review the opening three verses of Chapter 16, we can see a list there that includes most of the great virtues adhered to by Yudhiṣṭhira, which are given the joint designation of *daivī sampad*, the way of the gods. And this is followed up in verse 5 of that chapter with the words, *daivī sampad vimokṣāya*, the *daivī sampad* leads to liberation from rebirth. The point is clearly made.

And as a final note, one will naturally enough ask how it can be that Kṛṣṇa on the one hand urges Arjuna to wage war, *tasmād yudhyasva bhārata*,[149] and at the same time advocates adherence to the principle of *ahiṁsā*, as he does on three occasions.[150] The solution to this conundrum is again to be found within the doctrine of *karma-yoga*, action free of desire. If we look at the history of the world, and the world as it is today,

149 2.18.

150 13.7, 16.2, and 17.14.

we can observe that acts of violence at a personal, religious, communal, and national level, are almost always committed as a result of either anger or a desire for land, power, and scarce resources. All such acts of violence are prohibited by the *Gītā*'s emphasis on motive, and it is only where protection is to be granted to those in need that violence is permitted for persons who take action without any sense of anger or desire for personal gain. It is in this way that the *Bhagavad-gītā* again seeks a reconciliation between differing ideals of *dharma*, in this case between the precept of *ahiṁsā* and the need to protect those who would otherwise be brutalised by persons who are wicked, powerful, and aggressive.

Discussion Topic: *Dharma*

Here are some questions you might care to ponder after completing this chapter:

- Is Yudhiṣṭhira right in his constant insistence on adherence to *dharma*?
- What is more important in life, the *dharma* of pure virtue, the *dharma* of social and familial duty, or the *mokṣa-dharma*?
- To what extent can the *sanātana-dharma* of pure virtue be reconciled with the *mokṣa-dharma*? Is morality distinct from spirituality?
- How important is ritual as an element of *dharma*?
- When Kṛṣṇa says in the Gītā (4.8) that he has appeared to sustain *dharma*, what does he mean?

VI
Religious Philosophy and Yoga Practice

As has been mentioned before, the *Mahābhārata* is widely known purely in terms of the central narrative of the conflict between the Kauravas and the Pāṇḍavas, culminating in the great battle at Kurukṣetra. This is certainly the principal theme of the work as a whole, but for this study of the *Mahābhārata*, I want to consider the text in its entirety; this must include the extensive passages of religious, ethical, and practical instruction that it contains, which collectively comprise almost half of the total number of chapters. So in these final two chapters I want to move the focus of the discussion away from the central narrative in order to provide some greater insight into the pattern of teachings that are also presented to the reader at different points within this vast work. These passages of instruction occur repeatedly throughout the progression of the narrative, but it is after the battle is over that the *Mahābhārata* begins to take the form of an exclusively didactic work. Within the 353 chapters of the *Śānti-parvan* (Book 12), 185 chapters (168–353) form what is known as the *Mokṣa-dharma-parvan*, and it is to this collection of religious and philosophical discourses that we will be turning our attention in this chapter.

This lengthy passage of the *Mahābhārata* is of particular significance for any understanding of Indian religious thought, as it is here that we find the earliest known teachings on the philosophy of the Sāṁkhya system and the practice of the techniques of Yoga. After a change of direction in the teachings contained in the *Anuśāsana-parvan* (Book 13), which will be reviewed in the next chapter, this line of instruction is resumed within the *Aśvamedhika-parvan* (Book 14) wherein Kṛṣṇa reprises his role as the imparter of wisdom to Arjuna. This passage begins with Arjuna informing Kṛṣṇa that he has forgotten most of the teachings of the *Bhagavad-gītā*, and requesting Kṛṣṇa to instruct him in the same way that he did at Kurukṣetra. Kṛṣṇa's response is to present Arjuna with a passage known as the *Anugītā* (literally, the follow-on *Gītā*), which covers thirty-five chapters of the *Aśvamedhika-parvan* (Chapters 16–50). In fact, the content of the *Anugītā* bears only a passing resemblance to the *Bhagavad-gītā* and is far more closely aligned to the Sāṁkhya and Yoga teachings located in the *Śānti-parvan*.

The *Mahābhārata* and Indian Religious Thought

If we take a step back and consider early Indian philosophy as a whole, we can see that those systems that adhere to the Vedic traditions fall roughly into three categories: first, the Nyāya-Vaiśeṣika system, which found its primary location within the Śaivite traditions; secondly, the various schools of Vedānta, all of which look to the Upaniṣads and *Bhagavad-gītā* as authoritative sources and claim that these works establish the primary principles of their doctrines; and finally Sāṁkhya and Yoga, the central precepts of which are set out in two later philosophical treatises, the *Sāṁkhya-kārikā* and the *Yoga Sūtras*. What is significant for our purposes here, however, is that just as Vedānta looks to the Upaniṣads as its primary source of revelation, so the *Mahābhārata* provides an equivalent primary source for Sāṁkhya and Yoga. On this basis, it is appropriate to once again assert the significance of the *Mahābhārata* in understanding the development of Indian religious and philosophical thought as a whole.

It is certainly the case that today and for some centuries past, Vedānta has been the dominant doctrinal system in Indian religious thought, but it would be a mistake to underestimate the significance of Sāṁkhya teachings, which have profoundly influenced those traditions based on Vaiṣṇava theism. Moreover, Vedānta has to a significant degree absorbed Sāṁkhya notions, in part because of the prominent position of Sāṁkhya ideas within the *Bhagavad-gītā*, and in part because of the extent to which Vedānta has embraced Yoga teachings such as those found in the *Yoga Sūtras*.

It is not possible here to provide anything but the barest outline of the complexities of Sāṁkya, but a brief overview of the central ideas will be helpful for any consideration of these passages of the *Mahābhārata*. The Sāṁkhya system seeks to analyse the nature of the material world by isolating and enumerating the elements of which it is comprised. It is taught that the variegated world evolves by a natural process of development from out of a single, undifferentiated material substance. The number of elements arrived at by means of this analysis is twenty-four, including those which form the mental faculties of living beings, although matter, *prakṛti*, is essentially inert and devoid of life until such time as it comes into association with the twenty-fifth element, *puruṣa* or *ātman*, which is entirely spiritual and is the source and location of consciousness. Without the presence of *puruṣa*, matter is dull and inert, but when mind and body are in contact with *puruṣa* they display the symptoms of life just through the power of association.

This system of thought is not merely a means of understanding the world and our existence within it, but has a clear application in terms of an individual's spiritual progression. The aim of Sāṁkhya is to allow *puruṣa* to break free from its association with matter so that it no longer has to undergo suffering and rebirth. This goal of liberation is achieved through knowledge of our true spiritual identity as explained by Sāṁkhya analysis. The attainment of such knowledge, however, cannot be a purely intellectual process, and hence Sāṁkhya is inextricably linked to the Yoga practices that elevate the intellectual appreciation of the truth into experiential realisation. Sāṁkhya provides an analytical understanding of our true spiritual identity, but Yoga practice allows for the direct perception of the *ātman* through withdrawal of the external senses and intense internal meditation. The realisation of the spiritual identity acquired in this way liberates *puruṣa* from its unwanted association with matter and its experience of rebirth.

The teachings of Sāṁkhya and Yoga thus display many similarities with Advaita Vedānta, the crucial difference being that from the Sāṁkhya perspective each spiritual entity is eternally individual and there is no question of the absolute unity of *ātman* with Brahman as is taught in the Upaniṣads and the system of Advaita Vedānta. Moreover, the Vedāntic idea that the variegated world is only perceived as such because illusion covers the perception of absolute unity is also rejected. The world is absolutely real as we perceive it, for *prakṛti* is real and the variegated nature of the world around us is a reality based on the evolution of distinct elements from out of primal *prakṛti*. The spiritual teachings encountered in the *Śānti-parvan* and *Anugītā* almost universally espouse this Sāṁkhya and Yoga perspective rather than the idea of the absolute unity of all things as taught within the Upaniṣads.

Looking at those passages in more detail, we can observe the diverse nature of the ideas they present. First of all, there is an emphasis on withdrawal from interaction with the world, giving up strenuous endeavours for material success in the form of wealth or reputation, and simply accepting whatever fortune destiny may bring us. It is to be accepted that life in this world fluctuates between good and bad fortune, happiness and distress, but one should view these vicissitudes of life with a dispassionate gaze, being neither overly elated nor overly downcast. The *Mokṣa-dharma-parvan* also gives extensive consideration to the ethical and moral dimensions of the quest for liberation, placing primary emphasis on *ahiṁsā*, ensuring that one lives in such a way as causes as little suffering as possible to other living beings. There is also a sprinkling of Vaiṣṇava theism throughout this section of the *Mahābhārata*, but the primary emphasis is on the doctrines of Sāṁkhya and the associated practice of meditational Yoga.

For the main part of this chapter I want to look at a selection of passages that can be broadly classified under three headings: teachings on Sāṁkhya doctrine, teachings on Yoga practice, and teachings on proper conduct for those in pursuit of liberation. We will begin with a consideration of the ways in which Sāṁkhya ideas are presented within the *Mokṣa-dharma-parvan*.

Sāṁkhya Teachings in the *Mokṣa-dharma-parvan* of the *Mahābhārata*

When one studies the Sāṁkhya system, it is generally the case that one turns first to the *Sāṁkhya-kārikā* composed by Īśvarakṛṣṇa, perhaps in the fourth or fifth century ce, and the understanding of Sāṁkhya most commonly encountered will generally be based entirely on that work in order to present what appears to be a single unified system of thought. What we encounter within the *Mahābhārata*, however, are a number of different versions of Sāṁkhya, some of which are closely aligned with the *Sāṁkhya-kārikā* whilst others display notably distinct lines of thought.

The most obvious example of this is the question of the existence of God, for the usual view, based on the *Sāṁkhya-kārikā,* would be that Sāṁkhya is atheistic or non-theistic. But when we turn to the *Mahābhārata*'s *Mokṣa-dharma-parvan,* we will find clear evidence of theistic strands of Sāṁkhya, which stand in contrast to Īśvarakṛṣṇa's later exposition of the system. What seems clear from a careful review of these passages is that in its earlier stages of development, Sāṁkhya displayed a variety of loosely associated doctrinal strands that shared notable common features but were also clearly distinct in relation to some elements of their teaching.

So let us start off by reviewing a selection of passages in which key precepts of Sāṁkhya doctrine are presented by the different teachers cited by Bhīṣma in his instruction to Yudhiṣṭhira.

Manifestation of the World and the Evolution of Elements

This first extract is taken from Chapter 203 of the *Śānti-parvan* and forms a part of the instruction given by an unnamed *guru* to his disciple. Here we can note the use of the term *avyakta,* meaning invisible or non-manifest, being applied to *prakṛti* in its primal, undifferentiated state. *Avyakta* first gives rise to *buddhi,* and *buddhi* evolves into *ahaṁkāra;* from *ahaṁkāra,* the five great elements of space, air, fire, water, and earth come into being, each one evolving from its predecessor. From these first eight elements come sixteen more, the five senses, the five objects of perception, the five organs of action, and *manas* as the sixteenth. We thus arrive at the usual total of twenty-four, each one appearing by means of a transformation of its predecessor. We will look at what is meant by *buddhi, ahaṁkāra,* and *manas* later on when we consider passages discussing the mental faculties. A further significant point to note here is that whilst verse 23 might indicate a non-theistic form of Sāṁkhya, the first group of verses from the same chapter shows a clear orientation towards Vaiṣṇava theism. So although the assertion that Sāṁkhya is atheistic might be reasonable on the basis of the *Sāṁkhya-kārikā,* it cannot be applied to the totality of Sāṁkhya discourse.

> 7 The teacher said: You are a student of great wisdom. Listen now to the highest knowledge that is concealed within the Vedas. This concerns the self of all beings and represents the true worth of the *āgamas* [scriptures].
>
> 8 Vāsudeva [Viṣṇu] is everything that exists; he is the mouth through which all the Vedas emerge. He is truth, charity, sacrifice, tolerance, restraint, and honesty.
>
> 9 Those who fully comprehend the Vedas know that Viṣṇu is the timeless *puruṣa,* the non-manifest eternal Brahman who brings about both the creation and destruction of the world. Now hear from me the story of how he who is Brahman appeared as a member of the Vṛṣṇi tribe [Kṛṣṇa].
>
> 10 Viṣṇu is the god of gods and his power is without limit. When brahmins recite his glories, the account should be heard by other brahmins, but if a *kṣatriya* recites them it should be attended to by other *kṣatriyas*. You are righteous and thus also worthy, so now hear about that member of the Vṛṣṇi race who is in truth the Supreme.
>
> 11 He is the wheel of time that has neither beginning nor end and is marked by alternating states of being and non-being. Just like a wheel, it moves around the three worlds amongst all the living beings that exist therein.
>
> 12 He is the eternal Brahman which never decays, is never manifest in this world, and never meets with death. They say that Keśava [Kṛṣṇa], who is a tiger amongst men and the greatest of all persons, is in fact that Brahman.
>
> 13 That Supreme Being, the unchanging one, creates the

forefathers, gods, *ṛṣis, yakṣas, dānavas, nāgas, asuras,* and human beings.

14 The lord is also the creator of the Vedas and other scriptures, as well as the eternal forms of *dharma* practised within the world. At the time of destruction, he absorbs *prakṛti* and at the beginning of the *yuga,* he manifests it once again.

...

23 *Prakṛti* constantly brings forth this existence, which exists under the direction of the *puruṣa.* It is from this cause alone that the entire world proceeds on its course.

24 From a single lamp thousands of other lamps can be lit. In the same way, *prakṛti* brings forth this world but remains undiminished because its extent is without limit.

25 *Buddhi* [the intellect] is created when matter in its non-manifest state [*avyakta*] becomes active; *buddhi* gives rise to *ahaṁkāra,* the sense of ego. Space comes into being from *ahaṁkāra* and air is born from space.

26 Heat appears from air, water arises from heat, and Earth comes into being from water. These eight are the primal elements of *prakṛti;* the entire world rests upon them.

27 From this group of eight come the five knowledge acquiring senses, the five organs through which action is performed, and the five objects perceived by the senses. Their constant interactions produce the single entity that is *manas* [the mind]; hence this list is sixteen in total.

28 The ear, the skin, the eyes, the tongue and the nose are the five senses. The feet, the anus, the genitals, the hands, and the voice are the five organs through which action is performed.

29 Sound, touch, form, flavour, and aroma are the objects perceived by the senses. Roaming everywhere amongst

> them, *manas* should be understood as the consciousness that pervades all of these.[151]

In the next passage from Chapter 267 of the *Śānti-parvan* (*Nārada-devala-saṁvāda*), the famous sage Nārada is receiving instruction from another *ṛṣi* named Asita Devala. Again it includes an enumeration of elements, but here the list is notably different, with time replacing *avyakta*, and *citta* replacing *ahaṁkāra* as one of the three elements that comprise the mental faculties. *Ahaṁkāra* means the ego or sense of selfhood, but the meaning of *citta* is less clear and might be regarded as the 'thinking faculty' or 'thought processes' for want of any clearer alternative. There is a further complication in that *bhāva* and *abhāva*, being and non-being, are included in the initial group of eight so that the full enumeration does not come to the usual total of twenty-four. Here we also find *puruṣa* being referred to as *kṣetrajña*, the knower of the field, a term that is quite commonly employed in this way in Sāṁkhya treatises. We will also notice that this passage is quite assertively non-theistic, insisting that time alone is the instigator of the process of creation, indicating that this is a purely natural occurrence. My purpose in including this passage is not to create doubts and confusion, but simply to demonstrate the diversity of ideas within the Sāṁkhya expositions to be found in in the *Mahābhārata*.

> 4 Asita said: Time acts under the impulse of its own inherent nature. Those conversant with the elements of matter speak of 'the five great elements' through which time creates living beings.

---

151 *Śānti-parvan*, 203.7–14, 23–29.

5 Impelled by itself alone, it is time that creates the living beings by means of these great elements. There is no doubt that one who states that there is something beyond these elements is speaking falsely.

6 You should understand, Nārada, that by their very nature the five great elements are eternal, unchanging, and constant. They are masses of energy, which form a group of six when time is included with them.

7 The five elements are water, space, earth, air, and fire. No principle beyond these elements can be demonstrated. This point is above contention.

8 For, without doubt, neither by logical deduction nor reasoned argument can one assert that which does not exist You should understand living beings as evolving from these elements, which form their primary substance.

9 These five along with time and then the pure states of being and non-being comprise the eight eternal elements in terms of the creation and destruction of living beings.

10 By means of these elements, living beings emerge from a state of non-being into various forms of existence. And when a living being meets with destruction, it becomes nothing more than these elements in their five different forms.

11 A living being's body consists of earth, its hearing arises from space, the sun is its sense of sight, its breath is air, and its blood is derived from water.

12 Men of wisdom have identified the eyes, nose, ears, skin, and tongue as the five senses that acquire knowledge of the objects of perception.

13 They act by seeing, hearing, smelling, touching, and tasting. You can understand the qualities they perceive through logical deduction: the five senses act on five objects in five ways.

14 These qualities are form, aroma, taste, touch, and sound. These five are perceived by the five senses in five ways.

15 Form, aroma, taste, touch, and sound are indeed the objects of perception but the senses do not comprehend them. It is the *kṣetrajña* that comprehends them by means of the senses.

16 Beyond this group of senses is the *citta*, and *manas* is beyond this faculty. Beyond *manas* is *buddhi*, and the *kṣetrajña* lies beyond the *buddhi*.

17 The living being first becomes aware of different sensations by means of the senses. It next examines these objects with the *manas* and reaches a decision about them with the *buddhi*. In this way, *kṣetrajña* gains an understanding of all objects that are perceived through the senses.

18 Thus we now have eight elements: *citta*, the five senses, *manas*, and *buddhi*. Those conversant with the nature of a living being refer to these eight as the senses for acquiring knowledge.

19 Then there are the hands, the feet, the anus, the genitals, and the fifth here is the mouth. Listen now as these are declared to be the organs for performing action.[152]

In the final extract for this section, which is from Chapter 294 of the *Śānti-parvan* (*Vasiṣṭha-karālajanaka-saṁvāda*), the *ṛṣi* Vasiṣṭha is instructing a king named Karālajanaka, who may or may not be the father of Sītā from the *Rāmāyaṇa*. Here we have a pleasingly clear and succinct account of the origin of the world that is brought about by the evolution of elements from primal *prakṛti*, referred to again as *avyakta*. Here the term *mahat*, the great element, is used in place of

---

152 *Śānti-parvan*, 267.4–19.

buddhi as the first element to appear from the *avyakta*. This usage of terminology is quite frequently encountered in these passages, and what *mahat* really refers to is the substance of primal, undifferentiated *buddhi*, from which all the individual intellects of living beings appear. Initially *buddhi*, or *mahat*, is a single substance, and each living being is endowed with an individual manifestation of that substance in the form of its own reasoning faculties. This idea is particularly significant in considering certain passages of Patañjali's teachings in the *Yoga Sūtras*.

> 26 I have thus presented an accurate exposition of the teachings on Yoga. I will now speak about the system of knowledge known as Sāṁkhya, the teachings that analyse the nature of the world.
>
> 27 Those who are experts on *prakṛti* speak of *prakṛti* as the *avyakta*; this is the first principle. The *mahat* then emerges from the *avyakta* as the second principle, O best of kings.
>
> 28 We have heard that *ahaṁkāra* emerges from the *mahat* as the third principle. The teachers of Sāṁkhya then assert that the five elements emerge from *ahaṁkāra*.
>
> 29 Whilst these are the eight manifestations of *prakṛti*, there are sixteen further transformations. There are five primary qualities and five senses that perceive them.
>
> 30 Men of wisdom who understand the rules and precepts of Sāṁkhya and who constantly adhere to path of Sāṁkhya assert that this is the proper analysis of the material elements.
>
> 31 Each element is eventually withdrawn back into that from which it emerged. They are withdrawn in the reverse order from their creation and are created by the inner self.
>
> 32 The material qualities emerge in succession, one from the other, and are withdrawn in the reverse order. This

process takes place constantly, just as waves constantly emerge from the ocean and disappear back into it.

33 This is the process, O best of kings, by which the creation and withdrawal of matter occurs. After the withdrawal, matter exists as one substance, but when creation occurs it becomes manifold. This is the understanding reached by persons who comprehend the truth, O king.[153]

Twenty-Five or Twenty-Six Elements?

In most forms of Sāṁkhya analysis, the number of elements arrived at is twenty-four, to which is added the twenty-fifth element, variously called *puruṣa, ātman,* or *kṣetrajña,* the eternal spiritual entity that is our true identity, which imbues *prakṛti* with life and consciousness. This understanding underlies the fundamental dualism of Sāṁkhya thought with its rigid differentiation between *prakṛti* and *puruṣa,* matter and spirit, but in some passages we also find the idea of there being a twenty-sixth element that is not referred to at all in the *Sāṁkhya-kārikā.* This might perhaps be regarded as a further example of theistic Sāṁkhya, but let us look at a couple of passages that refer to the twenty-sixth in order to discover exactly how this idea adds a new dimension to Sāṁkhya analysis.

The first extract consists of verses also spoken by Vasiṣṭha as a part of his instruction to King Karālajanaka. The point of this passage is to explain the goal of the Sāṁkhya system, which is to allow the *puruṣa* to break free of its association with *prakṛti,* and thereby become liberated from suffering and rebirth. The process by which liberation is attained is that of knowledge and enlightened wisdom, encapsulated in the phrase *anyo 'ham,* 'I am different' used in verse 10. This highest revelation is also

153 *Śānti-parvan,* 294.26–33.

presented by Patañjali in the *Yoga Sūtras* as the ultimate goal achieved through Yoga practice, the *viveka-jñāna* or *viveka-khyāti,* which means knowledge of the distinction.

Puruṣa in its state of bondage is designated as the twenty-fifth principle, which is not usually perceived by people of this world because it is beyond the range of the mind and senses. Verses 7, 8, 16, and 17 also describe a twenty-sixth principle, beyond even the twenty-fifth, and it seems fairly clear from these verses that a distinction is being drawn between *puruṣa* in its embodied state, the twenty-fifth, and *puruṣa* in its liberated state when its unwanted association with *prakṛti* is broken, the twenty-sixth. As stated above, this distinction between the embodied *puruṣa* and the liberated *puruṣa* does not form a part of the more orthodox form of Sāṁkhya, as seen in the *Sāṁkhya-kārikā,* and its presence here again demonstrates the diversity of Sāṁkhya thought in this early period.

> 6–7 Although endowed with consciousness, the living being cannot comprehend the twenty-fifth, the great *ātman,* which is the twenty-sixth when entirely free of blemish, fully enlightened, without limit, and eternal.
>
> 8 This is an entity of mighty effulgence. It alone always comprehends both the twenty-fifth and the twenty-fourth principles, for it pervades both the perceptible and imperceptible realities.
>
> 9 A living being does not comprehend the existence of Brahman as entirely separate from *avyakta,* my child. And neither does he perceive the twenty-fifth as distinct from the twenty-four elements.
>
> 10 When the conscious living being understands the true nature of the *ātman* and realises, *anyo 'ham* 'I am different from this world', then, although existing in association with *prakṛti,* it is capable of perceiving the nature of the *avyakta.*

11 When it comprehends that higher mode of understanding, which is pure and free from blemish, it then attains the enlightened state, which is the twenty-sixth principle, O tiger amongst kings.

12 It then casts off the *avyakta*, which is subject to creation and destruction. Being free of attributes itself, it then understands that *prakṛti* is the principle that possesses attributes though it is bereft of consciousness.

13 Thus through its perception of the *avyakta*, this living being comes to exist as a single entity. Attaining this state of separation from matter, the liberated one then reaches the state of existing as the *ātman*.

14 They speak of the *ātman* as a part of this world, even though it exists beyond this reality, and is untouched by old age and death. Although it is never truly connected with matter, O respectful one, it takes up residence within this domain, and hence men of wisdom speak of there being a total of twenty-five elements.

15 The conscious principle is never truly connected with these elements, my child, and when it gains enlightenment it fully transcends the elements. It then quickly moves beyond even the state of being that is characterised by enlightenment.

16 Possessing wisdom, and being free from old age and death, he then understands, 'I am that twenty-sixth principle.' There is no doubt that by its own strength alone it attains unity with that principle.

17 Though it gains enlightenment through contact with the enlightened state that is the twenty-sixth principle, this entity is also subject to ignorance. Therefore, in accordance with the teachings of Sāṁkhya and *śruti*, it is spoken of as having different forms of existence.[154]

---

154 *Śānti-parvan*, 296.6–17.

In the next short passage, the speaker is Yājñavalkya and the recipient of the teachings is a celestial *gandharva* named Viśvāvasu. Here we find an explanation for why it is that some teachers of Sāṁkhya include a twenty-sixth principle in their analysis of everything that exists. Again it is not a theistic perspective, the point being that in its embodied state *puruṣa* cannot be regarded as absolutely distinct from *prakṛti*, for it is still subject to the influence of *prakṛti* and affected by its transformations. For this reason, some *ṛṣis* emphasise the twenty-sixth beyond the twenty-fifth, for it is only when *puruṣa* is entirely liberated from its association with *prakṛti* that the dualism at the heart of Sāṁkhya teachings is fully apparent.

> 72 As a fish is carried by the movements of the water, so the twenty-fifth proceeds according to the movements of *prakṛti*. The existence of the twenty-fifth is understood as being exactly like that of the fish. Because of its association with *prakṛti*, it has an attachment for *prakṛti* like that of the fish for water, and hence its understanding of its existence is just like that of the fish.
>
> 73 When the essential unity is not recognised, the living being sinks down in the ocean of time, but when its sense of individuality is overcome, it emerges from the ocean of time.
>
> 74 When a brahmin comes to the realisation, 'I am one thing and this world is something different', he then exists apart from matter and can perceive the twenty-sixth principle.
>
> 75 The inferior substance is one thing, O king, and the twenty-fifth principle is something different. But because they perceive the latter's existence within that inferior substance, some holy sages regard them as one.

> 76 For this reason, they do not praise the twenty-fifth principle as the infallible entity. Oppressed by fear of repeated birth and death, O Kaśyapa, such pure souls who follow the paths of Yoga and Sāṁkhya instead perceive the twenty-sixth principle and devote themselves to that.
>
> 77 When a person who exists apart from matter perceives the twenty-sixth principle, he is then indeed a person of wisdom who has knowledge of all things. Such a person never again experiences rebirth.[155]

Prakṛti and Puruṣa: The Dualism of Sāṁkhya Teachings

The fundamental precept of Sāṁkhya thought is the absolute distinction between that which is material and that which is spiritual, between *prakṛti* and *puruṣa*. Various passages of the *Mahābhārata*'s philosophical treatises discuss this precise point, but, as we shall see, this rigid dualism is qualified to some extent by the fact that in its embodied state *puruṣa* is still influenced by *prakṛti* to the point where there is some question as to whether the two are entirely distinct. We will examine two passages from the *Śānti-parvan* here.

The first passage is from Chapter 187 of the *Śānti-parvan,* entitled the *Adhyātma-kathana,* the treatise on the nature of the self. This passage may in fact be one of the earliest contained in the *Śānti-parvan,* and appears to represent an earlier stage in the development of Sāṁkhya thought. Here we find the oft-cited examples of the fly in the fruit and the fish in water, which are used to demonstrate the simultaneous distinction and unity of *prakṛti* and *puruṣa* (here referred to as *kṣetrajña* and *ātman*). Despite the state of union in which they co-exist, the two are entirely distinct, for *prakṛti,* including the mental

---

155 *Śānti-parvan,* 306.72–77.

faculties of a human being, is non-sentient, whilst *puruṣa* is the source of consciousness in a living being and the true perceiver of the manifest world.

> 37 Now note the distinction between the material existence and the *kṣetrajña,* both of which may be subtle by nature. It is this, one manifests qualities and the other does not manifest qualities.
>
> 38 The co-existence of these two is like that of the *udumbara* fruit and the fly living within it, which always exist in a state of union and yet retain distinctive identities.
>
> 39 In terms of their inherent nature, the character of the two is entirely distinct though they remain in a constant state of union. They are like a fish and the water it swims through, which always remain united.
>
> 40 The qualities present in the world do not perceive the *ātman* but the *ātman* perceives all the qualities of existence. The *ātman* is the perceiver of the qualities and always regards itself as the one that has generated them.
>
> 41 The senses, including the *buddhi* as the seventh amongst them, are by themselves inactive and devoid of knowledge. The *paramātman* is like a glowing lamp that acts through these senses to gain illumination of the world.
>
> 42 It is material nature [*sattva*] that manifests the qualities of the world, whilst the *kṣetrajña* merely observes them. This is the only true point of contact between *sattva* and *kṣetrajña.*[156]

156 *Śānti-parvan,* 187.37–42.

This next passage is again taken from the teachings presented by Yājñavalkya, in this case to King Janaka, and here he is discussing the subtle nature of the relationship between *prakṛti* and *puruṣa*. They are clearly distinct each from the other, because *prakṛti*, here referred to as *avyakta*, is non-sentient, whilst *puruṣa* is the conscious principle that gives life to inert matter. However, because it is the proximity of *puruṣa* that causes non-differentiated *prakṛti* to evolve into the elements that comprise the manifest world, *puruṣa* can also be said to exist as a part of *prakṛti* and must be included as the twenty-fifth element in the enumeration. In verse 12, it is stated that *avyakta* is a single principle because all the elements and all the variegated forms visible in this world are ultimately nothing but *prakṛti*. By contrast, there is an infinite number of individual spiritual entities existing in various life forms, and so *puruṣa* is said to exist in a variety of different ways.

> 1 Yājñavalkya said: My dear master of this house, that which is devoid of qualities cannot be made into something that possesses qualities. So learn from me in precise detail about that which possesses qualities and that which is devoid of qualities.
>
> 2 The great souls, sages who perceive the truth, explain it in this way: that which possesses qualities is permeated by the *guṇas* [fundamental qualities], whilst that which is devoid of qualities is free of these *guṇas*.
>
> 3 The *avyakta*, which is by nature pervaded by the *guṇas*, moves into association with the *guṇas* and appropriates them for itself. This principle is by nature devoid of consciousness.

4 The *avyakta* cannot comprehend, but the *puruṣa* is by nature the knower. He always carries the understanding, 'There is nothing superior to myself.'

5 For this reason, the *avyakta* must be without consciousness. Being both eternal and imperishable, the other principle, *puruṣa*, is clearly distinct from the *avyakta*, which is subject to transformation.

6 When, due to ignorance, the *puruṣa* repeatedly brings into being the manifestation of different attributes, and when it does not comprehend its own true nature, then it is referred to as an element of *avyakta*.

7 Because of its being the origin of the material elements, *puruṣa* is said to be of the nature of these elements, and because of its being the origin of different life forms it is said to have the nature of these creatures.

8 Because of its being the origin of various manifestations of *prakṛti*, it is said to be of the nature of *prakṛti*, and because of its being the origin of the seeds of life, it is said to be of the nature of these seeds.

9 Because it is the source of the attributes of this world, the living being is said to exist in relation to the process of creation, and because of its being the instigator of their destruction, it is also said to exist in relation to the process of destruction.

10 So on the one hand it arises from a source, exists in relation to *prakṛti*, and undergoes destruction, and yet on the other it is merely the witness, it is entirely separate from matter, and it has awareness of this distinction.

11 Therefore pure-hearted sages whose knowledge of spiritual doctrines has freed them from passion conceive of it as the eternal, non-manifest principle existing in a non-eternal state. This is what we have heard.

12 Those whose existence rests solely on knowledge and who possess compassion for all beings assert that the *avyakta* is a single principle whilst there are multifarious manifestations of *puruṣa*.

13 In fact, *puruṣa* is distinct from the *avyakta*, which is the impermanent principle that is perceived to be permanent. The living being appears in this world just like the green stalk of a reed.

14 One should recognise that the fly is one thing and the *udumbara* fruit in which it lives is another, for the nature of the fly is not affected by its existence within the *udumbara* fruit.

15 Similarly, the fish is one thing and the body of water it lives in is known to be another, for the true nature of the fish does not become affected by its contact with the body of water.

16 The fire is one thing and the cooking pot is always another. Now try to approach an understanding of this point: the fire does not have its nature affected by its close contact with the pot.

17 It is well-known that the lotus is one thing and the water is another. The lotus is not affected by its contact with the water.

18 Conjunction together with separation constantly takes place in all these examples, but the common people cannot always see the point as it should be understood.

19 And those who see things in a different way do not gain a proper understanding from these examples. They must repeatedly enter the visible world, which is a terrible place, a hell devoid of happiness.

20 This Sāṁkhya doctrine that has been taught to you is the ultimate analysis of the reality we encounter. By analysing the world in this way, the adherents of Sāṁkhya are able to attain a position of isolation from material existence [*kevalatā*].

21 There are, however, others conversant with the truth and I shall now move on to discuss their doctrine: the teachings on the different forms of Yoga.[157]

The Three Guṇas

Another significant feature of Sāṁkhya teachings is the idea of there being three *guṇas*, or essential qualities, which pervade *prakṛti* in all its different forms. The principal feature of the understanding of the *guṇas* relates to the influence they exert over the lives of every person, being causal factors in the development of differing states of mind, and hence the actions all of us perform. The *guṇa* known as *sattva* is said to promote purity, goodwill, and enlightened wisdom, *rajas* impels a person towards action, passion, and the fulfilment of worldly desires, whilst *tamas* is of the nature of darkness, carelessness, ignorance, indolence, and indifference. It is by cultivating *sattva* that a person makes progress towards spiritual enlightenment, but ultimately *sattva* is also a cause of bondage, and so one must seek to transcend all three of the *guṇas*.

157 *Śānti-parvan*, 303.1–21.

In the following passage, from Chapter 205 of the *Śānti-parvan*, the unnamed *guru* instructs his disciple about the nature of the *guṇas* and the influence they exert in shaping the varied dispositions of different individuals. The instruction given to the disciple here is that he should be an observer of the interaction of the *guṇas* within his own mind rather than participating fully and living in relation to their constant fluctuations.

> 17 Living beings are deluded by the qualities of *sattva*, *rajas*, and *tamas*, and because of this ignorance they revolve constantly through the cycle of existence.
>
> 18 One should therefore closely observe the faults that arise within oneself due to ignorance, and one must always give up the sense of ego, the *ahaṁkāra* that is born of ignorance.
>
> 19 The great elements, the senses, the qualities of *sattva*, *rajas*, and *tamas*, as well as the three levels of the universe, and the Deity who is its master, all rest on this *ahaṁkāra*.
>
> 20 In this world, time exerts its control over everything, causing the qualities of each season to appear in turn; similarly, one should understand that the *ahaṁkāra* present in all creatures is the factor that causes them to proceed through life.
>
> 21 One should know *tamas* as the dark quality that deludes the living beings; it is born of ignorance. All the joy and misery that such beings encounter are bound to the three *guṇas*. Now you may learn about these as they pertain to *sattva*, *rajas*, and *tamas*.
>
> 22 The infatuation that comes from delight, happiness, freedom from doubt, determination, and memory are known as the qualities of *sattva*. The following are the qualities of *rajas* and *tamas*:

> 23 These are lust, anger, negligence, greed, stupidity, fear, indolence, despondency, grief, dissatisfaction, arrogance, contempt, and vulgarity.
>
> 24 When one has considered the severity or weakness of these faults and others as well, one should review them one by one, noting the extent of their presence within oneself.[158]

The Mind and Mental Faculties of a Living Being

A highly significant feature of Sāṁkhya doctrine is the analysis it provides of the workings of the mental faculties in a living being. This is even more important for teachers of Yoga practice who need to gain a detailed understanding of the workings of the mind, which the techniques they offer are designed to bring under control. Most treatises on Sāṁkhya describe what we know as the mind as the *manas*, *ahaṁkāra*, *buddhi*, and five senses. The senses are usually understood as external organs like the ears or eyes, but the senses also operate on a mental level ensuring that perceived sensations are categorised by the mind. *Ahaṁkāra* is usually translated as the ego or the sense of ego, and it really refers to the consciousness of selfhood that is present in all the movements of the mind. We have a permanent sense of self-identity that relates to the body and mind of the present embodiment, and this pervasive feature of the mind is named as *ahaṁkāra*.

When perceptions are brought into the mind a process of identification and recognition takes place so that we can know exactly what it is we are smelling, hearing, touching, seeing, or tasting. When the mind is engaged in this process of identification, based on past perceptions, it is referred to as *manas*. However, the mind also has the power of reflection,

---

158 *Śānti-parvan*, 205.17–24.

consideration, decision-making, and the forming of ideas, often based on the recognition of perceptions performed by *manas*. When the mind is reflecting and making conscious decisions it is known as *buddhi*, and it is *buddhi* that is most commonly identified as oneself. When one asks oneself questions, ponders on right and wrong, or on philosophical ideas, the mind is *buddhi*. And when I ask myself 'Who or what am I?' the immediate answer will be related to *buddhi*, the self I live with moment by moment.

The Sāṁkhya treatises of the *Mahābhārata* also include an analysis of these functions of the mind, though not always in the same form, so let us now briefly consider several passages that focus on this topic.

The following verses form a part of an extensive passage of instruction given by Vyāsa to his son Śuka known as the *Śukānupraśna*. There are a number of interesting features here, not least of which is the manner in which *ahaṁkāra* is overlooked and replaced by *hṛdaya*, the heart, demonstrating again that Sāṁkhya appears in a number of different forms at this stage in its development. It seems likely that *hṛdaya* refers to the emotions, but it is impossible to be certain about that. The omission of *ahaṁkāra* might represent a differing analysis of the mind, or it might just be because the emphasis here is on mental activity, whilst *ahaṁkāra* is a pervasive rather than an active faculty.

Most of the focus here is on the role of *buddhi*, which is shown to take on different forms in relation to the sense it is operating through, the point being that when we look at an object, *buddhi* becomes the seer, and when we listen to a sound, *buddhi* becomes the hearer. It is also *buddhi* that undergoes the transformations of the mind experienced due to feelings of happiness or distress, but *buddhi* is also closely associated with the *ātman* so that it appears to be the self of a living being.

This relates again to the question of the nature of the association between *prakṛti* and *puruṣa*; how is it that an entity that is purely spiritual undergoes and experiences transformations that occur entirely within the domain of matter? The answer given here is that *buddhi* absorbs the characteristics of *puruṣa* so that it appears to be the true self, and this sense of identity means that *puruṣa* experiences transformations that in reality relate only to *buddhi*. So when it is said that *puruṣa* wrongly identifies itself with *prakṛti*, what is really meant is that *puruṣa* wrongly identifies itself as *buddhi*. There are also some preliminary hints of Yoga practice here, as it is said that the senses must be restrained so that *buddhi* can rise above its usual association with *manas* and engage itself in the yogic pursuit of enlightened wisdom.

1 Vyāsa said: *Manas* displays the existence we perceive, whilst *buddhi* draws conclusions about this information. The heart recognises what is pleasing and what is unattractive. Thus the impulse towards action has three features.

2 The objects they perceive are superior to the senses, and *manas* is superior to these objects. *Buddhi* is superior to *manas*, but the *ātman* is known to be superior to *buddhi*.

3 *Buddhi* is the self of a human being, and *buddhi* shares the identity of the *ātman*. When it interacts with the perceived existence, then it becomes *manas*.

4 Because each of the senses has its own separate existence, *buddhi* undergoes some slight modifications. When hearing sounds, it is the sense of hearing, and when experiencing sensations of touch, it is referred to as the sense of touch.

5 When seeing objects, it is the sense of sight, when tasting flavours, it will become the sense of taste, and when smelling aromas, it is the sense of smell. Thus the *buddhi* is transformed in various ways.

6 They refer to these transformations as the senses. *Buddhi* is the invisible controller within the senses. Whilst it remains within a person, *buddhi* exists in three different conditions.

7 Sometimes it gains pleasure, sometimes it is sorrowful, and sometimes it encounters neither happiness nor distress.

8 *Buddhi* is composed of reflections, and yet it goes beyond the three recognised states of mind. It is like the ocean, the master of the rivers, which throws up waves and overcomes its mighty shores.

9 When *buddhi* comes to desire anything, then it becomes *manas*, which through the *buddhi* can gain knowledge of the different senses in which *buddhi* resides. The senses are powerful forces that must be completely subdued.

10 If one does not order each of the senses in the correct manner, *buddhi* exists within *manas* as thoughts of a general nature. *Rajas* then arises following on from the presence of *sattva*.

11 And all such states of existence are within these three qualities. Thus they pursue their specific objects of enjoyment as the spokes follow the revolving rim of a chariot wheel.

12 In order to gain enlightenment, a man should act through his senses, led by the *buddhi*. Each of the senses unites with its own specific object, whilst remaining indifferent to what is perceived.[159]

The next short passage forms a part of the instruction given by Asita Devala to Nārada, and here we are given a further insight into the different functions of each of the mental faculties. Here we see again that *ahaṁkāra* is left out of

---

159 *Śānti-parvan*, 240.1–12.

the analysis, possibly for the reason mentioned above in that it does not play a direct role in the acquisition of knowledge through perception. In place of *ahaṁkāra,* we have *citta* as the third constituent of the mind, and this replacement of *ahaṁkāra* can be witnessed in a few other passages, as well as in the later teachings of the *Bhāgavata Purāṇa* (3.26.14). Verse 17 provides a clear definition of the respective functions of *manas* and *buddhi,* the former identifying the nature of sensory perceptions and then *buddhi* reflecting on the information thus acquired. The exact role played by *citta* in this process is unclear and it may be that it just means the condition of conscious awareness that allows *manas* and *buddhi* to perform their respective functions. Beyond the senses and the mind there is *puruṣa,* here designated again as *kṣetrajña,* which is the presiding entity on behalf of which all the mental faculties are active. The mind and senses appear to be constantly active in acquiring knowledge and reflecting on its significance, but of course all of this activity is only possible due to the remote presence of *kṣetrajña,* the source of life.

> 12 Men of wisdom have identified the eyes, nose, ears, skin, and tongue as the five senses that acquire knowledge of the objects of perception.
>
> 13 They act by seeing, hearing, smelling, touching, and tasting. You can understand the qualities they perceive through logical deduction: the five senses act on five objects in five ways.
>
> 14 These qualities are form, aroma, taste, touch, and sound. These five are perceived by the five senses in five ways.
>
> 15 Form, aroma, taste, touch, and sound are indeed the objects of perception, but the senses do not comprehend them. It is the *kṣetrajña* that comprehends them by means of the senses.

> 16 Beyond this group of senses is the *citta,* and *manas* is beyond this faculty. Beyond *manas* is *buddhi,* and the *kṣetrajña* lies beyond the *buddhi.*
>
> 17 The living being first becomes aware of different sensations by means of the senses. It next examines these objects with the *manas* and reaches a decision about them with the *buddhi.* In this way, *kṣetrajña* gains an understanding of all objects that are perceived through the senses.
>
> 18 Thus we now have eight elements: *citta,* the five senses, *manas,* and *buddhi.* Those conversant with the nature of a living being refer to these eight as the senses for acquiring knowledge.[160]

Liberation from Rebirth

As has been mentioned several times, the ultimate aim of all Sāṁkhya teachings is to provide the knowledge by which *puruṣa* can escape from the suffering of perpetual rebirth. It is the realisation *anyo 'ham,* 'I am something else' which is the key to liberation, as expressed here in the words of Vasiṣṭha, who is instructing King Janaka.

> 42 The Sāṁkhya teachers provide a proper enumeration of the twenty-four material elements, but in addition to their explanation of matter they also discuss the twenty-fifth element that transcends all material categories.
>
> 43 This twenty-fifth element is understood as the conscious principle in its unenlightened state. But when it comprehends its own true nature it then exists alone, free from any connection with matter.
>
> 44 I have now given you a precise explanation of the proper doctrine of Sāṁkhya. Those who understand this teaching, as I have explained it, obtain a state of equanimity.

---

160 *Śānti-parvan,* 267.12–18.

45 A proper understanding of the nature of *prakṛti* is referred to as the true doctrine. *Prakṛti* consists of material elements, but one who understands himself to be unconnected with these elements exists as a being apart from them.

46 When the self frees itself from attributes, it never appears in this world again. Because of its indestructible nature, it is not subject to any other cause, and is unchanging.

47 Those who perceive only one type of substance do not have a proper understanding. Again and again, O scorcher of the foe, they return to the realm of matter.

48 But there are others who understand everything that exists. Being enlightened about everything, they never again exist within the manifest world and they are never constrained by its control.

49 'Everything' is said to mean the *avyakta*, but 'everything' also includes the twenty-fifth element. No fear exists in those who acquire this knowledge.[161]

Yoga Teachings in the Śānti-parvan

I want to move on now to consider the teachings on Yoga included in the *Mahābhārata*'s *Śānti-parvan*, but we should be aware that any distinction drawn between Sāṁkhya and Yoga is of limited significance, for in most respects they form two strands of the same overall system. Here is what Yājñavalkya has to say on that subject.

1 Yājñavalkya said: I have presented here knowledge of Sāṁkhya. Now learn from me an understanding of the

161 *Śānti-parvan*, 294.42–49.

Yoga system. I will present these teachings exactly as I have heard and understood them, O best of kings.

2 There is no knowledge equal to that of Sāṁkhya, there is no power equal to that of Yoga. They both demand the same lifestyle and it is understood that both lead to a state beyond death.

3 Men who possess but limited intelligence see the two systems as distinct, O king, but after reaching a final conclusion we see them as one system.

4 Whatever is perceived by the followers of Yoga is also recognised by the followers of Sāṁkhya. One who regards Sāṁkhya and Yoga as a single system has a proper understanding.[162]

Yoga Teachings in the Mokṣa-dharma-parvan

Most people today are very familiar with Yoga practice, and millions across the world have attended classes on Yoga and taken up the practice with varying degrees of commitment. The forms of Yoga typically practised today, however, are primarily centred on *āsanas* and other bodily postures, whereas the ancient system of Yoga, as taught in the *Yoga Sūtras*, *Bhagavad-gītā*, and here in the *Mahābhārata*, is very much a Yoga of the mind. Despite the prevailing emphasis on postural Yoga, various forms of meditation do still form a significant feature of contemporary practice, and the *Yoga Sūtras* is highly regarded as a foundational text.

Hence the passages of instruction on Yoga practice within the *Mahābhārata* are particularly important in understanding the development of Yoga, as these passages almost certainly

162 *Śānti-parvan*, 304.1–4.

predate the *Yoga Sūtras* and are in fact the earliest treatises on Yoga that we have access to today. As was the case with our consideration of Sāṁkhya teachings, the presentation of passages giving instruction on Yoga practice is inevitably selective simply because of the volume of material available. In this chapter, the translations themselves provide the clearest insight into the points under discussion, and I will refrain from indulging in excessive commentary, apart from where points of particular importance are to be highlighted.

What is clear from these passages is that the principal aim of the Yoga techniques taught in this earlier period is to gain direct, experiential knowledge of the presence of the spiritual *ātman* at the very core of our being. The Sāṁkhya treatises provide a theoretical explanation of the distinction between the material embodiment and the true self, and the role of Yoga teachings is to provide a means by which the conclusions of that theoretical discourse can be directly perceived and experienced. Hence we will repeatedly encounter the principal idea of practising intense meditation by fixing the mind upon the *ātman,* the innermost self.

We will begin by making reference to the point made at the end of the previous section regarding the essential unity of Sāṁkhya and Yoga. In this first extract, which is taken from a passage entitled the *Yoga-kathana,* we encounter a slightly different perspective, which emphasises the distinction between them based on the theism of Yoga and the non-theism of Sāṁkhya. From verse 7, we can also identify the idea that whilst Sāṁkhya is an essentially theoretical system, based on knowledge of specific texts, the knowledge attained by followers of Yoga comes through direct experience. The presentation here is made by Bhīṣma in response to a question from Yudhiṣṭhira.

> 1 Yudhiṣṭhira said: My dear grandfather, please instruct me about the distinction between Sāṁkhya and Yoga.

Everything is known to you, O best of the Kurus, for you possess knowledge of all subjects.

2 Bhīṣma said: Those brahmins who follow Sāṁkhya praise the Sāṁkhya system, whilst those who adhere to Yoga praise the Yoga system. In order to elevate their own faction, they present various arguments to show that theirs is the superior path.

3 'How can one who does not believe in the Deity gain liberation?' In this way, O vanquisher of the foe, those men of wisdom who follow the path of Yoga use sound arguments to establish the superiority of their system.

4 Those brahmins who follow the Sāṁkhya system also make their assertions with sound reasoning, saying, 'In this world, one who understands all states of existence and remains unattached to the objects of pleasure,

5 Is quite clearly liberated when he departs from the body. It cannot be otherwise.' Men of great wisdom propound this Sāṁkhya doctrine as a system directed towards liberation from rebirth.

6 One should accept the reasoning of one's own faction, for its teachings are beneficial and have the same aim as the other. The ideas set forth in such teachings should be accepted by persons such as yourself who can receive good instruction.

7 The followers of Yoga base their conclusions on direct perception whilst the Sāṁkhyas are guided by scripture. My dear Yudhiṣṭhira, it is my opinion that both these systems teach the truth.

8 Both forms of knowledge, O king, are approved of by myself and by other learned men. When adhered to according to their scriptures, they lead one to the highest destination.

> 9 O sinless one, both Sāṁkhya and Yoga place the same emphasis on purity, compassion to other living beings, and accepting vows of austerity. It is in terms of doctrine that differences emerge between them.[163]

After this introduction on the distinctions between Sāṁkhya and Yoga, Bhīṣma then eulogises the empowerment of the adepts that comes as a direct result of their success in their yogic endeavours. In this next extract from the same chapter, the direction of the discussion changes as more detail is given about the specific techniques to be undertaken, and again we will notice that the primary focus is on gaining the ability to fix the mind unwaveringly on a particular point so that it can explore the inner self without distraction and thereby locate the presence of the *ātman* as the true spiritual identity of a living being. It is this ultimate realisation that brings liberation from rebirth. There might be some suggestion that verses 39–41 are making reference to the presence of the subtle *cakras* within the body, but on balance this seems unlikely as there is little or nothing to indicate any form of tantric influence on these chapters of the *Mahābhārata*, or indeed anywhere within the whole body of the work.

> 28 There can be no doubt, O king, that a *yogin* who possesses such power and has conquered the bonds that tie him to this world has gained control over his own liberation from rebirth.
>
> 29 O lord of the people, I have thus explained the powers that are gained through Yoga. I will now speak further in order to indicate to you its more subtle features.
>
> 30 In the state of meditation, my lord, the concentration of the mind (*dhāraṇā*) is absorbed (*samādhāna*) in the *ātman*.

163 *Śānti-parvan*, 289.1–9.

Now hear from me about these subtle features of Yoga, O best of the Bharatas.

31 As a careful archer who concentrates his mind succeeds in hitting his target, so there is no doubt that a *yogin* who properly follows his discipline will gain liberation from rebirth.

32 A person who fixes his mind unwaveringly on the pot filled with oil he is carrying can carefully climb up a stairway whilst keeping his mind set on the task.

33 In the same way, O king, the *yogin* who properly directs his unwavering mind purifies his inner self so that it shines like the sun.

34 By concentrating carefully, O Kaunteya, a helmsman swiftly guides his ship across the vast ocean to the town that is its destination, O king.

35 Similarly, one who knows the truth concentrates his mind [*samādhāna*] on the *ātman* through the disciplines of Yoga, and, after quitting his body, O king, he attains the position that is hardest to attain.

36 Yoking fine horses to the carriage, the charioteer who concentrates fully on his task swiftly carries the archer to the place he desires, O best amongst men.

37 In the same way, O king, the *yogin* who regulates his mind by different forms of concentration [*dhāraṇā*] swiftly attains the highest state, as an arrow swiftly finds its target when it is released.

38 That *yogin* who fixes his mind on the *ātman*, and then remains in that state without wavering, destroys all his wickedness, as a fisherman kills fish, and attains a state beyond decay.

39–41 O possessor of unlimited power, the *yogin* who remains intent on the great vows of Yoga and thereby unites

> the subtle mind with the *ātman* in the navel, in the throat, in the head, the heart, the chest, the flanks, the eye, the sense of touch, and the nose, acquires knowledge without blemish and quickly burns to ashes the results of his previous pure and impure acts. Following this highest form of Yoga, O lord of your race, he can attain liberation from rebirth whenever he desires it.[164]

Chapter 188 of the *Śānti-parvan* forms a passage entitled the *Dhyāna-yoga,* the Yoga of meditation, and again it is Bhīṣma speaking directly here without referring to any earlier discussions between particular individuals. One might say that the main point of emphasis here is on *pratyāhāra,* the withdrawal of the senses from external perceptions, although, of course, it is this process of withdrawal that facilitates the internal focus of the mind in meditation. Verse 15 refers to *vitarka, vicāra,* and *viveka* as primary forms of meditation, indicating that one begins with processes of conscious reflection, which are ultimately transcended, a point that will be familiar to those who have made a study of the *Yoga Sūtras,* which employs the same terminology.

Bhīṣma is also anxious to make the point that this is a difficult and gradual process, simply because the mind has such a pronounced tendency to focus on outward perceptions. As is stated in the *Bhagavad-gītā,*[165] this form of yoga is very hard to master, but one must remain resolute in one's practice, repeatedly drawing the mind back from its external peregrinations to fix it in meditation. Here there is no mention of the *ātman* as the object of meditation, but the goal of liberation is clearly stated through the use of the word *nirvāṇa,* a term frequently associated with Buddhism but used equally within other Indian schools of thought.

---

164 *Śānti-parvan,* 289.28–41.

165 *Bhagavad-gītā,* 6.35–36.

1 Bhīṣma said: Now, Pārtha, I will teach you about *dhyāna-yoga,* the yoga of meditation, which can be divided into four types. After understanding this science, the highest amongst the *ṛṣis* attain a state of perfection that never ends.

2 The great *ṛṣis* who are *yogins* are satisfied by wisdom alone and their minds are focused on reaching the state of *nirvāṇa*. They always behave in such a way that their meditation can be successfully performed.

3 When they are liberated from the miseries of repeated birth and death, Pārtha, they never return to this world. With the miseries of rebirth cast aside, they can then exist in accordance with their true nature.

4 They are liberated beings, free from worldly dualities, who never deviate from the quality of *sattva*. They always dwell in places where there are no material entanglements or disputations, and which create a tranquil state of mind.

5 There, absorbed in silent recitation, the sage fixes his mind in meditation on a single point. He sits like a log of wood, compressing all his senses into a single substance.

6 With his ear he perceives no sound; with his skin he is unaware of any touch. With his eye he sees no form; with his tongue he perceives no taste.

7 During his practice of meditation, one who knows the path of Yoga will also remain unaware of any aroma. Filled with spiritual potency, he no longer desires any object that agitates the five senses.

8 Having brought the five senses together within his mind, the man of wisdom should then take control of the wandering mind as well as the five senses within it.

9 The mind does not depend on anything but itself. It has five gates and is always restless. From the outset, the wise man who is undeviating on the path of meditation should direct the mind inwards.

10 When the practitioner combines the senses and the mind together as one substance, this marks the first stage of the path of meditation I am teaching.

11 Although the adept's mind, the sixth element, has previously been brought under complete control, it may ignite once more into a state of agitation, just like lightning flashing from within a cloud.

12 The consciousness of one on the path of meditation is just like a drop of water moving in all directions as it sits trembling on a leaf.

13 The mind remains fixed on its course of meditation for a short time but then it takes off once more, just like the wind as it sweeps along its course.

14 Without disappointment at the setback, and setting aside his distress and all sense of hostility, one who understands this *dhyāna-yoga* should remain calm and bring his mind under control once more through renewed practice of meditation.

15 In the beginning stage, the powers of reflection, deliberation, and discrimination [*vicāra, vitarka,* and *viveka*] progressively appear as the primary meditation for the sage who is practising inner contemplation.

16 Even when disturbed by the mind, he must continue his practice of inward contemplation. The sage should never fall prey to disappointment but should continue to make the endeavours that will ultimately bestow great benefit.

17 Piled up heaps of soil, ashes, and dung do not immediately become merged together when they are soaked by water.

18 Slowly and gradually they all merge into one substance, but while they are only partially moistened there will still be parts that are dry like powder and devoid of water.

19 In the same way, one should slowly draw together all the senses into one combined substance and gradually withdraw them from their objects. When held together in this way, that group of senses will then become pacified.

20 When, through his own resolve, he is able to keep his mind and five senses fixed on the path of meditation, O Bhārata, the adept then pacifies them by means of constant Yoga practice.

21 Neither through human endeavour nor any gift of destiny can one obtain joy like that of one who controls his mind.

22 Filled with this joy, *yogins* will then take further delight in their practice of meditation. In this way they reach the state of *nirvāṇa* that is free from any blemish.[166]

The next extract is from a lengthy passage of instruction in the *Śukānupraśna, Śānti-parvan,* Chapter 232, delivered by Vyāsa in response to questions from his son, Śuka, who is well-known as the principal speaker of the *Bhāgavata Purāṇa*. Again the most salient feature of the teachings on Yoga practice is acquiring the ability to fix the mind on a single point without any form of deviation or distraction. According to verse 15, one may begin by focusing the mind on any object one chooses, but we must presume that this is simply the means by which one gains mastery over the mind, and that once this ability is acquired, the adept then applies it to realisation of the *ātman,* as indicated in verses 16, 18, and 19.

Another interesting feature of this passage is the reference to the *yogin*'s acquisition of magical abilities, the *vibhūtis*

166 *Śānti-parvan,* 188.1–22.

outlined in the third chapter of the *Yoga Sūtras*. Vyāsa does not describe these powers in anything like the same detail as Patañjali, but he does confirm the point that such *vibhūtis* are not the true goal of Yoga, and must be set aside rather than indulged in. We can also observe that in Vyāsa's view, the intense dedication to Yoga presented here is for renunciants, the wandering *sādhus* who have given up intimate association with human society and developed a mood of complete world-indifference. Such persons should seek out a remote spot such as a temple, mountain cave, or deserted house, where they can engage in extensive periods of meditation without fear of disturbance. This might, however, be due to the fact that Vyāsa's instruction is directed specifically at Śuka, who has already adopted this lifestyle.

> 15 One who understands the science of Yoga should first of all take possession of his mind [*manas*], just as a fisherman will first seize a dangerous fish. Then he may take possession of his hearing, then his sight, and then the senses of taste and scent.
>
> 16 After bringing the senses under control, the sage should keep them stationed firmly within the *manas*. Only after these inclinations have been removed can *manas* be fixed in meditation on the *ātman*.
>
> 17 After bringing the five senses to a state of union by means of this knowledge, the sage should keep them stationed firmly within the *manas*. *Manas* is the sixth element amongst the senses. Brahman becomes apparent when all six of them remain within the *ātman*, and there become inactive.
>
> 18 Then, by his own powers, he perceives the *ātman* within, appearing like blazing flames without any smoke, like the sun shining with a brilliant effulgence, or like a flash of lightning in the sky. Because of the all-pervasive nature of the *ātman*, all things in all directions can be perceived within it.

19 Wise brahmins who are great persons and who are resolute, endowed with knowledge, and attached to the welfare of all beings, perceive the *ātman* within.

20 By thus adhering to the regulations of Yoga, and dedicating the prescribed time to such practice, he enters a state of communion with the undecaying self, whilst sitting alone in a secluded place.

21 The *yogin* will develop the following abilities: the power of delusion, wandering at will, and self-transformation; the power to create wonderful scents, sounds, sights, tastes, and touches, as well as heat and cold; the ability to merge oneself with the wind;

22 The ability to comprehend hidden things, and to cause misfortune for others. After developing these powers through his practice of Yoga, one who properly understands this science should first ignore them, and then through his own abilities turn them back to their source.

23 On the peak of a mountain, in a crematorium, or in front of a tree, the self-controlled sage should continue his progress in Yoga three times a day.

24 Subduing his senses, he should be like a man in a crowd carrying a pot on his head, keeping his mind always fixed on one point and never allowing it to waver.

25 When practising Yoga, he may focus on any object by means of which he can bring the restless mind under control, and then he should not deviate from that object of concentration.

26 Keeping his mind fixed on one point, he should resort to deserted mountain caves for his residence, or else the temples of the gods, or abandoned houses.

27 He should not show affection towards any other person with his words, deeds, or thoughts. He should be indifferent towards the food he eats, and should remain unmoved whether or not he receives something to eat.

> 28 He should maintain the same state of mind towards one who praises him and one who abuses him, and should not contemplate how to bring them prosperity or misfortune.
>
> 29 He should not rejoice on acquiring things, nor feel anxiety when nothing comes his way. He should be equal to all beings, and live in the same manner as the wind.
>
> 30 If a holy *sādhu* who regards all beings as himself and looks upon everything with equal vision engages in this practice for six months without deviation, he transcends the sacred sounds of the Vedas.[167]

The next passage is an extract from the teachings delivered by Vasiṣṭha to King Karālajanaka, as recounted in the *Vasiṣṭha-karālajanaka-saṁvāda, Śānti-parvan,* Chapter 294 by Bhīṣma to Yudhiṣṭhira. It might be significant to note that there is a later work entitled the *Yoga Vasiṣṭha,* where again the *ṛṣi* Vasiṣṭha delivers teachings on Yoga, although I am not inclined to attach too much significance to that connection. Here again the emphasis is on *dhyāna,* meditation, which is said to involve both intense internal concentration and the practice of *prāṇāyāma,* control of the inward and outward breaths. Verse 8 asserts that *prāṇāyāma* is *sa-guṇa,* involving material qualities, whilst concentration is *nir-guṇa.* It is not clear exactly what is meant by this statement, but the idea may be that *prāṇāyāma* is a physical process utilising the material body, whereas *ekāgratā manasaḥ,* fixing the mind on a single point, relates to a spiritual or even mystical experience. The point here is that once again the primary object of that fixed concentration is the *ātman,* the true self, direct experience of which is the ultimate goal of Yoga.

By way of comparison with Patañjali's *aṣṭāṅga-yoga,* one might define the fixed concentration of the mind referred to

167 *Śānti-parvan,* 232.15–30.

in verse 8 as a form of *dhāraṇā* rather than *dhyāna*, though in actuality the two are closely linked, whilst verses 14 to 16 are clearly describing the practice of *pratyāhāra*, by which the senses are withdrawn from the external mode of perception that is their usual field of activity. The process of *pratyāhāra* that is typically presented in these passages involves the withdrawal of the five senses back into the *manas* so that there is only a single element within this part of the mind, and here again this seems to be what is being referred to.

Another interesting point to notice here is that *manas* and *buddhi*, the two main components of our mental faculties, are the means by which knowledge of the *ātman* is attained when they are withdrawn from external activity and applied to the task of inward meditation (verse 23). Hence we are to understand that the externally focused mind is the cause of the continuing bondage of the *ātman* in this world, but when properly applied the mind can also be the means by which liberation is attained. And, finally, I was also struck by the phrase *yogam etad dhi yogānāṁ manye yogasya lakṣaṇam* in verse 25, as this indicates that the true mark of Yoga is the practice of practitioners, and not necessarily that which is defined in textual sources. This again relates to the understanding that Yoga is primarily based on practice and personal experience, rather than being defined by reasoned explanations or written manuals. The adepts in Yoga use these as a preliminary guide, but ultimately find the form of Yoga that brings success at a personal level.

> 6 Vasiṣṭha said: Very well, I will speak on the subjects you have asked about. But first, great king, hear from me a separate account of *yoga* practice.
>
> 7 Meditation [*dhyāna*] is certainly the most effective *yoga* technique employed by the *yogins*. Persons who know the Vedic teachings assert that there are two types of meditation.

8 These are the fixing of the mind on one point and the regulation of the breathing process [*prāṇāyāma*]. *Prāṇāyāma* employs material qualities but concentration of the mind is performed without any such qualities.

9 There are only three times when a *yogin* may desist from his practice, O lord of your people: whilst he is urinating, defecating, or eating. He should apply himself to it at all other times.

10 Either by mental control or by the twenty-two forms of breathing exercise, a holy sage should first withdraw the senses from their objects and then progress to that which lies beyond the twenty-fourth element.

11 Using the techniques of Yoga as his means, the learned sage should impel himself towards that constant ageless entity described in the teachings of wise men.

12 We have heard that by using these techniques one can be conscious of the *ātman* at all times. It is certain that this object can be reached only by one whose mind is not fixed on anything inferior, and not by any other person.

13 Remaining free of all attachments, eating only small amounts, and controlling the senses, he should concentrate his mind on the *ātman* at dusk and at dawn.

14 To do this, O Lord of Mithilā, he should suppress the senses with his mind [*manas*], and then use his intellect [*buddhi*] to make his mind steady, remaining as motionless as a rock.

15 Enlightened persons who understand the precepts and regulations of Yoga practice should remain steady like a pillar and motionless like a mountain. Then it can be said that they are practising Yoga.

16 In that state he no longer hears, smells, tastes, or sees; he has no awareness of sensations of touch, and his mind no longer wanders after different objects.

17 He no longer desires anything at all, and, like a plank of wood, he has no conscious thoughts. Men of wisdom assert that such a person is truly engaged in Yoga whilst still existing within *prakṛti*.

18 He then appears like a lamp burning in a windless place, never flickering or wavering, and going only upwards and never sideways.

19 When he gains such vision, he may then behold that which persons like me refer to as the innermost *ātman* situated in the heart; it is the known and it is also the knower, my child.

20 The *ātman* is perceived within the *yogin's* own being like the seven-flamed fire devoid of any smoke, like the sun with its spreading rays, or like a flash of lightning.

21 Those great souls who are resolute and possess great wisdom are brahmins who exist in the domain of Brahman. They perceive that which never takes birth from a womb and is by nature immortal.

22 They speak of it as being smaller than the smallest object and greater than the greatest object. It is present within all beings, remaining constant but unseen.

23 When illuminated by the *manas*, this creator of worlds may be seen through the wealth possessed by the *buddhi*. Untouched by ignorance, my child, it remains in a state that is beyond the great darkness of this world.

24 Those who comprehend the truth and are learned in the Vedas speak of it as that which dispels the darkness. It is uncontaminated and untouched by ignorance; it has no individual attributes and is therefore known as that which has no attributes.

25 I consider that the form of Yoga actually practised by the *yogins* is the true indication of Yoga. It is by this means that they perceive the true object of perception, the ageless *ātman* that is the highest principle.

> 26 I have thus presented an accurate exposition of the teachings on Yoga. I will now speak about the system of knowledge known as Sāṁkhya, the teachings that analyse the nature of the world.[168]

The next extract, from the *Yājñavalkya-janaka-saṁvāda, Śānti-parvan,* Chapter 304, in which Yājñavalkya offers teachings on Yoga to King Janaka, displays clear similarities to the previous passage of instruction delivered by Vasiṣṭha, and it may be that one of them is derived from the other, or else that they both drew upon the same earlier source. Here again we find the view that there are two forms of Yoga, although here the concentration of the mind referred to by Vasiṣṭha is designated as *dhāraṇā*. And again it is said that *prāṇāyāma* is *sa-guṇa,* with attributes, whilst *dhāraṇā* is *nir-guṇa,* devoid of attributes. Yājñavalkya also emphasises the practice of *pratyāhāra,* withdrawing the senses back into the mind so that they come to exist as a single entity united with *manas*. In verse 21, it is mentioned that the adepts in Yoga develop this technique to such an extent that even loud sounds of singing and music cannot penetrate their consciousness, which remains entirely fixed on internal perception.

In addition to the enactment of the *pratyāhāra* that withdraws the senses back into the mind, we are told that the *yogin* withdraws each element of the mental faculties back into its predecessor, ultimately taking the whole of the mind back into primal *prakṛti* and thereby reversing the process of creative evolution set forth in Sāṁkhya teachings, by which the world and living beings emerge into a state of manifestation. The indication is that it is in this way that the *yogin* breaks the association of *puruṣa* with *prakṛti* and thereby attains liberation from rebirth.

---

168 *Śānti-parvan,* 294.6–26.

This liberated state is referred to here as *kevala*, separation, which is equivalent to the *kaivalya* that forms the title of Patañjali's fourth and final chapter. The object of the *dhāraṇā* is *puruṣa* (verse 17), and the fixed concentration that is required for full success in the yogic endeavour is facilitated by the *pratyāhāra* that prevents distractions arising from external sources through the senses. And, finally, once again we are told that the true definition of Yoga is whatever practice the adepts undertake; *kim anyad yoga-lakṣaṇam*, 'What else could be the defining characteristic of *yoga*?' Yājñavalkya rhetorically asks at the conclusion of his speech.

> 5 You should understand that Yoga practices involve the regulation of the bodily airs and the senses, destroyer of the foe. By this means the *yogins* travel within their bodies through the ten directions.
>
> 6 At the point of death, my child, they employ Yoga techniques with their eight subtle qualities to wander throughout the worlds, O sinless one, renouncing the pleasures of life.
>
> 7 Men of wisdom say that a Yoga that has eight qualities is found in the Vedas. They describe only the subtle science that has eight qualities and no other form of Yoga, O best of kings.
>
> 8 However, they also say that the Yoga practice that is supreme amongst all forms of Yoga is of two types. According to the teachings of the scriptures, these are practice involving qualities and practice that is devoid of such qualities.
>
> 9 These two forms of Yoga are concentration of the mind [*dhāraṇā*] and regulation of the breath [*prāṇāyāma*], O king. *Prāṇāyāma* is the practice involving qualities whilst concentration of the mind is practice devoid of qualities.
>
> 10 When one observes the exhalation of the breaths, O lord of Mithilā, there may arise an excess of wind in the body and one should then refrain from this practice.

11 For the first regulative practice of the night twelve exercises are recommended. Then after sleeping in the middle period of the night, twelve exercises are recommended for the practice before dawn.

12 There is no doubt that one who is peaceful at heart and self-controlled, who lives alone, finds pleasure within his own self, and is enlightened, should engage his very being in this Yoga practice.

13 In this way, he should put aside the five types of impediment caused by the five senses: sound, touch, form, flavour, and aroma.

14 He should restrain the process by which the senses are repeatedly aroused and then become still, O Lord of Mithilā; he should then concentrate the totality of the senses within the *manas*.

15 *Manas* should then be placed within *ahaṁkāra*, O king, *ahaṁkāra* within the *buddhi*, and *buddhi* within *prakṛti*.

16 After processing the mental faculties in this way, he may then engage in meditation [*dhyāyeta*] on the one that stands alone, free of any taint, unlimited, pure, and flawless.

17 This is the abiding *puruṣa*, the indivisible reality that is beyond both old age and death. It is eternal and unchanging, the Lord, the imperishable Brahman.

18 One should understand the characteristics of the adept in Yoga practice, great king. Such a person has the quality of serenity, like that of a contented soul who sleeps easily.

19 A lamp filled with oil burning in a windless place does not waver and has its flame pointed upwards. The wise speak of the *yogin* as being like such a lamp.

20 When raindrops fall from the clouds upon a stone, they do not have the power to wear it down. Such also is the mark of a *yogin*.

> 21 He is not disturbed even by the sound of conches and kettledrums, or by a range of songs and musical instruments. This is the mark of one who is truly absorbed in Yoga.
>
> 22 A person holding in his hands a vessel filled with sesame oil whilst mounting a flight of steps will certainly be afraid if threatened by men armed with swords.
>
> 23 But if such a person possesses self-control he will not spill a single drop from the vessel due to fear of those men. So it is with one who has a higher purpose and fixes his mind on one point alone.
>
> 24 This is due to his senses being fixed and held in a state of inactivity. One should understand these as the characteristics of a sage who engages in Yoga practice.
>
> 25 Such a *yogin* perceives Brahman, that which is supreme and unchanging, like a blazing fire situated in the midst of the greatest darkness.
>
> 26 After adhering to such practice for a long period of time, the *yogin* gives up his body unobserved and attains a state of dissociation from matter [*kevala*]. This is the teaching of the eternal *śruti*.
>
> 27 This then is Yoga as practised by the adepts in Yoga. What else could give a proper indication of Yoga? When they have mastered this science, men of wisdom think that they have attained their goal.[169]

The final extract on Yoga is taken not from the *Śānti-parvan* but from the section of the *Aśvamedhika-parvan* (Book 14) entitled the *Anugītā*, in which Kṛṣṇa, at Arjuna's request,

169 *Śānti-parvan*, 304.5–27.

rehearses some of the instruction he imparted earlier in the *Bhagavad-gītā*. In fact, the teachings on Yoga presented here are closer to the *Śānti-parvan* passages than to those in Chapter 6 of the *Bhagavad-gītā*, but at the same time they do display some distinctive features that set this passage somewhat apart from the insights given by Vasiṣṭha and Yājñavalkya.

Here again, we have the constantly recurring theme of Yoga being the ability to fix the mind on the *ātman* in order to gain direct, experiential knowledge of the highest spiritual truths; and here also we have reference to the supernatural powers that transport the *yogin* to a state of existence beyond even the control of the gods. Verses 31 to 35 are rather unusual inasmuch as they present a specific form of practice for one engaged in meditation. The practitioner is to envisage the body as his own abode and then fix the mind on various parts of the body, thereby establishing the absolute distinction between the *ātman* and its physical embodiment, between the seer and the seen, the *draṣṭṛ* and the *dṛśya* in the words of the *Yoga Sūtras*. One might wonder why there is no mention of *prāṇāyāma* in this extract, as there is in the earlier passages we looked at, the answer being that in the following chapters of *Anugītā*, Kṛṣṇa provides an extensive description of the airs present within the body and the process of *prāṇāyāma* by means of which they are controlled.

14 Now then I shall reveal to you the supreme teaching on Yoga, which stands above all other teachings. On comprehending this wisdom, even in this world, the *yogins* are able to perceive the *ātman* in its perfect state.

15 Now you may learn about this teaching from me, as I perceive it. I will reveal the gateways, passing through which one perceives the *ātman* within oneself.

16 After compressing the senses together, he should fix the mind [*manas*] in concentration on the *ātman*. One may

begin to engage in this practice of Yoga after first undertaking harsh acts of austerity.

17 Performing such austerities, one gives up material aspirations and becomes free of pride and egotism. Applying the *manas*, the wise brahmin then perceives the *ātman* within himself.

18 If such a righteous sage is able to make contact with the *ātman* within his own being, then, remaining constant in his good conduct, he perceives the *ātman* within his own being.

19 The regulated practitioner of Yoga remains always in control of himself, for he has conquered the senses. Such a practitioner properly perceives the *ātman* by means of his own faculties [*ātmanā*].

20 As a person may see someone in a dream, and exclaim, 'It is he', even though he has no visual form, so it is that the practitioner of Yoga properly perceives the *ātman*.

21 Or as one can see the inner stem when it is drawn out from a reed, so the *yogin* perceives the *ātman* as separate from his body.

22 They say that the reed is one's body whilst the inner stem represents the *ātman*. This is the matchless teaching revealed by those who understand the science of Yoga.

23 When an embodied being engages in Yoga, and properly perceives the *ātman*, then no one has power over him, not even he who is the Lord of the threefold universe.

24 He then moves from one body to another exactly as he wishes. Having cast aside old age and death, he neither rejoices nor laments.

25 Having control over his own existence, such a practitioner of Yoga can manifest the divine nature of the gods. And when he gives up the temporary bodily form, he then achieves the unfading Brahman.

26 Even when these worlds are destroyed, no fear arises within him. And although other living beings must endure affliction, he is not afflicted by anything at all.

27 One who engages himself in Yoga is not disturbed by these terrible afflictions of suffering and grief, which are born of attachment and affection. He is untouched by desire, his mind is at peace.

28 Weapons cannot pierce him; for him, death does not exist. Nowhere in the world is there anyone more joyful than him.

29 It is only when he properly engages in Yoga, and perceives the *ātman* within his own being, that he cannot be touched even by Indra, the performer of a hundred sacrifices.

30 One should never become indifferent in any way with regard to one's practice of Yoga. Now hear how a person who is exclusively committed to the proper practice should engage in Yoga.

31 Thinking of a region previously seen, he should then reside in the eastern part. The mind should be fixed on the interior of his residence, and not be allowed to wander outside.

32 Remaining within that residence, he should live in that abode. There the mind should be fixed in that abode, along with all its external movements.

33 He should conceive of that entire abode as being situated within the body. The mind may wander within that body but it must not move externally in any way.

34 Residing in a silent, uninhabited forest, he should restrain all of his senses and fix his mind one-pointedly, keeping it entirely within the body.

35 He should fix his concentration on the teeth, the palate, the tongue, and the neck, as well as the heart, and the veins around the heart.[170]

Ethical Perspectives in the *Mokṣa-dharma-parvan*

I mentioned previously that the spiritual quest for liberation produced a particular perspective on *dharma*, which would, of course, be designated the *mokṣa-dharma*. This idea of *dharma* would primarily take the form of the lifestyle and practice advocated in the teachings on Yoga previously considered, but it also embodies a clear ethical perspective, which insists that the highest spiritual goals can only be achieved by those who conduct their lives in a particular manner in relation to other living beings. The ideal way of life that forms an intrinsic part of the *mokṣa-dharma* centres primarily on acts of universal compassion and on *ahiṁsā*, never causing harm to any other living being.

The *mokṣa-dharma* taught within the *Śānti-parvan* exposes the inherent tension between the path of *nivṛtti*, renunciation, and that of *pravṛtti*, the performance of ritual acts. This tension exists firstly in relation to the goals that are sought through these two ways of spiritual life, for the *pravṛtti* rituals aim primarily at improving one's position in this world, whilst the *nivṛtti* of *mokṣa-dharma* aims at the wholesale transcendence of the world. From an ethical perspective, however, the main focus of the tension is on the violent slaughter of animals that formed

---

170 *Aśvamedhika-parvan*, 19.14–35.

a part of the Vedic ritual. Such acts of violence stand in marked contradiction to the ideal of *ahiṁsā,* and the teachers of *mokṣa-dharma* are not backward in their condemnation of such rites.

So I want to conclude this chapter with a brief glance at one of the passages in which this challenge to Vedic ritualism is asserted by advocates of *ahiṁsā*. This is from the teachings delivered by Tulādhāra to Jājali, which occupy Chapters 253 to 256 of the *Śānti-parvan*. Of significance here is the fact that whilst Jājali is a brahmin who has undertaken severe acts of austerity, Tulādhāra is a merchant from the city of Vārāṇasī who has a clear understanding of the path to liberation and is an ardent advocate of the precepts of compassion and *ahiṁsā*.

What I think is particularly interesting about this chapter is the connection Tulādhāra makes between living in a state of compassion towards other beings and the spiritual quest for liberation. He thus draws together *dharma* and *mokṣa,* and shows that they are in fact inseparable. This point is first made in verses 16 to 18, and then, following on from verse 28, he expands on what he means in those three verses. In the following chapter, Chapter 255, he insists that the Vedic ritual must be conducted without animal slaughter, but his initial emphasis on *ahiṁsā* relates to the cruelties inherent in animal husbandry as well as the exploitation of labour by greedy, heartless persons who have no interest in *dharma*. The points made here by Tulādhāra surely have a strong resonance in the present day in terms of the abuse of animals in the agriculture industry, as well as the oppression of workers who are forced to live in a state of poverty, victimised by employers whose avarice appears to have no limit.

> 16 When a person no longer feels any fear, when no fear arises because of him, and when he has neither desire nor hatred, he has certainly achieved perfection, and he is indeed a brahmin.

17 When he never creates any evil circumstances for any living being with his actions, thoughts, or words, he then reaches the level of brahman.

18 Then there is neither past nor future, and no *dharma* at all. One who is never an object of fear for any living being obtains such a state, which is beyond fear.

...

28 By freeing others from fear in this world one can achieve whatever is to be gained by means of austerities, sacrifices, charity, pious words, and the pursuit of knowledge.

29 Anyone who brings the gift of fearlessness to all living beings in this world has offered all the prescribed sacrifices and thereby obtains that same gift of fearlessness. There is no *dharma* superior to *ahiṁsā* towards all living beings.

30 That person from whom no living being ever experiences fear does not feel fear from any living being, great sage.

31 But that person who brings fear to the world, like a snake entering a house, does not obtain the state of *dharma* either in this world or the next.

32 Even the gods are bewildered by the path followed by a living being who is the self of all beings. Such a person sees all beings as the same. Although such a person has no permanent status, the gods still seek to attain his position.

33 They say that when the gift of fearlessness is granted to living beings it is the greatest of all gifts. I am speaking the truth, Jājali. Have faith in my words.

34 After enjoying good fortune, a person then meets with misfortune again. After observing how the results of ritual acts become exhausted, people try to guard themselves against such misfortune.

35 Even though *dharma* is subtle, Jājali, nothing happens in this world without a prior cause. The precepts of *dharma* have been created here, relating to both the past and the future.

36 But because it is so subtle, it is impossible to fully comprehend the science of *dharma*. Noting the many contradictions in the rules of *dharma*, a person then starts to recognise other modes of conduct.

37 There are men who castrate animals and some who pierce their noses. These beasts bear heavy burdens and these men bind them and hold them captive.

38 After putting an end to their lives, they then consume these animals. How is it that you never condemn such persons? Men also devour other men by exploiting their service.

39 Through beatings, bondage, and oppression, they make their slaves work day and night. You know yourself the pain of being beaten and whipped.

40 The entire celestial host resides in these living beings within their five senses – the sun, the moon, the wind god, Brahmā, Prāṇa, Kratu, and Yama.

41 But after trading in living beings, what hesitation would they feel in selling the flesh of those that are dead? What about trading in oil or ghee, O brahmin, or honey, liquids, or herbs?

42 Fully aware of how dear they are to their mothers, men often capture animals that have grown up happily in places free of biting insects, and then take them away to muddy fields covered in sharp grass.

43 Some animals suffer the torment of being made beasts of burden, and others are treated in ways that violate the

rules of *dharma*. I do not think that even the slaying of the child in the womb is any worse than such behaviour.

44 Even though their conduct is so cruel, they think that farming is a righteous profession. They use the wooden plough with its tip of iron to afflict the Earth and the creatures that live in the soil. Now look at these oxen, Jājali, bound to the yoke in this way.[171]

Discussion Topic: Sāṁkhya and Yoga

Here are some questions you might care to ponder after completing this chapter:

- What does the *Mahābhārata* mean by the term Yoga when it gives teachings on this subject in the *Śānti-parvan*?
- According to the *Mahābhārata*, what is the relationship between Yoga and Sāṁkhya?
- What distinctions between Sāṁkhya and Yoga should we be aware of?
- Why does the *Mahābhārata* speak of 23, 24, 25, and 26 elements at different points in the Sāṁkhya teachings included in the *Śānti-parvan*?
- According to the teachings of the *Mahābhārata*, what is prime goal of Yoga practice?

171 *Śānti-parvan*, 254.16–18, 28–44.

VII
THE *ANUŚĀSANA-PARVAN*

For this final chapter our discussion moves on to the thirteenth book of the *Mahābhārata*, the *Anuśāsana-parvan*. Here we find a continuation of the extensive forms of instruction imparted by Bhīṣma to Yudhiṣṭhira that covered almost all of the *Śānti-parvan*, though here the topics considered are far more varied than those on the duties of a king and the path to liberation contained within the *Śānti-parvan*. We have already considered some of the passages of the *Anuśāsana-parvan* when we looked at teachings on the role and status of women and then on the manner in which Śiva is represented as the one Supreme Deity, but in this chapter I want to review a further selection of chapters that Bhīṣma presents in response to Yudhiṣṭhira's questions.

Some of the passages in this thirteenth book take the form of *dharma-śāstra* in relation to subjects such as the four *varṇas*, marriage, inheritance, and the role of women. At other points, we have passages of the highest significance for both Vaiṣṇava and Śaivite theism, including the *Viṣṇu-sahasra-nāma-stotra* (Chapter 134) and the *Śiva-sahasra-nāma-stotra* (Chapter 17), the thousand names of Viṣṇu and Śiva, which are still frequently memorised verbatim by temple priests and used as a part of their rituals.

In considering how to structure this chapter, it quickly became apparent that I would have to be selective as to the topics considered simply because of the extensive nature of the *Anuśāsana-parvan,* which contains a total of 154 chapters, and the range of ideas it offers the discriminating reader. The process of selection is inevitably subjective, but I have tried consistently to focus on chapters that appeared to offer teachings that will be of interest to the modern reader, and which shed considerable light on the development of Indian religion in general. So to start off with, let us turn our attention to the vexed question of destiny and free will. What power do we have to exert control over our lives and our actions in light of the view that all things occur as a direct result of destiny, shaped by the *karma* we have accrued through past actions? Chapters 1 and 6 of the *Anuśāsana-parvan* address that question directly, though the answers given might be regarded as somewhat contradictory. This is rather typical of the *Mahābhārata,* which has a strong tendency to offer both sides of a debate without always presenting a clear cut determination as to which view is correct.

Destiny, Human Endeavour, and Free Will

Destiny: The Determinist View

At the start of the first chapter of the *Anuśāsana-parvan,* we find Yudhiṣṭhira still lamenting and condemning his own wickedness in causing death, destruction, and grief by waging war at Kurukṣetra. In response, Bhīṣma relates to him a clearly allegorical story about the manner in which a sagacious lady named Gautamī reacted to the death of her young son due to the bite of a serpent. A hunter who has witnessed this tragic event captures the snake and brings it to Gautamī so that she can find some comfort by revenging herself on the creature. Gautamī, however, rejects this idea, saying that the snake is not responsible, for the death of her son was due to the destiny he carried with him; killing the serpent will just cause another creature to suffer and will not restore her son to her. The child's death at this place and time was always certain to happen, and a righteous person never seeks vengeance or harbours hatred towards any being. No one benefits from the infliction of harsh punishments, whilst forgiveness is a meritorious act that brings future benefits, as *karma* unfolds.

The hunter disagrees. What Gautamī is saying may have some merit in abstract, philosophical forms of discourse, but he is a practical man and from a practical perspective those who do harm to others must be punished. Executing violent miscreants is itself a meritorious act for it protects others from any future misdeeds of these wrongdoers. At this point, the serpent joins the conversation and, perhaps not surprisingly, confirms the view that Gautamī has presented. He is not to blame, he says, for he was just the instrument employed by Death, Mṛtyu, to carry out its purpose. A potter uses a wheel to make a pot and a man may use a rod to strike another, but the wheel is not the maker of the pot and the rod is not to be blamed for the act of violence. It is the instigator, in this case Mṛtyu, who is the primal cause of the tragedy, and the instrument, in this case himself, is not the true cause. The hunter accepts this view in part, but still insists that even though the snake was not the primary cause, it was still a secondary cause and as such is worthy of blame and punishment.

At this point, Mṛtyu, death himself, enters the conversation and similarly seeks to absolve himself from blame for the death of the child. Mṛtyu admits that the serpent acted under his instigation, but he himself was also just a secondary cause, for he was compelled to end the boy's life due to the force of Kāla, time or destiny, which propels all beings through life, just as the wind moves clouds through the sky. Neither he nor the snake are free agents, but are forced to act under the compulsion of destiny. Once again, the hunter will not accept this declaration of innocence on the part of the instrumental factors; although Kāla may be the ultimate cause, as instrumental causes both the serpent and Mṛtyu are also blameworthy.

Now Kāla appears on the scene, and likewise declares his innocence in the matter. It is true that time and destiny are the causal factors for all events that occur, but destiny itself is formed by the previous acts of each living being. Therefore none of them assembled there are truly to blame, for the tragedy witnessed by the hunter was due entirely to the past actions of the young boy and his mother. Gautamī accepts this verdict as the true understanding, and the hunter then releases the serpent from its captivity. Just like the serpent, Bhīṣma says, Yudhiṣṭhira was not the true cause of the tragedy at Kurukṣetra, but was simply an instrument in the hands of insurmountable time.

The chapter thus offers us a deeply deterministic view of life by which no individual can be held responsible for his or her own actions, as all the joys and misfortunes that befall living beings are predestined due to the *karma* each of us has accrued through previous deeds; and this *karma* can never be avoided by any form of endeavour. With regard to Bhīṣma's view of the slaughter that has just occurred on the battlefield, one is reminded of Kṛṣṇa's words in the *Bhagavad-gītā* where he declares that he himself is time, *kālo 'smi;*[172] the warriors present there have already been slain by Kṛṣṇa in this form of time even before the conflict erupts, *mayaivaite nihatāḥ pūrvam,* and Arjuna is to be just an instrument in the hands of time, *nimitta-mātraṁ bhava savyasācin.*[173]

172 *Bhagavad-gītā,* 11.32.

173 *Bhagavad-gītā,* 11.33.

The Power of Human Endeavour

This perspective based on absolute determinism is not the end of the debate, however, and in Chapter 6 of the *Anuśāsana-parvan,* we find this view of destiny and human endeavour qualified to a considerable degree. The chapter opens with Yudhiṣṭhira questioning Bhīṣma as to whether destiny, *daiva,* or human endeavour, *puruṣa-kāra,* is of greater significance in shaping the fortunes of life. In response, Bhīṣma cites a passage of instruction delivered by the deity Brahmā to the *ṛṣi* Vasiṣṭha on that very subject.

Brahmā begins his discourse with the metaphor of a field and the farmer who seeks to grow crops in it. A field will never produce a crop without the farmer's endeavour in sowing the seed, and in the same way destiny does not produce the result one desires unless one makes the necessary endeavour, *puruṣa-kāreṇa vinā daivaṁ na sidhyati.*[174] The field is like our destiny and human endeavour is like the sowing of the seed; the results we enjoy are to be understood as arising from a combination, *saṁyoga,* of these two factors, *kṣetra-bīja-saṁyogāt tataḥ sasyaṁ samṛdhyate.*[175] There seems to be an inversion of the metaphor in these verses, but the point is made clearly enough: our experiences in life, and the results we achieve, arise from a combination of our destiny shaped by past *karma* and the endeavours we make to achieve those results.

From this point on, Brahmā places a consistent emphasis on the necessity and the efficacy of human endeavour in achieving a desired outcome. The achievement of desired results through appropriate action can be perceived constantly in life, as we strive and often succeed in acting in a way

---

174 *Anuśāsana-parvan,* 6.7.

175 *Anuśāsana-parvan,* 6.8.

that produces the desired outcome; righteous action brings joy to others, whilst iniquitous deeds lead inevitably to the suffering of living beings. Resolute action will certainly bring the desirable things of life to one who performs such action, and one who refrains from such action will never achieve such a result simply by relying on destiny, *na daivād*.[176] Moreover, destiny itself is shaped by human action, for righteous acts in the here and now ensure the propitious nature of one's future destiny; *puruṣa-kāra* is the source of *daiva*.

If one's destiny in life is unfavourable, this may limit one's ability to achieve the desired results, but without endeavour it is certain that such results will not be achieved. Destiny is certainly one factor in the progression of an individual's life, but without proper endeavours being made destiny alone will never bring success or prosperity. It is to be recognised that one is one's own friend and also one's own enemy, for each person creates his or her own future destiny through the type of action they choose to pursue. Virtue (*puṇya*) is the refuge of the gods, and all things can be attained through virtuous deeds; if a person is determined to follow the path of *puṇya* and restrain all wicked impulses, then such a person's endeavours will never be thwarted by the force of destiny, *kiṁ daivaṁ prakariṣyati*.[177]

Brahmā then cites examples of great kings of the past who have achieved success through vigorous endeavour, including the Pāṇḍavas, whose regaining of their kingdom could only be achieved because of the committed actions they performed to achieve that goal. Destiny alone could not have yielded that result without being combined with endeavour. A fire is transformed into a mighty conflagration when fanned by the wind; in the same way destiny becomes fully apparent only when it is enhanced

176 *Anuśāsana-parvan*, 6.12.

177 *Anuśāsana-parvan*, 6.29.

by association with action. The effulgence of a lamp becomes dim when it is bereft of oil; in the same way, even though one's destiny may be entirely favourable, if endeavour diminishes the influence of that destiny it will also fade away. And even if destiny has bestowed a righteous nature on a person, if that person chooses to stray from the path of virtue, destiny has no power to keep her or him on the proper path, for destiny follows behind actions, as disciples follow the lead of their *guru*.

We might well feel that these two passages stand in direct contradiction to each other, but I think it is more a difference of emphasis. In the first of them, we can see that Gautamī's insistence on the power of destiny is largely confirmed, although the dissenting voice of the hunter cannot be entirely dismissed. From this perspective, destiny, as shaped by previous acts, is the primary factor in our lives, and however much we may endeavour to change the preordained course of our existence, the force of past *karma* is so overwhelming that there is little we can do to resist the progression of inevitable events.

In Chapter 6, however, we find an alternative line of thought in the debate on this issue. Brahmā does not deny the influence of destiny, but he places a greater emphasis on the efficacy of vigorous human endeavour. All of us are certainly subject to the influence of past *karma*, but our efforts in the here and now are equally or more significant in shaping the course of our lives. Here the metaphor of the field and the sowing of seeds is particularly instructive, indicating as it does that the course of everyone's life is shaped by a combination of destiny and the efforts we make. The lines of the metaphor are somewhat blurred, as it is not entirely clear whether it is the field or the sowing of the seed that represents human endeavour. The message, however, is absolutely clear. A person's destiny may be unfavourable, but by making the appropriate efforts, a positive outcome in life may still be achieved; and from the other side, one may be blessed with a most propitious destiny, but if one refrains from all endeavours, then one will not be able to reap the full rewards to be derived from past righteous acts.

The Virtuous Act of Charitable Giving

One of the major topics considered by the *Anuśāsana-parvan* is the giving of gifts in charity, with twenty chapters (58 to 77) being devoted to teachings delivered by Bhīṣma on this subject. We will be aware that unlike the *Mokṣa-dharma* section of the *Śānti-parvan,* the *Anuśāsana* is generally focused on ritual acts and the rewards such acts bring in this world rather than on means by which the practitioner can transcend this existence and achieve liberation from rebirth. Acts of charity, however, have a position in both patterns of religious teaching. Giving away one's possessions to those in need signifies a transformation of consciousness away from a preoccupation with self-interest towards a form of enlightened wisdom that is the key to spiritual liberation. Hence the act of giving is both a part of the path to spiritual awakening and also a characteristic mark of one who has made progress in that direction. For this reason, *dāna,* charity, is often referred to in the *Śānti-parvan* as a key element of the *mokṣa-dharma* that forms the path to liberation. Here in the *Anuśāsana-parvan,* by contrast, we encounter numerous assertions to the effect that charitable giving is an act of *puṇya,* piety, which nullifies negative *karma,* brings good fortune in life, and elevates the giver towards a more desirable form of rebirth.

Praise of Charity as the Essence of Righteous Living

One must add, however, that this distinction is less than absolute, and we can observe that many of the verses included in these chapters praise acts of charity as supreme amongst all forms of *dharma*. This is particularly the case in Chapters 58 and 59, which form a general introduction to the wider discourse on acts of charity. Bhīṣma begins this line of teaching with the following statement:

> 3 Freeing all beings from fear, and showing compassion for anyone in distress, one should give whatever is sought after by a person in need who asks for help.
>
> 4 That which is considered purely as a gift when given away is the best form of charity. Once it has been given, that gift then follows the giver, O best of the Bharatas.[178]

Bhīṣma continues by stating that the giver of charity is loved by all, both in this world and the world to come. Even persons who have been inimical in the past should be given assistance if they are suffering from difficult circumstances; one who acts in such a way is indeed the best of all people, *puruṣa-sattama*.[179] Even if they do not ask for help, one should seek out those who are destitute and emaciated by hunger, and provide all the help one is able to give. A person who does not ask for charity may be regarded as superior to one who does ask, but charity should always be given whether or not it is asked for. Such acts of kindness are the highest expression of *dharma*, so one should give charity to anyone who asks, *ānṛśyaṁsaṁ paro dharmaḥ yācate yat pradīyate*.[180]

Gifts of Food and Other Forms of Charity

In the following chapters, Bhīṣma reviews the different forms of charity that may be given, discussing each object in

---

178 *Anuśāsana-parvan*, 58.3–4.

179 *Anuśāsana-parvan*, 58.10.

180 *Anuśāsana-parvan*, 59.6.

turn. First of all, he refers to gifts of land (Chapter 61), then gold, ghee, wood for making a sacrificial fire, an umbrella to give protection from the sun and rain, a cart, shoes, sesame for the *śrāddha* rites, clothing, jewels, and lamps. All these items are suitable gifts to be given to those in need, but the main emphasis in these chapters is on gifts of food and gifts of cows. There is also extensive discussion of suitable recipients for charitable donation and on this subject we find extensive eulogy of the brahmins in society, who should have all their needs catered for by gifts from kings and other wealthy persons.

It is in this assertion that extensive charity should be provided for the brahmanical communities that we see clearly the ritual nature of such giving. This insight is particularly reinforced in Chapter 63, which lays out the different constellations under which charity should be given, the type of charity to be given under each, and the desirable results gained by the giver who presents gifts at each of these auspicious times. And in these chapters we also find extensive descriptions of the celestial regions to which the generous donor may expect to be elevated in the afterlife, and the pleasures that may be enjoyed therein.

It is not the case, however, that brahmins are represented as being the only suitable recipients for gifts of charity. In Chapter 62, Bhīṣma states that food should not only be given to mendicant *sādhus* who have renounced the world, but also to those who live by eating dogs, and even to the dogs themselves, though not at the same time one presumes, *api śva-pāke śuni vā*.[181] Gifts given to brahmins will bring the greatest rewards in terms of future *karma*, but a gift of food made to a *śūdra* will also yield great good fortune in terms of the karmic reaction,

181 *Anuśāsana-parvan*, 62.13.

annaṁ śūdre mahā-phalam.[182] This good fortune takes the form of prosperity and a pleasing family life in this world and elevation to higher worlds in the afterlife, and as we read through these chapters we find equal emphasis being placed on charity and compassion as *dharma,* and on the great rewards attained in the future by persons who make such gifts.

As mentioned earlier, most attention is paid in this passage to charity in the form of food and cows. It is said that whenever a hungry person asks for food his request must always be granted and, moreover, food should be given to those in need even where no such request is made. One must seek out those emaciated by hunger and ensure that their suffering is eased by gifts of food. It can be seen that food brings life and strength to a living being, and life is everyone's dearest possession. Therefore the giving of food in charity is the essence of true *dharma,* as Bhīṣma explains:

> 6 It is due to food that the strength and energy of living beings constantly increases. Therefore Prajāpati has said that there is nothing superior to giving food in charity.
>
> 7 You have already heard about the auspicious speech of Sāvitrī, O son of Kuntī, given at the time offerings were made to the gods. You have heard why that speech was made and how it was presented, O man of great wisdom:
>
> 8 'The gift of food made by any person is in fact a gift of life, and there can be no gift in this world that is superior to the gift of life.'[183]

As is so often the case in our study of the *Mahābhārata,* we will surely recognise the significance these verses hold for the modern world.

---

182 *Anuśāsana-parvan,* 62.17.

183 *Anuśāsana-parvan,* 66.6–8.

Giving Cows in Charity

It is in Chapters 67 to 78 that Bhīṣma turns his attention to the giving of cows as gifts of charity, and this passage is combined with a glorification of cows that emphasises the sanctity of these creatures. This discussion includes a delineation of the different types of cows that should be given away, with a warning that one should never give cows that are too old to give milk and hence bring no benefit to the recipient. There is also an extensive account of the great future rewards awaiting those who make gifts of cows as well as a presentation of the story of the unfortunate King Nṛga, who accidently gave the same cow to two different brahmins (Chapter 69).

The idea of the cow as a sacred animal will be discussed shortly, but here we can note that there is a stern warning given against making such gifts to anyone who may slaughter cows, or anyone who is a *nāstika,* a non-believer, presumably because such persons do not show cows the reverence due to them. It is also said that cows should never be given to a person who trades in animals, and again one presumes that this is because it is understood that such traders may either slaughter the cows themselves or else sell them on to others who will slaughter them. It seems likely that these prohibitions are directed against a false form of charity whereby cows that are no longer able to provide milk are given away to those who indulge in animal slaughter so that the giver no longer has to provide for animals that have ceased to bring any monetary profit. The warning is severe, for it is said that anyone who makes gifts of cows in this way is destined not for realm of the gods attained by legitimate donors, but for the regions of hell (Chapter 65, verses 49–50).

The High Status Accorded to Brahmins

The Social Elite of the Mahābhārata

At various points throughout the *Anuśāsana-parvan*, Bhīṣma emphasises the high status of the brahmins and the reverence to be shown to them by all other sections of society. The brahmins are the intellectual and spiritual elite who offer enlightened guidance and conduct rituals to ensure the wellbeing of other persons and of society as a whole. It is members of the royal order in particular who are urged to accept the superior position of the brahmin class and to ensure that all their needs are provided for through extensive gifts of charity. We are thus offered a vision of the ideal society in which there is a dual elite that gives practical and spiritual leadership, thereby ensuring the prosperity of a kingdom or community, and within that elite it is the brahmins who are to be accepted as holding the higher position. This idea of there being a combined political and spiritual elite governing society is one that will be readily identifiable in many nations throughout the world, particularly, though not exclusively, in earlier periods of history.

Schooled as it is in the ideals of democratic governance, the modern mind will naturally tend to resist this view of a social structure dominated by designated elites, particularly where membership of the elite groups is based on birth alone. Nonetheless, we might reflect on the fact that all societies are dominated by elite groups and that the ideal of that elite consisting of those who possess wisdom, and are disinterested in power and wealth, is one that makes a pleasing contrast to contemporary elitism, which is generally based on inherited wealth or else shallow reputation and celebrity. We might indeed applaud the notion of a social elite consisting of those who are most honest, selfless, and devoid of hankering for power and status, cleaving instead to the pure virtue of *sanātana-dharma,* but we will simultaneously be aware that all social elites have an inherent tendency towards corruption and self-interest.

Moreover, the idea that the royal order will accept the supremacy of another, and potentially rival, social class is one that appears overly idealistic, and there are numerous examples in the *Mahābhārata* and Purāṇas which reveal that the harmonious relationship extolled by Bhīṣma in the *Anuśāsana-parvan* often fell short of the reality, the most obvious example being that of Rāma Jāmadagnya, a brahmin who is said to have waged war on the ruling class and slaughtered numerous kings and princes.

An analysis of social structures suggests that real power resides within the economic system, and as the royal order possessed the military strength to exert control over the economic systems of India in the time of the *Mahābhārata,* one inevitably feels that brahmanical authority was constantly under threat; once again there are several accounts in the *Mahābhārata* and Purāṇas of wicked kings who displayed contempt for the brahmins. Despite the fact that in most of the chapters of the *Anuśāsana-parvan* it is Bhīṣma, a *kṣatriya,* who is the speaker, we can be fairly sure that the final author was himself a brahmin. Hence it is not unreasonable to suspect that the effusive praise of the brahmin class, and the insistence on their social preeminence, is in part polemical and designed to ensure that the high status of the brahmins was not impinged upon by kings besotted by their own exhibitions of power and wealth.

The vision of an ideal society we are presented with here is from a peculiarly brahmanical perspective, and it may well be that this vision was not universally shared. It is certainly the case that in more recent centuries there have been numerous examples of the abuse of their status by brahmanical communities seeking material gain from their position, and viewing those perceived as having a lower status with contempt. The ideas we encounter in the *Anuśāsana-parvan*, however, do not reflect these more contemporary deviations, and the picture presented is of an ideal brahmanical culture free of any such blemishes.

The Supreme Status of the Brahmins

As we have already noticed when reviewing Bhīṣma's instruction on gifts of charity, the highest karmic benefit is said to be gained by those who make gifts to brahmins. However, it is in Chapters 33 to 36 of the *Anuśāsana-parvan* that Bhīṣma presents his most thoroughgoing eulogy of brahmins. The passage in question begins as follows:

> 1 Yudhiṣṭhira said: What is the most important of all the duties to be carried out by a king, grandfather. What is the form of action by performing which a king gains both this world and the next world?
>
> 2 Bhīṣma said: This is the highest duty for a king who has just been installed on the throne and who seeks unlimited happiness, Bhārata: it is conforming to the will of the brahmins. He should always worship those elderly brahmins who are well-versed in the Vedas.
>
> 3 Through words of kindness, through gifts of food, and by offering his respects, he should revere those brahmins who reside in both the towns and in rural areas, and who are well-versed in sacred texts.
>
> 4 He should be constantly aware that this is the highest duty of a king. He must give protection and succour to the brahmins equal to that given to his own self and his own sons.
>
> 5 There are some amongst them who are the most worthy of veneration, and he must be certain to worship brahmins of this type. When such brahmins are able to live contentedly, then the whole kingdom flourishes.

> 6 These brahmins must be adored, shown all respect, and protected, just as one would one's own father. The welfare of the world rests upon such brahmins, just as the welfare of living beings depends upon Indra.[184]

Bhīṣma then warns against the dangers of angering brahmins. Their spiritual potency is such that their anger will bring all manner of misfortune down upon anyone who causes them offence. Brahmins engage in many different occupations, such as agriculture, acting, dancing, and begging, whilst some become thieves or engage in deceit, *corāś cānye 'nṛtāś cānye tathānye naṭa-nartakāḥ;*[185] others who are highly blessed perform priestly functions on behalf of others, *purohitā mahā-bhāgā brāhmaṇāḥ.*[186] Their influence is such that if they praise a man, he will certainly prosper, but if they criticise his conduct, then his worldly endeavours are doomed to fail. It is because there are no brahmins amongst them that races such as the Yavanas, Pulindas, and Śakas are regarded as people of the lowest status. The most heinous crime a person can commit is killing a brahmin, and even speaking harsh words critical of a brahmin is a great sin.

Great happiness in the world to come is guaranteed for any person who throughout his life gratifies brahmins with gifts, respect, and worship, but one who disturbs or insults brahmins will certainly undergo suffering in the afterlife. A virtuous king should rule his domain in accordance with the instructions given him by his brahmin advisors, for it is they who possess the greatest wisdom. Bhīṣma then gives examples of kings of the past whose conduct angered the brahmins and

184 *Anuśāsana-parvan*, 33.1–6.

185 *Anuśāsana-parvan*, 33.11.

186 *Anuśāsana-parvan*, 33.14.

were destroyed utterly as a result of the conflicts that took place between the two branches of the ruling elite, for the brahmins possess a potency that is far more destructive than the martial prowess of any king. In a conversation with the Goddess of the Earth, Kṛṣṇa once asked how a householder can become free of the karmic influence of any unrighteous acts he may have performed, to which the Earth replies that purity can most easily be attained by service rendered to the brahmins, *brāhmaṇān eva seveta pavitraṁ hy etad uttamam.*[187]

The Good Fortune of Being Born as a Brahmin

Bhīṣma concludes his teachings on this subject by stating that anyone who takes birth as a brahmin is greatly fortunate, for brahmins are revered by all living beings and are always the first to be served with food in any assembly. They are the well-wishers of the world and bestow blessings on those who show them respect. Still, however, there are some persons who challenge the status of brahmins, and they will suffer misfortune due to the curse of a brahmin. Such brahmins should try to avoid taking up the professions of the *śūdra,* which involve service to others, and should live by studying sacred texts and performing rituals for wealthy patrons. By living in such a way, devoid of malice or greed, a brahmin can attain the greatest benefit, both in this world and in the realm of the gods. Different brahmins display different natures; some are like lions, some are like tigers, some are like boars, and some are like elephants, whilst there are others who are as gentle as cotton. In all cases, however, anyone who causes distress to brahmins will inevitably suffer the direst consequences. In the

187 *Anuśāsana-parvan,* 33.21.

final chapter of this passage, Chapter 36, Bhīṣma recounts the story of a conversation between Indra and a mighty *asura* named Śambara in which Indra asks Śambara how he has achieved the great prosperity and good fortune he displays. As one might expect by this point, Śambara replies that it is all due to the respect he shows to brahmins and to the humble manner in which he learns from them and follows their instructions. This alone is the cause of all the success he has achieved in life.

A Brahmin by Birth or by Qualities?

One might feel a little uneasy about the idea presented in these chapters of the elevation of one social class to a position of such marked preeminence, and one question that will inevitably arise relates to the criteria employed to establish which persons are to be accepted as brahmins. Essentially, is it merely birth in a brahmin family, or is it the qualities displayed by individuals that determine whether or not they are to have that topmost designation bestowed upon them? If we take the *Mahābhārata* as a whole, then we will encounter contrary views on this question. Within the *Anuśāsana-parvan*, however, we find Yudhiṣṭhira questioning Bhīṣma directly on this very topic and receiving an unequivocal response:

> 2 If one is a *kṣatriya*, a *vaiśya*, or a *śūdra*, how does one attain the status of a brahmin? Explain that to me, O best of kings.
>
> 3 If one wants to attain the status of a brahmin, is that to be achieved through great acts of austerity, through ritual acts, or through the study of sacred texts. Instruct me on this matter, grandfather.
>
> 4 Bhīṣma said: The status of a brahmin is very difficult to achieve for members of the three other *varṇas*, headed by the *kṣatriyas*, for this is the highest position that can be attained by any living being, Yudhiṣṭhira.

> 5 Only after transmigrating through numerous forms of rebirth, and being reborn again and again, can a living being finally take birth in the form designated as a brahmin.[188]

It seems almost certain that what Yudhiṣṭhira is inquiring about here is the possibility of a person born in one of the other social classes achieving brahmanical status by dedicating himself to different religious practices. In response, Bhīṣma insists that it is birth alone that defines an individual as a brahmin and he follows this assertion by telling the story of Mataṅga, who was born into a brahmin family but displayed none of the qualities of a brahmin. Finally the truth is revealed. Mataṅga was not born as a brahmin, but was conceived due to his mother's infidelity with a man of lower birth.

This idea that *varṇa* status is determined solely by birth finds some confirmation in the *Bhagavad-gītā,* where Kṛṣṇa tells Arjuna that the nature he is born with is that of a warrior. He cannot change that identity and hence he will be forced to wage war by his own inherent tendencies that are a fundamental element of the *kṣatriya* nature with which he was born.[189] As mentioned above, however, this is not the sole view on this question expressed within the *Mahābhārata.*

When Bhīma is captured by King Nahuṣa, who has been cursed to take the form of a mighty serpent, Yudhiṣṭhira frees his brother by answering questions put to him by Nahuṣa (*Āraṇyaka-parvan,* Chapter 177). One of the questions asked is, 'Who is a brahmin?', to which Yudhiṣṭhira responds by saying that when the attributes of truthfulness, charity, forbearance, virtue, kindness, self-control, and compassion are seen in a person, that person is to be recognised as a brahmin, *sa*

---

188 *Anuśāsana-parvan,* 28.2–5.

189 *Bhagavad-gītā,* 18.59.

brāhmaṇa iti smṛtaḥ.[190] Nahuṣa responds by pointing out that such qualities can be found in persons of all four *varṇas,* to which Yudhiṣṭhira replies with the following verse:

> *śūdre caitad bhavel lakṣyaṁ dvije tac ca na vidyate*
> *na vai śūdro bhavec chūdro brāhmaṇo na ca brāhmaṇaḥ*
>
> If these characteristics appear in a *śūdra,* that
> person is not a *śūdra,* and if they are absent in a brahmin,
> then that person is not a brahmin.[191]

A little further on in the *Āraṇyaka-parvan,* the following verse is spoken in a conversation on the subject of *dharma* between a brahmin and a hunter:

> *yas tu śūdro dame satye dharme ca satatotthitaḥ*
> *taṁ brāhmaṇam ahaṁ manye vṛttena hi bhaved dvijaḥ*
>
> If there is a *śūdra* in whom the attributes of self-control, truthfulness, and *dharma* constantly appear, then I regard such a person as a brahmin. He is a brahmin by dint of his conduct.[192]

In the *Śānti-parvan,* this more liberal perspective is confirmed by Kapila, the founder of the Sāṁkhya system, who speaks the following verses to a ritualistic brahmin named Syūmaraśmi, confirming that the status of a brahmin is based on good qualities and spiritual realisation rather than birth:

> 29 If a person dresses without any upper garment, lies down to sleep without any cover, uses his arms as his pil-

190 *Āraṇyaka-parvan,* 177.16.

191 *Āraṇyaka-parvan,* 177.16.

192 *Āraṇyaka-parvan,* 206.12.

low, and possesses peace of mind, the gods understand that such a person is a brahmin.

30 If by living alone a sage enjoys pleasure that is equal to all the pleasures enjoyed in marriage and never allows his mind to dwell on the happiness that others enjoy, the gods understand that such a person is a brahmin.

31 If a person understands this entire world in terms of *prakṛti* and the transformations of *prakṛti*, and knows the destination of all beings, the gods understand that such a person is a brahmin.

32 If a person has no fear of any other living being, is not feared by any living being, and exists as the self of all beings, the gods understand that such a person is a brahmin.[193]

So what are we to make of these apparently contradictory views expressed by authoritative teachers? Here I think we must again be aware that the emphasis within the *Anuśāsana-parvan* is on ritual *dharma* pertaining to this world, whereas Kapila and Yudhiṣṭhira tend towards the *sanātana-dharma* that is based on pure virtue and looks towards spiritual enlightenment rather than material gain. We have already noticed the inherent tension between these two tendencies designated as *pravṛtti*, where the emphasis is on ritualised religion, and *nivṛtti*, which is based on the renunciation of such acts in pursuit of the higher goal. The view that a brahmin is to be identified by birth alone is the perspective of the ritualists, whilst the emphasis on pure virtue and enlightenment as the essential criteria represents the perspective of *nivṛtti*, as well as Yudhiṣṭhira's constant tendency towards the *dharma*

193 *Śānti-parvan*, 261.29–32.

of pure virtue. As we have seen on numerous occasions, the *Mahābhārata* is quite happy to live with this tension, and, indeed, uses it effectively to enhance the teachings it offers in both narrative and didactic form.

Ahiṁsā and Vegetarianism

Throughout the *Mahābhārata*, we encounter an emphasis on the principle of *ahiṁsā*, which essentially means refraining from any form of speech or practice that causes harm to another living being. The phrase *ahiṁsā paramo dharmaḥ*, *ahiṁsā* is the highest form of *dharma*, is found repeatedly in various passages in the different *parvans* of the work, but especially when it is the *dharma* of pure virtue or else the *mokṣa-dharma* that is the speaker's principal theme. The following verse, spoken by the enlightened Tulādhāra, epitomises the ideal of *ahiṁsā* from the perspective of *mokṣa-dharma*:

> *yadā na kurute bhāvaṁ sarva-bhūteṣu pāpakam*
> *karmaṇā manasā vācā brahma saṁpadyate tadā*

> When he is never the cause of any harmful condition for
> any living being with his actions, thoughts, or words,
> then he has realised Brahman.[194]

The word *ahiṁsā* is in fact a negative noun with the literal meaning of avoiding *hiṁsā*, which means harm to others, but it should not be understood entirely in that sense, which might be taken as simply avoiding harmful deeds without taking any form of positive action, or acts of kindness, to help other beings. A fuller explanation of this point is provided in a later text, the *Liṅga Purāṇa*:

---

194 *Śānti-parvan*, 254.17.

> *ātmavat sarva-bhūtānāṁ hitāyaiva pravartanam*
> *ahiṁsaiṣā samākhyātā yā cātma-jñāna-siddhi-dā*

> Acting towards all living beings as one would for oneself, and dedicating oneself to their welfare; this is what is designated as *ahiṁsā* and it brings about knowledge of the *ātman*.[195]

We have noted on a number of occasions the *Anuśāsana-parvan*'s tendency towards ritualism and ritual *dharma*, so it may come as some surprise to find that the most strident advocacy of *ahiṁsā* is contained within this thirteenth book of the *Mahābhārata*. At the start of Chapter 114, Yudhiṣṭhira asks about the form of conduct that is superior to all others and is instructed on that subject by Bṛhaspati, the priest and *guru* of the celestials:

> 1 Yudhiṣṭhira said: *Ahiṁsā*, Vedic ritual, meditation, control of the senses, acts of austerity, rendering service to one's *guru*: which of these is the best practice for any person?

> 2 Bṛhaspati said: All of these represent the different gateways of *dharma* for all persons. Listen now as I discuss these six, all of which are certainly praiseworthy, O best of the Bharatas.

> 3 Now I will speak of that which is supremely beneficial for any living being. If a man seeks to achieve the highest goal, he should follow the *dharma* of *ahiṁsā*.

> 4 Being constantly aware of the three faults [*doṣa*] that exist in all beings, and bringing the forces of desire and anger under control, a person then achieves all success in life.

195 *Liṅga Purāṇa*, 8.12.

> 5 A person who seeks only his own pleasure and in doing so strikes down harmless creatures, using a rod to afflict them, will find no joy in the world to come.
>
> 6 But that person who regards the welfare of other beings as equal to his own, who puts aside that chastising rod, and who has conquered his anger, will experience joy in the world to come.
>
> 7 Such a person sees the existence of all other living beings as the same as his own existence. Even the gods are confused about the path followed by such a person. They desire to follow that path but are unable to perceive it.
>
> 8 One should never act towards another living being in a manner different to how one behaves towards oneself. This is the very essence of *dharma*; the opposite course arises solely from selfish desire.
>
> 9 In relation to refusal and giving, in terms of joy and misery, and of things that are pleasing and displeasing, a person who acts towards others as he would towards himself has achieved the proper outcome.
>
> 10 A person behaves towards others in the same manner that the other person behaves towards him. This is the rule of equivalence that prevails in the domain of living beings, and it is on the basis of this principle that *dharma* has been precisely explained to you.[196]

Bṛhaspati here quite clearly elevates *ahiṁsā* beyond all other forms of religious or spiritual practice, but he does not entirely lose sight of the ritualistic theme of the *Anuśāsana-parvan*, for there is still reference made to elevation in this world by means of superior rebirth. One of the main goals sought through the Vedic ritual is the attainment of a position in this world whereby

196 *Anuśāsana-parvan*, 114.1–10.

one gains prosperity, progeny, and good fortune. Here it is asserted that this same result is achieved through adherence to the precept of *ahiṁsā*. There is a 'rule of equivalence' amongst living beings, and hence it is to be understood that all beings will reciprocate if one displays a disposition that is resolutely benign. *Ahiṁsā* is to be accepted because it is a part of the spiritual path that brings liberation and because it is an essential element of *dharma,* but also because it brings great rewards in both this life and the world to come.

Three Forms of Ahiṁsā

In Chapter 115, Bhīṣma follows on from Bṛhaspati's introduction to the topic by explaining that *ahiṁsā* is to be understood as existing in four forms. *Ahiṁsā* is certainly the supreme feature of *dharma* and in fact all other forms of *dharma* are contained within *ahiṁsā,* just as the footprints of all other animals are contained within the marks left by a serpent. Therefore, *lokeṣv ahiṁsā tu nirdiṣṭā dharmataḥ parā,* throughout the worlds, *ahiṁsā* is recognised as supreme amongst all forms of *dharma.*[197] The first three of the four forms of *ahiṁsā* are said by Bhīṣma to be *ahiṁsā* of action, *ahiṁsā* of words, and *ahiṁsā* of the mind, and amongst these three *ahiṁsā* of the mind is the most important, for when *ahiṁsā* is established in the mind, it will quickly become manifest in a person's words and deeds.[198]

The Fourth Form of Ahiṁsā: Abstention from Meat

Bhīṣma then turns his attention to the fourth kind of *ahiṁsā,* which is abstention from eating meat, and it is this topic that dominates the remainder of this passage, which

197 *Anuśāsana-parvan,* 115.6.

198 *Anuśāsana-parvan,* 115.8.

continues through Chapters 116 and 117. What follows in these chapters is a remarkable diatribe against eating meat, which is put forward as the most overt violation of the principle of *ahiṁsā*. There is quite considerable attention paid to the negative *karma* that is accrued from any form of indulgence in animal slaughter, but the main emphasis is on the moral precepts at stake, as Bhīṣma repeatedly rails against the cruelty of pursuing self-interest at the expense of the lives and welfare of other living beings. He starts off very much in that vein, by asserting that eating the flesh of an animal is the same as eating the flesh of one's own son (v 10). Such cruel practices inhibit mental awareness, *cittaṁ nirudhyate*, for even speaking words approving of meat eating is a sinful act that prevents any form of elevation in the next life.

Eating Meat Slaughtered by Others

At the start of Chapter 116, Yudhiṣṭhira raises further questions regarding the propriety or otherwise of eating meat. First of all, he refers to the fact that Bhīṣma has previously stated that meat should be offered and then eaten as a part of the *śrāddha* rites performed on behalf of departed ancestors. Is this injunction now to be superseded by the higher principle of *ahiṁsā*? And is the violation of the principle of *ahiṁsā* performed by a person who kills the animal himself and eats the flesh, by one who slaughters the animal for others, by one who eats the flesh of an animal slaughtered by others, or by one who merely purchases the meat? Who is it that actually incurs the sin arising from the eating of meat? Then again, if meat is a source of energy and nourishment, how does one who refrains from eating meat gain longevity, bodily strength, or physical development?

Bhīṣma's initial response to these questions is a reassertion of the precept of *ahiṁsā* as the supreme manifestation of *dharma*, the highest vow one can accept in life, *vrataṁ śreṣṭham* (v 19).[199] Life is as dear to all other beings as it is to oneself; even enlightened sages fear death, so how much more so is this the case for innocent creatures slaughtered by wicked persons (v 23).[200] Indeed, those who eat meat are just like *rākṣasas*, evil spirits of the night. Turning to directly address Yudhiṣṭhira's questions, Bhīṣma then cites the opinion of Mārkaṇḍeya. That renowned *ṛṣi* has asserted that the person who purchases meat, the person who slaughters the animal, the person who cuts up the flesh, the person who keeps the animals captive, and even one who merely approves of the practice, are all culpable, as well as the person who eventually eats the flesh of living beings, and all will have to endure the negative *karma* that arises when harm is done to others.

Eating the Flesh of Animals Offered in Sacrifice

Turning then to the question about meat offerings as a part of the *śrāddha* rites, Bhīṣma gives a slightly equivocal response by saying that there is a much lesser fault when meat is eaten in these situations, *alpa-doṣam iha jñeyam*.[201] He then makes it clear, however, that Vedic rites involving animal slaughter should never be performed by one who is seeking higher spiritual goals, *na tu mokṣa-kāṅkṣinām*.[202] He also reaffirms a point we have heard before by stating that animal sacrifice is a later addition to the pristine Vedic revelation, and that in ancient times the offerings consisted

---

199 *Anuśāsana-parvan*, 116.19.

200 *Anuśāsana-parvan*, 116.23.

201 *Anuśāsana-parvan*, 116.43.

202 *Anuśāsana-parvan*, 116.49.

of grains of rice rather than animals, *purā-kalpe nṛṇāṁ vrīhi-mayaḥ paśuḥ.*[203]

This innovation is explained by reference to the story of King Vasu, who was asked to arbitrate in a dispute amongst *ṛṣis* over whether animal sacrifice is an authentic part of the Vedic ritual. Although Vasu knew well enough that grains alone constitute a proper offering, he gave a false decision by saying that animal sacrifice should be performed. It is because of these deceitful words that meat has become a part of the offerings in the *śrāddha* rites. A fuller version of this story is told in Chapter 324 of the *Śānti-parvan,* from which we learn that the dispute was actually between the gods who favoured animal sacrifice and the *ṛṣis* who were opposed to it. Vasu gave his false verdict because he favoured the gods from whom he was expecting a rich reward, whereas in fact he was cursed by the *ṛṣis* for his duplicity and forced to dwell in a pit in the ground.

Eating Meat, Vegetarianism, and Karma

Chapter 117 opens with Yudhiṣṭhira showing that he has been persuaded by Bhīṣma's arguments on this subject and asking about the positive results achieved by abstaining from meat in terms of one's future *karma.* His grandfather begins by once again stating his abhorrence of eating the flesh of an animal; there is no one more vile, he says, and no one more cruel than one who plunders the flesh of another living being in order to enhance the flesh of his own body.[204] There is nothing more dear to a living being than its life, and with this in mind one should behave towards other beings as one would wish others to behave towards oneself.

---

203 *Anuśāsana-parvan,* 116.53.

204 *Anuśāsana-parvan,* 117.10.

He then, perhaps surprisingly, qualifies this statement by saying that eating the flesh of animals offered in a *yajña* is acceptable, as is meat acquired by *kṣatriyas* who go to the forest to hunt. The latter point is explained on the basis that hunting involves equal danger for the hunter and the hunted. As it is deer that are spoken of as the animals killed in this way, this point may appear to be rather insubstantial (although students of British history may be aware that one of the sons of King William I was killed whilst hunting in the New Forest when he rode into an overhanging branch). Overall though, a person must show compassion towards others, *tasmād dayāṁ naraḥ kuryāt,*[205] as those who eat meat will suffer the most terrible karmic consequences. In fact, in a future life the animal one is eating today will exist in a form that allows it to consume one's own body in that future life.[206]

The passage as a whole then concludes with Bhīṣma's final eulogy of the precept of *ahiṁsā*:

> *ahiṁsā paramo dharmaḥ: Ahiṁsā* is the highest form of *dharma*.
>
> *ahiṁsā paro damaḥ: Ahiṁsā* is the highest form of self-mastery.
>
> *ahiṁsā paramaṁ dānam: Ahiṁsā* is the supreme act of charity.
>
> *ahiṁsā paramaṁ tapas: Ahiṁsā* is the highest form of austerity.
>
> *ahiṁsā paramo yajñaḥ: Ahiṁsā* is the best of all *yajñas*.

---

205 *Anuśāsana-parvan,* 117.11.

206 *Anuśāsana-parvan,* 117.33.

> *ahiṁsā paraṁ balam: Ahiṁsā* is the greatest strength.
>
> *ahiṁsā paramaṁ mitram: Ahiṁsā* is the greatest act of friendship.
>
> *ahiṁsā paramaṁ sukham: Ahiṁsā* is the greatest joy.
>
> *ahiṁsā paramaṁ satyam: Ahiṁsā* is the supreme truth.
>
> *ahiṁsā paramaṁ śrutam: Ahiṁsā* is the ultimate revelation.
>
> No other form of ritual, vow, or pilgrimage is equal in merit to *ahiṁsā*, and one who adheres strictly to this principle is the father and mother of the world.[207]

One might find it surprising to encounter a passage of this type within the *Mahābhārata*, particularly with regard to the strident tone with which Bhīṣma condemns eating animal flesh. *Ahiṁsā* is frequently represented as being the highest point of dharmic living, but the advocacy of vegetarianism as a universal precept is certainly unusual at this point in the development of the Vedic tradition. The ritualistic tendencies of the *Anuśāsana-parvan* are not entirely abandoned here, however, both in terms of the frequent references to the wonderful karmic results acquired through abstention from meat, and the partial caveats inserted in relation to brahmanical rituals and *kṣatriya* customs.

In fact, Chapter 117 has a rather confusing tone to it, as it oscillates between absolute condemnation and the legitimation of eating meat in certain circumstances. Here one feels that the passage may have been interpolated, or else that there was a reluctance to entirely condemn traditional

207 *Anuśāsana-parvan*, 117.37–41.

practices in a manner that Buddhists or Jains might have tended towards. As can be observed on a number of occasions throughout the work, the mood of change and reformation is in the air when the *Mahābhārata* is being composed, but there is no appetite here for stepping entirely beyond the parameters of Vedic orthodoxy. Reinterpretation rather than rejection is the course to be followed.

Rituals and Offerings

Throughout the *Mahābhārata*, the religious ritual that is repeatedly referred to is the Vedic *yajña* consisting of offerings made into the sacred fire and carried to the Vedic deities by the fire-god, Agni. In the central narrative, this type of ritual comes to the fore most notably with regard to the *rājasūya-yajña* (*Sabhā-parvan*) performed by Yudhiṣṭhira to confirm his preeminent position over all other kings, and the *aśvamedha-yajña* (*Aśvamedhika-parvan*) he performs after the battle in order to atone for the sins he perceives himself as having committed in waging war against his enemies. Similarly, where collective rituals are referred to in didactic passages, particularly with regard to the duties of a brahmin, it is the Vedic *yajña* that is consistently mentioned.

We do, however, also find occasional reference to *devatāyatana* and *deva-gṛha*, both of which mean 'houses of the gods', which might suggest the worship of sacred images that is now commonly practised in temples all over India. In actuality, it is unlikely that these are references to temples or places of communal worship, and what are being referred to here are probably household shrines such as are to be found in many Hindu homes today. We must be aware that whilst the *yajña* is the ritual of the Vedic tradition, temple building and image worship are based on the teachings of the Āgamas and Tantras, a series of texts that stand somewhat apart from the Vedas, and were probably composed at a later date. As the *Mahābhārata* stands firmly within the Vedic tradition, we should not be surprised to find scant reference to such ritual acts.

If we continue our consideration of the ideas encountered in the *Anuśāsana-parvan,* however, we do find quite detailed discussion of ritual acts somewhat distinct from the type of *yajña* more frequently referred to elsewhere. Chapters 87 to 92 provide extensive instruction on the proper means of performing the *śrāddha* rites, in which offerings are made to the *pitṛs,* the ancestors and forefathers, and then in Chapter 101 Bhīṣma discusses the proper ways in which flowers, incense, lamps, and food should be offered to the gods.

When considering the *śrāddha* rituals, we must first notice that the term *pitṛ* refers not only to a person's parents, grandparents, and other ancestors, the *mānuṣya-pitṛs,* but also to a category of deities who are said to be the original progenitors of humanity, the *deva-pitṛs.* In the *Dharma-khaṇḍa* of the *Garuḍa Purāṇa,* a later text, we find detailed instruction about death, transmigration, *śrāddha* and funeral rites, *karma,* ghosts, hauntings, and exorcisms, all of which relate to the *mānuṣya-pitṛs,* but the passage here in the *Mahābhārata* is primarily concerned with the rituals by which worship is offered to the *deva-pitṛs,* and is therefore rather different from the Purāṇic exposition, even though the subject is designated by the same term, *śrāddha.* Let us now consider the main points to be noted within Bhīṣma's instruction on these ritual acts:

1. As is usual for the introduction of a new topic, the passage begins with a question from Yudhiṣṭhira to Bhīṣma, and the wording of that question is quite significant in providing an insight into the type of rituals he is inquiring about. Specifically, the question posed is about the type of *havis,* or offerings, that should be presented to the *pitṛs,* which gives a clear

indication that the rituals in question are not those typically performed on behalf of immediate ancestors, but are more closely associated with the Vedic *yajña*, the difference being that the recipients of the offerings made into the sacred fire are the *deva-pitṛs* rather than the *devas* themselves. It is also apparent that whilst the rituals outlined in the *Garuḍa Purāṇa* are performed for the benefit of departed ancestors in whatever form they may now be existing, the worshippers of the *deva-pitṛs* execute the rites with the expectation of worldly gain by dint of the blessings bestowed upon them by these celestial progenitors. Hence throughout this passage we read of the desirable results gained by the worshipper through different types of offering made at different times of the year.

2. In response to Yudhiṣṭhira's question, Bhīṣma first states that in the ritual of *yajña* the initial offerings should be made to the *pitṛs* and only when this is complete should offerings be made to the Vedic deities. He then lists the different benefits gained by means of the *śrāddha* rites performed in the afternoon of each day of the waxing moon: sons, daughters, wives, horses, goats, fame, and prosperity. Only the fourteenth day is prohibited, and during the period of the waning moon *śrāddha* rites should be executed only on the tenth to the thirteenth days.

3. Responding to a further question from Yudhiṣṭhira (Chapter 88), Bhīṣma then lists the type of offerings that should be made to the *pitṛs* along with the duration for which they remain satisfied by each. Citing Manu as his authority, he begins by referring to offerings consisting of sesame seeds, but quickly

moves on to list various types of animals that may be presented for slaughter and sacrifice: fish, sheep, rabbits, goats, pigs, birds, deer, antelopes, wild oxen, buffaloes, rhinoceroses, or dairy products.

4. The chapter then takes a rather surprising twist, which may be a later addition, as it is said that a man should try to beget sons who can make annual offerings on his behalf in Gayā on the anniversary of his death. To this day, Gayā, in Bihar state, is still revered by Hindus as the best location for *śrāddha* rites to be performed on behalf of departed parents.

5. In Chapter 89, Bhīṣma continues his discourse on the benefits of performing the *śrāddha* rites, here following a similar theme to that pursued in Chapter 87 as he outlines the benefits attained by persons who perform the ceremony under the different constellations. And once again these are presented in terms of offspring, good health, animals, and prosperity, rather than any overtly spiritual benefits.

6. At the start of Chapter 90, Yudhiṣṭhira enquires about the different types of brahmins who should be fed and made beneficiaries of largesse after the *śrāddha* ceremony is complete, and in response Bhīṣma offers extensive lists first of those who should be excluded and then of those who should be invited to attend. The list of those to be invited is very much as one would expect, but the list of those to be excluded is rather surprising due to the range of deviant conduct that was apparently indulged in by individuals who are elsewhere eulogised as 'gods amongst men'. These include cheats, fraudsters, abortionists, thieves, adulterers, astrologers, and palmists, as well

as those who sell *soma*, an intoxicating ritual drink, and even those who practise medicine. The brahmins who should be invited are those who are most learned in the teachings of the Vedas and most expert in the Vedic ritual, as well renunciants and practitioners of the techniques of Yoga. The invitations should be made on the basis of the brahmin's proficiency in Vedic learning and priestly duties, and never simply because a brahmin happens to be one's friend.

7. Responding to a further question from Yudhiṣṭhira, Bhīṣma tells him of how the *śrāddha* rites were initiated in ancient times (Chapters 91 and 92). Here attention is very much focused on the rituals performed for the benefit of the *mānuṣya-pitṛs* in their future lives, and it is made clear that it is not just one's parents who should be the recipients of the offerings, but any family member who has died. The original performance of the rituals was devised and enacted by a *ṛṣi* named Nimi whose son had died as a result of performing harsh acts of austerity, and it was for the benefit of this departed son that the *śrāddha* rites were first performed. Concerned that he may be initiating a non-orthodox practice, Nimi seeks guidance from his own father, Atri, who assures him that these rituals were originally ordained by Brahmā himself and are properly performed when offerings are made into the sacred fire.

8. As was mentioned above, the predominant form of religious ritual referred to within the *Mahābhārata* is the Vedic *yajña* in which offerings to the Vedic deities are made into the sacred fire. We find no mention of any of the principal characters in the narrative

> engaging in the temple worship that is today central to Indian ritual life. The occasional references to *deva-gṛha*, houses of the gods, cannot be overlooked, but there is to nothing to indicate that these forms of worship were enacted on the scale indicated by the Tantras and Āgamas.

In Chapter 101 of the *Anuśāsana-parvan*, however, we do find teachings on ritual offerings that appear somewhat equivalent to the forms of worship enacted today in temples throughout India and across the world. No reference is made to sacred images, but the chapter focuses on offerings of flowers, incense, lamps, and food (*bali*), and it may be presumed that there was some form of image or altar to which these offerings were presented. It seems unlikely, however, that what we encounter here is some form of proto-*tantra* that later developed into the elaborate temple rites revealed in the Āgamas. Where offerings of flowers are discussed, the word *yajñiya* is used to indicate those that are most suitable, and this might be taken as indicating a connection to the Vedic ritual, but it is more likely that *yajñiya* is used here in a more general sense, meaning 'fit to be offered'.

It is stated that when the gods and other celestial beings are offered fragrant flowers, they become gratified with the worshippers and bestow blessings upon them in the form of worldly good fortune. Different types of *dhūpa*, incense, are also discussed, along with recommendations as to which of these are suitable for worship. Lamps should also be offered, of which those formed from ghee are the best, although those made using plant oil are also acceptable. Lamps made with the fat of animal carcasses should never be presented. It is then stated that a righteous householder should offer a portion of cooked food to the *gṛha-devatās*, the household gods, before taking his own meal. The offerings to the gods should consist of the very best food mixed with milk and curd, but if offerings are made to *yakṣas* or *rākṣasas,* fierce and potentially malefic entities, these should consist of blood and meat.

What then are we to make of this short treatise on ritual offerings? If we can disregard any suggestion that these rites are an extension of Vedic ritualism or an early form of tantric worship, I would suggest that it is more likely the case that what we can observe here is the elevation of what are essentially folk or village rituals; this suggestion is reinforced by the statement that the offerings should be made not just to gods, but also to lesser celestial beings such as *rākṣasas, yakṣas, uragas, gandharvas,* and *nāgas*. We might surmise that the rituals in question were to be performed in household temples, but against this view we find the statement that lamps are to be offered to the gods when going through mountains or forests, to sacred trees, or at a crossroads. It must be noted that the *Bhagavad-gītā* (9.26) also advocates offerings of a leaf, flower, fruit, or water to Kṛṣṇa, the Supreme Deity, thereby demonstrating that worship of this type is a feature of the highest expressions of spiritual devotion, but the emphasis in this chapter of the *Anuśāsana-parvan* suggests overwhelmingly that the rites advocated here do not hold that same elevated status.

The Sacred Cow

Reverence for the cow is one of the most significant marks of Indian religion, and in some respects Hinduism has been defined by this ideal. Today it has become an issue of intense political controversy as the Hindu majority in India seeks to make cow slaughter illegal, a policy that has been enacted in twenty of the twenty-eight states and deemed legal by the Supreme Court. The term 'sacred cow' has entered popular discourse as indicating an essentially worthless idea or object that is shown unwarranted respect and reverence, and is beyond rational criticism. Although first appearing in American sources, the origin and usage of the term would appear to be related to the imperialist ideology of the British Empire, which consistently sought to denigrate Indian culture and religion in order to provide a specious justification for dominance and exploitation.

The fundamental idea underlying India's reverence for the cow is, however, one that is surely worthy of a more balanced consideration, based as it is on the ideals of reciprocation, nurturing, and symbiosis, rather than the one-sided and frequently vicious exploitation of animals by the farming industry. Repeatedly we encounter the idea that respect is always due to cows because of the nourishment they can provide for human beings in the form of milk and other dairy products, and that this respect should be translated into a form of animal husbandry based on nurturing, protection, and reverence. The wider significance of this idea becomes even more apparent when we notice that the Sanskrit word for a cow, *go*, is also used to refer to the Earth itself, our ultimate source of life, and that the Earth Goddess is typically represented in the form of a cow. It is the one-sided exploitation of the Earth, devoid of any sense of respect or reverence, which has led us to the current environmental crisis. The ideal of the nurturing of the cow can hence serve as a remedy not just for the cruelty of animal husbandry but also as a model for a more reverential regard for the Earth and the natural environment. What is required is a change of attitude, and this transformation is exemplified by the Indian regard for cows based on mutuality rather than ruthless exploitation.

We have already noticed in the section about gifts of charity that concern was shown to ensure that any cows given away would never be slaughtered or mistreated by recipients of the gifts. And in the passage on the *śrāddha* rites that lists animals that may form a part of the offerings on behalf of the *pitṛs*, we might notice that the list includes *gavya*, meaning dairy produce, rather than cows themselves, thereby precluding cow slaughter from this otherwise rather gruesome series of recommendations. Moreover, along with *kṛṣi* and *vānijya*, agriculture and business, the *Bhagavad-gītā* (18.44) adds *gau-rakṣya*, protection of cows, to the duties of the *vaiśya* class, which presents a rather different perspective on dairy farming.

It is within the *Mahābhārata*'s *Anuśāsana-parvan*, however, that we find the most thoroughgoing discourse on the sanctity of cows, and the reverence that is to be shown to them. In Chapters 77 to 82, Bhīṣma moves on from his teachings on charity and presents a fairly lengthy passage that glorifies cows and explains their status as sacred animals. There are three principal themes pursued in this passage:

1. A glorification of the sacred identity of cows;
2. Stories that explain how it was that cows achieved their elevated status;
3. The desirable forms of rebirth achieved by persons who give cows in charity.

The following selection of verses from this passage clearly illustrates the mood of reverence that is encountered therein.

> 5 Cows are wonderfully fragrant, bearing the sweet aroma of the *guggulu* [myrrh] tree. Cows are the fundamental support of other living beings, and cows are the great source of good fortune.
>
> 6 Cows are the present and the future, and cows are the eternal source of nourishment. Cows are the very root of prosperity; a gift made to cows is never destroyed. Cows are a constant source of food, and provide the supreme sacrificial offering for the gods.

7 The Vedic chants of *svāhā* and *vaṣaṭ* are both established on cows. Cows are the true fruit of the *yajña*, and all such rituals are based on cows.

8 Every morning and every evening, at the time for the offerings, cows present the *ṛṣis* with the offerings they require, O best of men.

15 One should not go to sleep without first praising cows, and one should not rise from sleep without remembering cows. Morning and evening, one should offer respect to cows; prosperity is achieved through this practice.

16 One should never feel revulsion for the urine and stool of cows, and one should never eat the flesh of cows. One achieves good fortune in this way.

17 One should constantly sing the praises of cows, and never show cows disrespect in any way. If a person has unpleasant dreams, then he should sing the praises of cows.

18 One should always bathe using cow dung, one should sit down on a mat formed from dried cow dung, and one should never seek to avoid the saliva, urine, or stool of a cow.

22 'May cows with golden horns that produce copious amounts of milk approach near to me, just as rivers flow towards the ocean. Such cows are themselves known as *surabhi* [literally, fragrant] and are the offspring of Surabhi.

23 May cows always behold me; may I always look upon them. Cows are ours and we are theirs; we will be wherever there are cows.'

24 Each night and each day, in both good and bad times, and in times of great fear, a person reciting these verses is delivered from fear.[208]

---

208 *Anuśāsana-parvan*, 77.5–24.

12 One should constantly recite this prayer: 'They are our mothers, they have beautiful forms, they have many different forms, and they are the form of the world [*viśvarūpa*]. May such cows be ever near me.'

15 Bowing my head, I worship the cow, the mother of the world in the present and in the future, by whom this whole world is pervaded with its stationary and moving beings.[209]

...

2 Bhīṣma said: Cows are the great source of merit [*puṇya*] and prosperity [*artha*], and they are a source of deliverance for human beings. Through their milk and the ghee used for sacrificial offerings, cows provide sustenance for living beings.

3 There is nothing that is a greater source of righteousness [*puṇya*] than cows, O best of the Bharatas. In terms of purity and righteousness [*pavitra* and *puṇya*], there is nothing superior to cows in all the three worlds.

17 Those righteous persons, free of selfish greed, who make gifts of cows in charity are said to be virtuous in their deeds, and they are givers of all forms of charity. Such persons attain the pure land of the cows, O sinless one.

32 If a person renders service to cows and dwells amongst them, they become satisfied with him and award boons that are very difficult to obtain.

33 One should never feel hostility towards cows within one's mind, for they are the true source of happiness. With restraint and gentility of mind, one should always show them respect, and worship them with a display of reverence. It is in this way that one gains good fortune from cows.

---

209 *Anuśāsana-parvan*, 79.12, 15.

39 Cows are purity and righteousness; they are the highest source of supreme purity. By making a gift of cows to brahmins, a person reaches the realm of the gods.

40 Remaining pure at heart in the midst of cows, one should silently recite the Gomatī hymns of the Veda. It is by sipping pure water from the palm of the hand that one becomes purified and free of blemish.[210]

...

3 Amongst all forms of charity, the gift of cows is most highly esteemed. Cows are the best of all creatures, the most pure, and this is the most purifying of all deeds.

4 One should render service to cows in order to gain good fortune [*puṣṭi*] and for the sake of tranquillity [*śānti*] as well. They are the source of milk, curds, and ghee, which destroy the effect of all sinful deeds.

16 It is stated that cows form the body of the *yajña*, Vāsava, and cows are fame as well. Without cows, the *yajña* cannot proceed in any form.

17 Through their milk and the ghee offered in sacrifices, they sustain other living beings. Their male offspring facilitate the production of crops.

18 Cows facilitate the production of grain, and seeds of various types, on the basis of which *yajñas* can proceed, including all kinds of *havya* and *kavya* offerings made to the gods and to the *pitṛs*.

19 They are most righteous [*puṇya*], O lord of the gods, producing as they do milk, curds, and ghee. Moreover, they bear various burdens even when afflicted by hunger and thirst.

---

210 *Anuśāsana-parvan*, 80.2, 3, 17, 32, 33, 39, 40.

> 20 Through their actions they also sustain the holy sages and other living beings, O Vāsava. They innocently bear burdens, and as a result of their righteous deeds they constantly reside in a realm of existence higher than our own.
>
> 45 Any man who becomes devoted to cows can achieve whatever he desires. Women also who are devoted to cows will have all their desires fulfilled.
>
> 46 Those who desire a son will obtain a son, and a woman will obtain a husband. Those who seek prosperity will acquire wealth, whilst one who pursues *dharma* will obtain *dharma*.
>
> 47 One who seeks knowledge will gain knowledge, and one who seeks happiness will gain happiness. There is nothing that is difficult to obtain for one who is devoted to cows.[211]

What is clear from these verses is the sacred status given to cows, as well as the desirable rewards that are achieved by *go-bhaktas*, devotees of cows, and by those who make gifts of cows in charity. This is, of course, the *Anuśāsana-parvan*, and so the main emphasis is on elevation and good fortune in this world, which can be achieved through ritualised ways of life, in this case showing reverence for cows. It is also apparent that cows are not to be regarded as ordinary creatures of a lower order, like dogs or goats, but do in fact possess a celestial identity by means of which gifts are showered upon those who revere their sanctity.

In Chapter 78, Bhīṣma relates the story of how the cows that appeared at the time of creation performed acts of austerity, *tapas*, and were then blessed by Brahmā that all their future offspring would be sources of purity for all beings, and that

---

211 *Anuśāsana-parvan*, 82.3, 4, 16–20, 45–47.

those who worshipped them would be elevated to the celestial realm of Goloka in their next life. Then in Chapter 81 another story is told of how Śrī, the Goddess of Prosperity, also known as Lakṣmī, wished to become permanently present within cows. The cows, however, refused to accept her because they knew her to be *cañcalā*, never staying in one place or person for long. Śrī begs the cows to allow her to dwell within them, saying that she is happy to reside even within their stool and urine, and eventually they accept the sincerity of her words and allow her to be always present within their stool and urine. It is for this reason that these substances, which might otherwise be avoided, are to be regarded as a source of purity and good fortune. Thus we can observe that the elevated status of cows comes from the sacred identity of their ancestors, from the service they perform for humanity, because of the foodstuffs they give to humanity, and because they are the source of ghee offered in the *yajñas* that ensure the fertility and wellbeing of the world.

I started off this section by suggesting reasons why persons in the modern era might continue to accept the enduring significance of the Indian reverence for cows. This was based on the emphasis on reciprocation rather than exploitation, which can be applied to the Earth as a whole. This idea of reciprocation is succinctly expressed in the *Anuśāsana-parvan* with the words *gāvo 'smākaṁ vayaṁ tāsām*, the cows are ours and we are theirs.[212] In these chapters, however, we also find the idea of there being an inherent sacredness to cows that has been transmitted through the generations of cows since the time of the original creation. Hence the veneration of the cow can be understood in terms of rational analysis as well as faith in the ancient traditions that have been passed down over the centuries from the very earliest enunciation of the Vedic religion.

212 *Anuśāsana-parvan*, 77.23.

Discussion Topic:
The Anuśāsana-parvan

Here are some questions you might care to ponder after completing this chapter:

- Are individuals to be designated as Brahmins on the basis of birth or personal qualities and conduct?
- According to the *Mahābhārata*, do people have free will in the shaping of their lives, or is everything controlled by destiny based on past actions?
- What reasons does the *Anuśāsana-parvan* give for cows being regarded as sacred?
- Is the giving of charity purely a moral act, or does it have a spiritual significance?
- What reasons are given in the *Anuśāsana-parvan* for adhering to a strictly vegetarian diet?

Concluding Words

Such is the extent and scope of the *Mahābhārata* that in the course of this study we have now moved from the starting point of an epic narrative to a discussion of the sacred identity of cows with innumerable ideas and insights occurring in between. Whether it be the Critical Edition or one of the longer manuscripts, the sheer size of the *Mahābhārata* means that a detailed knowledge of all its books, chapters, and verses will be beyond the reach of most of those who take up the task of reading and studying the full text. Nonetheless, as with any great work of this type, there is much benefit to be derived from exploring its different sections and pondering deeply the ideas it lays out before us. Perhaps the most attractive and enlightening feature of the *Mahābhārata* is the multiplicity of views it offers to its readers, showing us contrasting ideals and inviting us to consider different sides of the debates it pursues. We are given much to ponder, but ultimately the choice of which path to follow is left up to ourselves, just as Kṛṣṇa says at the conclusion of the *Bhagavad-gītā, yathecchasi tathā kuru,* 'Now you must act in the way you see fit' (18.63).

The significance of the *Mahābhārata* also rests on the range of ideas that it draws within its vast purview. The *Mahābhārata* itself makes the bold assertion that 'what is not here does not exist', and while this is obviously to be regarded as something of an exaggeration, it has some validity in terms of the huge array of points of contemplation that the work offers its readers and students. It is reasonable to assert that the *Mahābhārata* is a prime source for most of the central themes of Indian religious and ethical discourse. Indeed, one might be justified in going further by saying that it is a presentation of great value for persons of all backgrounds, Indian or otherwise, who seek to better understand the decisions all of us must make in life. This point is particularly prevalent in the numerous discussions of *dharma* that appear and reappear throughout the eighteen *parvans*, offering us help, advice, and guidance as we try to live our lives in such a way that we attain the fullness of our humanity.

It is hoped that the present study gives at least some indication of the pattern of ideas to be encountered within the *Mahābhārata* along with a significant insight into the narrative, the characters, and the dilemmas they face. What is presented here shows us good and evil and many points in between, thereby demonstrating the truth of the oft-stated maxim, *dharmaḥ sūkṣmo 'sti, 'dharma* is subtle'. Readers of the text are urged to seek crucial balance in leading fulfilling and positive lives. The satisfaction of desires and the search for prosperity are to be balanced by the insistence on the primary status of *dharma* in human life. This point is emphasised by the extreme differences of character revealed within Yudhiṣṭhira and Duryodhana, and by innumerable words of instruction throughout the *Mahābhārata*. Though there is allowance for the pursuit of the selfish goals of life, this should never be at the expense of causing harm to other beings, and such pursuits should be counterbalanced by an equal preoccupation with seeking the welfare of others. The spiritual dimension of life is also brought to the fore and explored in some detail in the work. Yet even the quest for liberation from this world is not dissociated from *dharma*, for all forms of spirituality must have a basis in the ways in which one conducts oneself in relation to other living beings, displaying compassion and an outlook on the world that is utterly benign.

What then should be our conclusion about the *Mahābhārata*? There are undoubtedly many candidates for the accolade of 'greatest work of literature ever composed', but if such a title were ever to be awarded, my own view would be that the *Mahābhārata* would be one of the leading contenders. My hope is that the present work will have gone some way towards revealing the significance and subtlety of the ideas it has to offer all those who approach it with a mind open to stimulation and challenge.

But perhaps we should leave the final word to the *Mahābhārata* itself, which concludes with the following:

> *ūrdhva-bāhur viraumy eṣa*
> *na kaścic chṛnoti me*
> *dharmād arthaś ca kāmaś ca*
> *sa kim arthaṁ na sevyate*
>
> *na jātu kāmān na bhayān na lobhād*
> *dharmaṁ tyajej jīvitasyāpi hetoḥ*
> *nityo dharmaḥ sukha-duḥkhe tv anitye*
> *jīvo nityo hetur asya tv anityaḥ*
>
> With arms raised, I cry out, but no-one hears me. From *dharma* come both wealth (*artha*) and pleasure (*kāma*), so what purpose could be served by not adhering to *dharma*?
>
> One should never abandon *dharma* for the sake of pleasure, out of fear, or because of greed, nor even for the sake of life itself. *Dharma* is eternal, but joy and misery are not; the living being is eternal, but the cause of its existence here is impermanent.[213]

---

213 *Svargārohaṇa-parvan*, 5.49–50.

APPENDIX: GENEALOGICAL TREE OF MAIN *MAHĀBHĀRATA* CHARACTERS

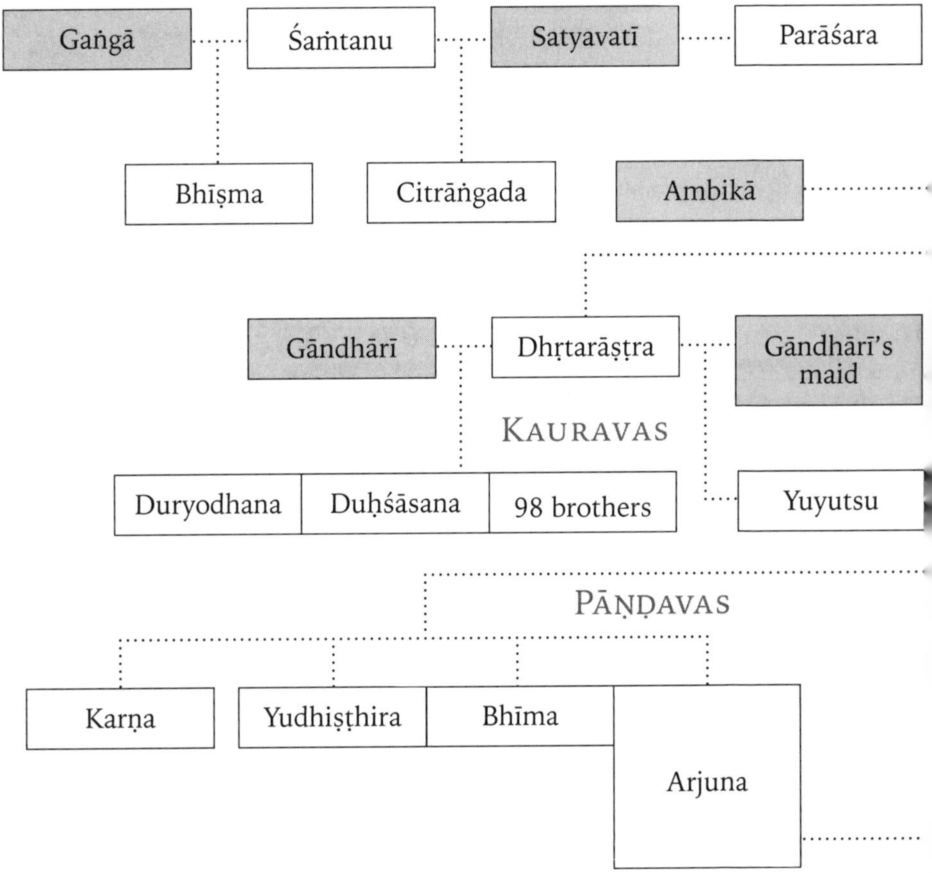

* Shaded box indicates female character; unshaded box indicates male character.

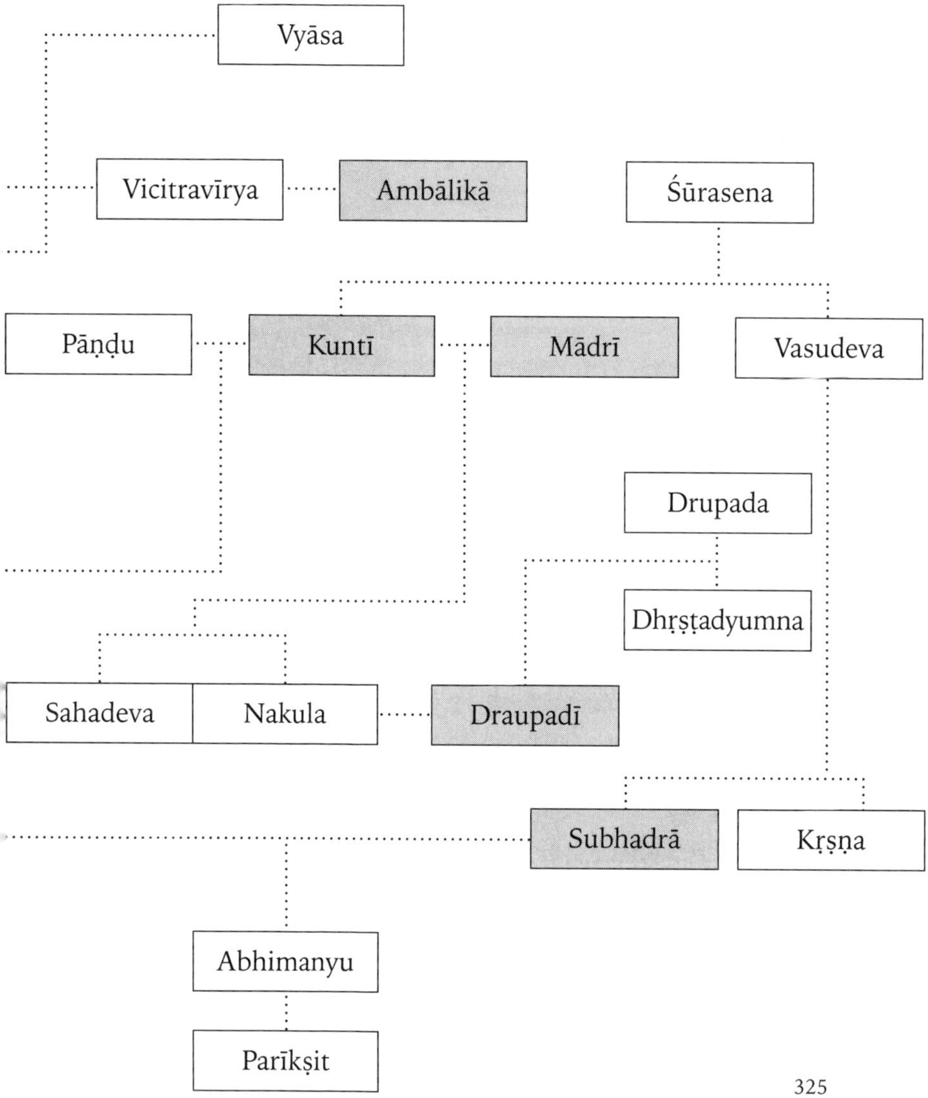
Vyāsa
Vicitravīrya
Ambālikā
Śūrasena
Pāṇḍu
Kuntī
Mādrī
Vasudeva
Drupada
Dhṛṣṭadyumna
Sahadeva
Nakula
Draupadī
Subhadrā
Kṛṣṇa
Abhimanyu
Parīkṣit

Bibliography

This Bibliography lists all the works cited in the text; those recommended for further study, along with some additional titles, are indicated with an asterisk. Links to further resources can be found at http://mahabharata-resources.org.

Critical Edition of the *Mahābhārata*

The Mahābhārata for the First Time Critically Edited. 19 vols., ed. Vishnu S. Sukthankar et al. Poona: Bhandarkar Oriental Research Institute. https://sanskritdocuments.org/mirrors/mahabharata/mahabharata-bori.html.

Complete English Translations of the Text

*Dutt, Manmatha Nath, trans. Mahābhārata: Translated into English with Original Sanskrit Text. 9 vols. Delhi: Parimal, 2006.

Ganguli, Kisari Mohan, trans. The Mahabharata of Krishna-Dwaipayana Vyasa, Translated into English Prose. Delhi: Munshiram Manoharlal, 2004; first published Calcutta: Bharata Press, 1883–1896. www.sacred-texts.com/hin/maha/index.htm.

Partial and Incomplete English Translations of the Text

*Fitzgerald, James L., trans. and ed. *The Mahābhārata,* Volume 7. Book 11, The Book of the Women; Book 12, The Book of Peace, Part One. Chicago: University of Chicago Press, 2004.

Johnson, W. J., trans. *The Sauptikaparvan of the Mahabharata: The Massacre at Night*. Oxford: Oxford University Press, 2008.

Lal, Purusottama. *The Mahābhārata of Vyāsa*. Calcutta, India: Writers Workshop, 1968.

The Mahabharata. Translated by Bibek Debroy. India Penguin, 2015.

*Narasimhan, Chakravarthi V. *The Mahābhārata: An English Version Based on Selected Verses*. New York: Columbia University Press, 1998.

*van Buitenen, J. A. B., trans. and ed. *The Mahābhārata*. 3 vols. Chicago: University of Chicago Press, 1973–1978.

*Wilmot, Paul, W. J. Johnson, Kathleen Garbutt, Alex Cherniak, Vaughan Pilikian, Adam Bowles, Justin Meiland, Kate Crosby, and Alexander Wynne, trans. *Mahābhārata*. Clay Sanskrit Library. New York: New York University Press, 2005–2009. https://claysanskritlibrary.org/volumes/about-mahabharata.

General Secondary Sources

*Brockington, John L. *The Sanskrit Epics*. Leiden, Netherlands: Brill, 1998.

Bronkhorst, Johaness. 'Manu and Mahabhārata'. In *Indologica,* T. Ya. Elizarenkova Memorial Volume, Book 2, edited by L. Kulikov and M. Rusanov, 135–156. Moscow: Russian State University for the Humanities, 2012.

Childs, Brevard. *Biblical Theology in Crisis*. Philadelphia: Westminster Press, 1970.

*Dandekar, R. N., ed. *The Mahābhārata Revisited*. New Delhi: Sahitya Akademi, 2011.

*Fitzgerald, James L. *'Mahābhārata'. In The Hindu World*, edited by Sushil Mittal and Gene R. Thursby, 52–74. New York: Routledge, 2004.

Fitzgerald, James L. 'Negotiating the Shape of "Scripture": New Perspectives on the Development and Growth of the *Mahābhārata* between the Empires'. In *Between the Empires: Society in India 300 BCE to 400 CE*, edited by P. Olivelle. Cambridge: Cambridge University Press, 2006.

*Hiltebeitel, Alf. *The Ritual of Battle: Krishna in the Mahābhārata*. Reading, UK: Ithaca Press, 1976.

*Hiltebeitel, Alf. *Rethinking the Mahābhārata: A Reader's Guide to the Education of the Dharma King*. Chicago: University of Chicago Press, 2001.

*Hopkins, E. Washburn. *The Great Epic of India: Its Character and Origin*. Delhi: Motilal Banarsidass, 1994; 1st ed. 1901.

*Rukmani, T. S., ed. *The Mahābhārata: What is not Here is Nowhere Else*. New Delhi: Munshiram Manoharlal, 2005.

*Sukthankar, V. S. *On the Meaning of the Mahābhārata*. Delhi: Motilal Banarsidass, 2016; 1st ed. 1942. Original text available at https://archive.org/details/in.gov.ignca.6570/mode/2up.

Sutton, N. *Religious Doctrines in the Mahābhārata*. Delhi: Motilal Banarsidass, 2000.

*van Buitenen, J. A. B. *The Bhagavad-gītā in the Mahābhārata*. Chicago: University of Chicago Press, 1981.

Glossary of Sanskrit Terminology

Advaita Vedānta: Indian philosophical system based on the Upaniṣads that propounds a doctrine of absolute non-dualism in relation to God, the world, and living beings.

Āgamas: Literally, what has been passed down. Usually refers to the Vedas or other sacred texts.

Ahaṁkāra: One of the three mental faculties. The sense of ego or 'I-ness' experienced by living beings. Can also mean pride or arrogance.

Ahiṁsā: Refraining from any action, words, or thoughts that cause harm to other living beings.

Āśrama: Place of spiritual practice for individuals or communities; one of the stages of a Brahmin's life: student, householder, forest dweller, and religious mendicant.

Asura: Powerful beings who are the constant enemies of the gods and seek to wrest control of the world from them.

Ātman: The spiritual entity that gives life to every living being.

Avatāra: Literally a descent; a manifestation of the Deity in this world.

Avyakta: Literally non-manifest; matter in its primal undifferentiated state.

Bhakti: Devotion to the Deity.

Brahman: The absolute reality that is the true identity of all that exists.

Buddhi: The element of the mental faculties that discriminates and makes decisions.

Dharma: Right conduct, social duty, religious ritual, or pure virtue. In philosophical discourse, *dharma* can refer to objects that are real, or else to the essential quality that defines an object.

Dharma-śāstra: Ancient texts that present rules and codes of conduct for different sections of society.

Dhyāna: Meditation, often connected to the Yoga systems.

Gandharva: Celestial beings that are particularly associated with music and dance.

Guṇa: A quality or more specifically a good quality. Matter is said to be pervaded by three *guṇas, sattva, rajas,* and *tamas* – purity activity, and the darkness of ignorance.

Kṣatriya: One of the four social classes, which is responsible for governance and military endeavours.

Kṣetrajña: Literally the knower of the field; an alternative term for the innermost self, or *ātman*.

Manas: That part of the mental faculties that identifies and classifies sensory perceptions.

Mokṣa-dharma: The mode of conduct, ways of life, and spiritual practices that lead to liberation from rebirth.

Nārāyaṇa: An alternative name for Viṣṇu.

Nāstika: A non-believer; one who does not accept the authority of the Vedas.

Nivṛtti: The spiritual path based on renunciation of the world and of religious rituals.

Parvan: A part or section; each of the eighteen books of the *Mahābhārata* is named as a *parvan*.

Prakṛti: Matter or nature; that out of which this world is formed.

Pravṛtti: The religious path of those who remain within the world and perform ritual acts.

Puṇya: Virtue; virtuous actions that produce positive future results.

Puruṣa: A person or man; term used in Sāṁkhya teachings to denote the spiritual entity that is the true self in all beings; an alternative term for *ātman*.

Rajas: Passion, activity; one of the three *guṇas*, or qualities, which pervade all things material.

Rākṣasa: A powerful demonic entity sometimes said to consume human flesh.

Ṛṣi: A spiritually enlightened individual; a celestial sage dwelling in the realm of the gods.

Sāṁkhya: Indian philosophical system that seeks to enumerate the elements of which matter is comprised and to rigidly differentiate the spiritual entity, *puruṣa*, from anything material.

Sattva: One of the three pervasive *guṇas* which shape everything material; purity, virtue, light, goodness. Can also mean existence.

Soma: The intoxicating or entheogenic beverage that is offered to the gods in the Vedic ritual; also a name for the moon.

Śrāddha: Rites performed for departed parents and ancestors.

Śruti: Literally that which is heard; a term used for the Vedic revelation.

Svarga-loka: The world of the gods.

Tamas: Darkness or ignorance; one of the three *guṇas* that pervade all things material.

Tīrtha: A ford or crossing place; a sacred site to which pilgrimages are made.

Upaniṣads: The sections of the Vedas which deal with spiritual and philosophical subjects.

Varṇa: One of the four social classes into which ancient Indian societies were divided.

Viśva-rūpa: The form of the Supreme Deity that is an embodiment of the entire created world.

Yajña: The Vedic ritual of making offerings into a sacred fire whilst the hymns of the Veda are recited.

Yakṣa: Celestial or earthly beings that can exert power and influence over humanity.

Yuga: The four great ages in Indian cosmology named Satya, Tretā, Dvāpara, and Kali. These revolve constantly over vast periods of time.

INDEX

B

C

D

Q

R

S

W

Y

MANDALA
An Imprint of MandalaEarth
PO Box 3088
San Rafael, CA 94912
www.MandalaEarth.com

Find us on Facebook:
www.facebook.com/MandalaEarth

Publisher Raoul Goff
Associate Publisher Phillip Jones
Publishing Director Katie Killebrew
Project Editor Amanda Nelson
VP Creative Chrissy Kwasnik
Art Director Ashley Quackenbush
VP Manufacturing Alix Nicholaeff
Sr Production Manager Joshua Smith

ISBN: 979-8-88762-077-0
ISBN: 979-8-88762-136-4 (Export Edition)

Manufactured in India by Insight Editions
10 9 8 7 6 5 4 3 2 1

Library of Congress Cataloging-in-Publication Data
Names: Sutton, Nicholas, author.
Title: Light on the Mahabharata : a guide to India's great epic / Nicholas Sutton.
Description: San Rafael : Mandala, [2024] | Series: The Oxford Centre for Hindu Studies Mandala Publishing series | Includes bibliographical references and index. | Summary: "In this in-depth, engaging guide to the Mahabharata, Hindu Studies scholar Nicholas Sutton explores the central messages of the work's core narratives and passages of instruction, demonstrating how the questions the text poses are as relevant today as they were to those who composed this mighty treatise on human existence"-- Provided by publisher.
Identifiers: LCCN 2024020012 (print) | LCCN 2024020013 (ebook) | ISBN 9798887620770 (hardcover) | ISBN 9798887621364 (hardcover) | ISBN 9798887620787 (ebook)
Subjects: LCSH: Mahābhārata--Criticism, interpretation, etc.
Classification: LCC BL1138.26 .S965 2024 (print) | LCC BL1138.26 (ebook) | DDC 294.5/923046--dc23/eng/20240625
LC record available at https://lccn.loc.gov/2024020012
LC ebook record available at https://lccn.loc.gov/2024020013

ROOTS of PEACE REPLANTED PAPER

Mandala Publishing, in association with Roots of Peace, will plant two trees for each tree used in the manufacturing of this book. Roots of Peace is an internationally renowned humanitarian organization dedicated to eradicating land mines worldwide and converting war-torn lands into productive farms and wildlife habitats. Roots of Peace will plant two million fruit and nut trees in Afghanistan and provide farmers there with the skills and support necessary for sustainable land use.

FSC www.fsc.org MIX Paper | Supporting responsible forestry FSC® C016779